Annual Editions:
Business Ethics, 26/e

Edited by Eric Teoro

http://create.mheducation.com

ISBN-10: 1259153320   ISBN-13: 9781259153327

Contents

Preface

In publishing ANNUAL EDITIONS we acknowledge and appreciate the important role played by the magazines, newspapers, Internet resources, and journals of the public press in providing current, first-rate educational information across a broad spectrum of interest areas. Many of the articles selected for inclusion in Annual Editions are appropriate and of significant value for students, researchers, policy makers, managers, and professionals seeking accurate, current material to help bridge the gap between principles and theories and the real world. These articles, however, become more useful for study when those of lasting value are carefully collected, organized, indexed, and reproduced in a low-cost format, which provides easy and permanent access when the material is needed. That is the role played by ANNUAL EDITIONS.

Welcome to the 26th edition of *Annual Editions: Business Ethics*. Since its inaugural issue, *Annual Editions: Business Ethics* has provided students and practitioners up-to-date articles to serve as a basis for analysis and discussion of business-related ethical issues, theories, and practices. This edition continues that legacy with a collection of articles covering a widearray of business ethics topics.

Ethics touches every facet of organizational life. Marketing managers and their staffs face ethical decisions regarding consumer research, privacy, product development, pricing, distribution, and advertizing. The financial sector faces challenges related to insider trading, risky financial products, money laundering, and "creative" accounting practices. Human resource and staff managers are confronted with decisions concerning layoffs, outsourcing, diversity and inclusion, employee safety, employee privacy, sexual harassment, and other forms of hostile environments. Executives in multinational companies must deal with varying cultures and ethical systems, which can produce inconsistent, and at times contradictory, ethically acceptable business practices.

In the midst of these ongoing ethical concerns, businesses today face additional ethical challenges as societal expectations regarding the nature of business changes. What role should businesses play in addressing societal problems? Note that this moves beyond a question of could to one that has moral imperatives. Do businesses have a responsibility to help solve discrimination, poverty, lack of education, and lack of access to basic life necessities? Do pharmaceutical companies, for example, have a responsibility to provide inexpensive or free drugs to individuals who do not have the means to pay the current market price? How should businesses interact with the environment? Is it sufficient for them to not cause harm, or do they have a responsibility to improve the environment given their resources? How do managers balance individual and organizational rights and responsibilities?

Who defines these rights and responsibilities? Questions like these become more complex for public companies in which executives and boards have fiduciary responsibilities to stockholders. Add to all of this, the ethical issues and dilemmas surrounding the use of technology, such as privacy, smart "autonomous" machines and systems, and the replacement of human workers, the contemporary business ethics setting can be a very confusing and challenging environment.

Accompanying the articles in this edition are resources to help students, practitioners, and researchers interact with the material more fully. Associated with each article are questions to generate discussion and analysis, and links to additional Websites for further investigation. This edition includes a topic guide to facilitate locating those articles most pertinent to a reader's needs, and a correlation guide to a couple of leading business ethics textbooks, enabling professors and students to reinforce learning by coupling real-world articles with theoretical insights. These resources can be found on Create Central at www.mhhe.com/createcentral.

It is our goal to continually improve *Annual Editions: Business Ethics*. We heartily welcome your comments, opinions, and recommendations as we strive to develop a text that will encourage and equip readers to uphold the highest standard of ethical business behavior.

Eric Teoro

Editor

Eric Teoro is the Chair of the Professional Studies Field and the Director of the Business Administration Program at Lincoln Christian University. He teaches several ethics courses including business ethics and leadership ethics. Eric's research interests are the cultivation of an ethical character, virtue ethics, business ethics, philosophy of business, and organizational trust. He has conducted business training in Ghana and China, and serves as a board member for the Greater Ashburn Community

Development Corporation and as the Education Officer for Aim to Work, not-for-profits serving one of Chicago's Southside neighborhoods. Prior to teaching, Eric worked in manufacturing and served in the United States Air Force.

Academic Advisory Board

Members of the Academic Advisory Board are instrumental in the final selection of articles for Annual Editions books and ExpressBooks. Their review of the articles for content, level, and appropriateness provides critical direction to the editor and staff. We think that you will find their careful consideration reflected here.

Januarius Asongu
Santa Monica University

Darrell Burrell
Florida Institute of Technology

Kenneth Harris, Jr.
Concordia University

Mahmoud Khaial
Keiser University

Tom Mahaffey
St. Francis Xavier University

Mary K. McManamon
Lake Erie College

Cheryl Moore
Argosy University

Carl Nelson
Polytechnic University

Joseph A. Petrick
Wright State University

Robert K. Rowe
Park University

Melodie M. Toby
Kean University

Joan Van Hise
Fairfield University

William Walker
University of Houston

Harvey J. Weiss
Florida National College

Jonathon West
University of Miami

Caroline Shaffer Westerhof
California National University

Unit 1

UNIT

Prepared by: Eric Teoro, *Lincoln Christian University*

Ethics, Values, and Social Responsibility in Business

Ethics can be defined as a body of moral principles or rules that govern behavior. It can also be defined as the area of study that examines ideas about moral principles. Business ethics considers the moral conduct of individuals within organizations, as well as the conduct of organizations as a whole. It must be remembered, though, that individuals establish the behavioral norms and cultures of organizations; so as one discusses business ethics at the corporate level, one is never far from discussing ethics at the individual level.

Values are beliefs about what is important in life, what one should hold in regard. In organizations, values are shared beliefs about what is good, what is important, and what is non-compromisable. Like ethics proper, values guide individual and corporate behavior. Social responsibility in business refers to the obligation that a business has to operate in a manner that will benefit society at large. Individuals and cultures can disagree regarding which principles are ethically good and normative, which values should be upheld, to what degree, if any, a business has social responsibility, and what social responsibility entails. Ethics is different from law. Not

every ethical standard has been codified in law, and history teaches us that not every law was grounded in ethics. Ethics, values, and social responsibility seek to do good, not out of legal compliance, but out of an inherent sense of moral responsibility, out of a belief that associated behaviors are simply the right things to do.

The eight articles in this unit provide an overview of ethics, values, and social responsibility in business. The essays provide guidance regarding ethical decision-making and the ethical challenges individuals face on a personal and corporate level, with suggestions on how to manage those challenges. They provide examples of individual and corporate misconduct while pointing out signs that such misconduct could be taking place. A couple of the articles focus on corporate social responsibility (CSR), helping readers define their orientation to CSR, and stressing the importance of CSR to many employees. Working through these eight articles will provide managers, employees, and students an introduction to the importance of business ethics, and provide several tools they can apply in their personal and professional lives.

Designing Honesty into Your Organization by Christian Mastilak et al.

5

Article

Prepared by: Eric Teoro, *Lincoln Christian University*

Designing Honesty into Your Organization

CHRISTIAN MASTILAK ET AL.

Learning Outcomes

After reading this article, you will be able to:

- Understand how perceptions of fairness impact dishonest behavior in organizations.

- Understand how the framing of organizational processes can lead to dishonest behavior.

- Take concrete, actionable steps to facilitate honest behavior on the part of employees.

The past decade has provided ample evidence that some people don't behave honestly at work. While it's easy to blame individual factors, such as greed or lack of an ethical compass, recent academic research paints a different picture. As a leader in your organization, you may have more influence than you realize about whether your employees act honestly or not. You can design honest behavior into an organization by using fair and properly aligned reward systems and simple communication strategies.

We know dishonesty is costly, and it may be on the rise. The Ethics Resource Center reports that the following percentages of employees surveyed in 2009 had observed these behaviors in the previous year: company resource abuse (23 percent), lying to employees (19 percent), lying to outside stakeholders (12 percent), falsifying time or expenses (10 percent), and stealing (9 percent). The Association of Certified Fraud Examiners suggests United States organizations may have lost as much as $994 billion to occupational fraud in 2008, and a PricewaterhouseCoopers global survey in 2009 suggests that recent economic pressures have increased the likelihood of fraud taking place. But how can this common problem be reduced?

Research suggests that integrity testing goes only so far in predicting honesty in the workplace. It turns out that most employees are neither consistent truthtellers who can be completely trusted in the absence of controls nor consistent liars who can never be trusted. This means preventing dishonesty isn't just a matter of finding the right people. Some factors can motivate employees to be closer to the truthtelling end of the scale. Specifically, research shows that honest behavior is influenced by employees' beliefs about whether they are being treated fairly, whether expectations of honest behavior have been made explicit, and whether organizational control systems reward dishonest behavior. This suggests that honest behavior can be designed into—or out of—an organization. In this article, we first discuss some of the research findings, then draw on them to develop practical suggestions for how managers can create an environment that both discourages dishonest behavior and enables honest behavior.

Why Do Employees Behave Dishonestly?

We broadly define dishonest behavior as making a report known to contain lies or taking an action known to be unauthorized for personal gain. This excludes accidental errors but includes a variety of behaviors common to accounting and finance functions. Most research in accounting has focused primarily on budgeting behavior, such as padding requests in order to keep the extra funds. But research on more direct forms of theft, such as stealing company property, has led to similar conclusions about why employees steal.

Admittedly, the reasons for dishonest behavior are many and varied. Much has been written about the fraud triangle and how the presence of pressure, opportunity, and rationalization increases the chance of fraud. We can't do justice to the entire topic here, but we can discuss some organizational design and control choices that affect people's behavior. Two common themes that surface are *fairness* and *frame*.

Fairness

For years, economic theory has rested on the assumption that two important desires drive people's behavior: leisure and wealth. Business schools teach future managers to assume that employees will avoid working hard and will lie to increase their wealth. These assumptions then show up in practice as internal control systems are developed to help prevent and detect lack of effort and dishonesty.

Recent academic research has identified two other desires that influence behavior: honesty and fairness. So it isn't simply that people want to be as rich and put forth as little effort as possible; rather, most people also care about being honest and want to ensure that their treatment and outcomes are reasonable compared to the treatment and outcomes of others. More importantly, these desires affect honesty in the workplace.

When employees believe they haven't received what they are due, they will look for ways to recover what they believe they're owed.

Several studies provide examples of how tradeoffs among desires for wealth, honesty, and fairness play out in organizational settings. Coauthor Linda Matuszewski conducted one such study with funding from the IMA® Foundation for Applied Research (now called IMA Research Foundation). Appearing in the 2010 issue (Volume 22) of the *Journal of Management Accounting Research*, "Honesty in Managerial Reporting: Is It Affected by Perceptions of Horizontal Equity?" is one of several studies in accounting in which student participants played the role of managers reporting to their employer. Participants knew the amount of actual costs that would be incurred on a project and were asked to submit a budget request. The employer would never know the actual costs. If the participant lied and the budget request exceeded actual costs, the participants kept the difference. This difference was personal gain for participants—at the expense of their employers. That is, the greater the lie, the more money the participants received.

Overall, Matuszewski's results are consistent with "Honesty in Managerial Reporitng," a study by John Evans, Lynn Hannan, Ranjani Krishnan, and Donald Moser in the October 2001 issue of *The Accounting Review.* Matuszewski's study shows that only a small proportion of people (15 percent) lied to maximize their wealth. A similar proportion of people were at the other end of the spectrum, with 19 percent behaving completely honestly. This left the vast majority (66 percent) in the middle—lying some and trading their desire to be honest against their desire for wealth.

At the two extremes, managers could assume the worst and develop expensive management controls to prevent and detect dishonesty, or they could assume the best and not develop any controls. Since most employees don't fall into either extreme, neither of these solutions is likely to be the most cost effective. Managers are left with the challenge of designing control systems for the majority of employees—those who have some desire to be honest but are also willing to lie to some extent. This is where the results of several other studies can be helpful, as they shed some light on factors within a company's control that influence whether an employee's behavior is closer to the honest or the dishonest end of the scale.

One factor is *vertical* fairness. This represents the relationship between employees and their organizations. In "Stealing in the Name of Justice: Informational and Interpersonal Moderators of Theft Reactions to Underpayment Inequity," Jerald Greenberg describes a study in which he promised two groups of research participants a certain level of pay for performing a low-skilled task (*Organizational Behavior and Human Decision Processes,* Volume 54, Issue 1, February 1993). Participants who were treated unfairly by being paid less than they were originally promised "stole" from the researcher, likely rationalizing that they were due the stolen amount. Participants who were given a reasonable explanation for why their pay was less than promised and received an apology from the researcher, however, stole less. Greenberg's work shows that an explanation and empathy can go a long way toward soothing hurt feelings—and reducing retaliation in firms.

Vertical fairness is critical—but it isn't the only element that matters. Look no further than *Strategic Finance's* Annual Salary Survey each June to know that horizontal fairness—how fairly people are treated compared to their peers—is also important. This was the main focus of Matuszewski's study, which demonstrated that participants' beliefs about changes in the *horizontal* fairness of their pay changed the honesty in their budgeting behavior. Participants in the study were paid a salary and received information about the salaries of other participants. When the horizontal fairness of pay declined, the change in honesty was the same, whether it occurred because of a decrease in the participant's own pay or an increase in others' pay. To make matters worse, this dishonest behavior is hard to undo. In Matuszewski's study, improvements in horizontal fairness resulting from decreases in others' pay didn't result in more honest behavior. Thus, being treated fairly right from the beginning is extremely important.

We aren't trying to minimize employees' personal responsibility for their actions. But research shows that when employees believe they haven't received what they are due, they will look for ways to recover what they believe they're owed. Accordingly, we believe that if top management designs fairness into its dealings with employees, it will eliminate this possible rationalization and cause employees to pursue honest behavior more frequently.

Frame

Another way to design honest behavior into organizations is to ensure that an organization clearly communicates that honesty is expected. When would an employee think that honest behavior isn't expected? Think of it this way: Imagine you're playing basketball. Is a head fake unethical? No, it's completely normal behavior because basketball is a competition, and misleading your opponent is expected. Imagine Kobe Bryant complaining that LeBron James cheated because he made a no-look pass. "Not fair! He looked the other way!" That isn't going to happen because Kobe understands they're competing against each other.

How is this relevant? Well, how often do your budgeting processes become framed as strategic competitions among employees and management rather than decisions with ethical implications? You're more likely to find dishonest behavior if employees believe that the budgeting process is expected to be competitive rather than collaborative, strategic rather than honest. That's what Frederick Rankin, Steven Schwartz, and Richard Young found in "The Effect of Honesty and Superior Authority on Budget Proposals" (*The Accounting Review,* July 2008). Participants completed a budgeting task similar to the task in Matuszewski's study. Those who were asked to honestly share their information about actual costs were more honest than those who were simply asked what portion of the profits should be returned to the company. This study suggests that, in the absence of formal controls, people will be more honest if you simply ask them to be!

Rankin, Schwartz, and Young's finding is particularly important given recent research about the costs and benefits of formal controls. In "When Formal Controls Undermine Trust and Cooperation," Margaret Christ, Karen Sedatole, Kristy Towry, and Myra Thomas suggest that employees sometimes view formal controls as a sign that employers question their competence and integrity, and this may undermine trust and cooperation (*Strategic Finance,* January 2008). To be clear, we aren't advocating doing away with all explicit formal controls. In circumstances in which formal controls aren't present or are too costly, Rankin, Schwartz, and Young show that some of the same benefits can be achieved by describing a task as an ethical dilemma, rather than a strategic competition, and asking for honesty.

Another effect that framing has in determining whether honest behavior is expected showed up in the large-scale fraud at Enron. Bennett Stewart suggests in "The Real Reasons Enron Failed" that Enron's managers were, in fact, paid to do dishonest things (*Journal of Applied Corporate Finance,* Volume 18, Issue, 2, Spring 2006). Stewart documents that performance at Enron was framed as an accounting game rather than as increasing the company's true economic value. In part, this involved manipulating internal performance measures to exclude any costs of capital. Stewart documents the use of EBITDA—the least accountable, most misleading indicator of corporate performance ever devised—by Enron executives who clearly knew better.

Why did they use this measure? Simple: Enron's performance measurement and compensation system, which included stock-based compensation, paid them to do so. Increases in Enron's stock price were driven in large part by—you guessed it—accounting performance. And we shouldn't be surprised when people do what firms pay them to do.

The greatest problem with poorly framed control systems is that, even when employees intend to be honest, a bad control system may discourage that employee from acting on that honest urge and *disable* that honesty. The challenge is for top managers to design control systems that *enable* honesty.

The Designed Honesty Model

Putting these research results together, we present the designed honesty model of organizational behavior (see Figure 1). The model shows that both fairness and frame contribute to designed honesty. Where should top management look to understand why employees aren't behaving honestly? That depends. If employees are grumbling about their working conditions or their pay—especially their pay relative to others within the organization—then they probably believe they aren't being treated fairly and may well be working the system to get what they believe is due them. On the other hand, if employees report conflicts between what they believe they should do and what they believe they're being asked and paid to do, then the culture and control system frame are probably the culprits, leading otherwise honest employees to feel like they are being encouraged to behave dishonestly.

The designed honesty model isn't intended to be complete—the factors that influence honesty and dishonesty are many and varied. As the research shows, most employees value honesty and fairness in addition to wealth and leisure and are influenced by all of these values when deciding whether to behave honestly. Since fairness and frame are within an organization's control to some extent, it's important for management to understand how these factors can contribute to honest behavior.

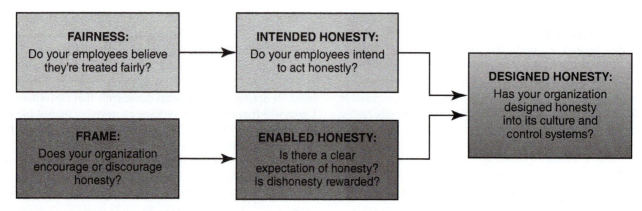

Figure 1   The designed honesty model.

Table 1   Six Key Steps toward Designing Honesty into Your Organization

1. Consider vertical and horizontal fairness when making compensation decisions
2. Fully explain compensation policies and procedures
3. Determine whether employees believe they are being paid fairly
4. Show (and feel!) empathy when tough compensation choices need to be implemented
5. Ask employees to be honest, and describe routine decisions as ethical dilemmas rather than strategic competitions
6. Review incentive plans to ensure they reward honest reporting of economic results

Therefore, in addition to attempting to hire the right people, we recommend that companies take the following steps to encourage employees to act on their intentions to be honest (see Table 1):

1. *Consider vertical and horizontal fairness when making compensation decisions.*

   Employees consider the fairness of their compensation from two perspectives—relative to their exchange with the company (vertical) and relative to the compensation of their peers (horizontal). Managers may be able to get a sense of the perceptions about the vertical fairness of compensation by considering employees' alternative employment opportunities. In today's culture of high turnover, it's reasonable to assume that employees are keeping their eye on the job market and asking "What could I make elsewhere?" But how often do managers consider their subordinates' opportunities when making compensation decisions? Incorporating this practice into the firm's periodic performance review system could help avoid the costs of dishonesty motivated by perceptions of vertical unfairness.

   From the horizontal perspective, although firms often have policies that discourage peers from sharing information about pay, we believe managers should assume that employees know how much money

their peers are making so should make an effort to compensate employees fairly compared to their peers.

2. *Fully explain compensation policies and procedures.*
   Fair doesn't necessarily imply equal. In cases where compensation isn't equal to an alternative employment opportunity or the pay a peer is receiving, detailed explanations may be especially important in helping employees evaluate whether their pay is fair. Communication strategies that help employees understand the justification for compensation policies can be extremely valuable. For instance, employees may be more likely to consider their compensation fair if managers explain the connection between the resources of their division and employee compensation.

3. *Determine whether employees believe they are being paid fairly.*
   Most large companies have periodic performance review systems in place, and it's through these systems that compensation decisions get communicated. Yet how many of these systems are two-way communication devices designed to determine whether employees believe they are being paid fairly? This data may be challenging to get, especially if employees fear

retaliation if they admit they don't believe they are being paid fairly. Managers may need to put themselves in their employees' shoes and pursue indirect methods for answering this question, such as anonymous surveys or hotline methods.

4. *Show (and feel!) empathy when tough compensation choices need to be implemented.*
Of course, managers won't always have the resources to give employees the compensation they want and feel they deserve. But empathy can have an impact on honesty, even when employees face an outcome they believe is unfair.

5. *Ask employees to be honest, and describe routine decisions as ethical dilemmas rather than strategic competitions.*
A logical first step in making it clear that you expect employees to be honest is the establishment of a corporate code of ethics, but even the best code won't be effective unless employees can see the connection between the code and their everyday activities. Think of it this way: Corporate planning doesn't stop with the development of a vision statement. Firms work toward the vision by identifying core competencies, developing organizational strategies, and translating these strategies into operating plans. In the same way, a company must develop strategies for ensuring honest behavior. The research suggests that one successful strategy would be to identify tasks that provide employees with opportunities to benefit from dishonesty and describe these tasks as ethical dilemmas rather than strategic competitions.

This suggestion is consistent with the findings in two 2011 studies published in the *Journal of Business Ethics* that identify factors that contribute to the effectiveness of corporate codes of ethics. Muel Kaptein found in "Toward Effective Codes: Testing the Relationship with Unethical Behavior" (Volume 99, No. 2, March 2011) that the quality of communication regarding a corporate code of ethics has a greater impact on reducing unethical behavior than the quantity of communication about the code. Put simply, it isn't enough to establish a code and talk about it a lot. The code must be accessible, clear, easy to understand, and useful for decision making. In the other study, "Determinants of the Effectiveness of Corporate Codes of Ethics: An Empirical Study" (Volume 101, No. 3, July 2011), Jang Singh found that a code's impact on behavior is determined in part by whether the code guides strategic planning and is useful in resolving ethical dilemmas in the marketplace.

6. *Review incentive plans to ensure they reward honest reporting of economic results.*
Both Kaptein's and Singh's studies also provide insight into the steps managers should take to ensure that their incentive plans promote honesty in the workplace. Singh found that codes are more effective when compliance with their provisions is a part of performance reviews and when there are real consequences for violations. Kaptein found that the most important factor in reducing unethical behavior was senior and local management's embedding of the corporate code of ethics within an organization. More specifically, employees are more likely to be honest when their managers are approachable positive role models who set reasonable performance targets that promote, rather than undermine, compliance with the corporate code of ethics. In addition, it's important that managers don't authorize violations of the code to meet business goals, are aware of the extent to which employees comply with (or violate) the code, and respond to violations appropriately.

To prevent the kind of financial reporting dishonesty that occurred at Enron and many other companies, we suggest that managers should also consider whether performance targets based on economic results are using measures less subject to manipulation than traditional financial accounting measures may be.

Steps Will Go a Long Way

While we can't guarantee that these steps will eliminate all dishonesty in the workplace, we believe that paying attention to the fairness of employees' compensation and highlighting the ethical dimension of certain decisions will go a long way toward designing honesty into your organization.

Critical Thinking

1. Why do some people behave dishonestly at work?
2. Using the Designed Honesty Model presented in the article, develop your own model and explain its strengths and weaknesses compared to the model presented in the article.
3. Pick out one of the "six key steps" toward designing honesty in an organization. Build arguments for and against the key step.
4. If you are a student in a class, engage in a debate for/against with another student concerning the key step you selected.

Create Central

www.mhhe.com/createcentral

Internet References

Forbes

http://www.forbes.com/sites/joefolkman/2013/11/18/how-to-make-your-organization-more-honest/

Houston Chronicle: Small Business

http://smallbusiness.chron.com/managerial-ethics-36425.html

Switch and Shift

http://switchandshift.com/honesty-the-secret-to-successful-organizations

CHRISTIAN MASTILAK, PhD, is an assistant professor of accountancy and business law in the Williams College of Business at Xavier University and a member of the North Cincinnati Chapter of IMA. You can reach Christian at (513) 745-3290 or mastilakc@xavier.edu. LINDA MATUSZEWSKI, PhD, is an assistant professor of accountancy in the College of Business at Northern Illinois University and a member of the Rockford Chapter of IMA. You can reach Linda at (815) 753-6379 or lmatus@niu.edu. FABIENNE MILLER, PhD, is an assistant professor of accounting in the School of Business at Worcester Polytechnic Institute and a member of the Worcester Chapter of IMA. You can reach Fabienne at (508) 831-6128 or fabienne@wpi.edu. ALEXANDER WOODS, PhD, is an assistant professor of accounting in the Mason School of Business at The College of William & Mary. You can reach Alex at (757) 221-2967 or alex.woods@mason.wm.edu.

Mastilak, Christian; Matuszewski, Linda; Miller, Fabienne; Woods, Alexander. From *Strategic Finance*, December 2011. Copyright © 2011 by Institute of Management Accountants-IMA. Reprinted by permission via Copyright Clearance Center.

Article   Prepared by: Eric Teoro, *Lincoln Christian University*

The CSR Litmus Test

Ask yourself some questions before blithely tossing around the term "Corporate Social Responsibility."

CHRIS MACDONALD

Learning Outcomes

After reading this article, you will be able to:

- Understand your own definition of corporate social responsibility (CSR).

- Question the value of CSR as a concept.

- Question what responsibilities businesses should fulfill.

I've complained *ad nauseum* about the fact that there's no clear, agreed-upon definition of CSR (Corporate Social Responsibility). Many definitions say something about "social contribution" or "giving back to the community." But just what that amounts to is up for grabs. It might mean something trivial, or it might mean something unfairly burdensome. In a forthcoming short article in *Canadian Business,* I riff on a recent *Globe and Mail* story about a South African winery that is working hard to face up to its slave-holding past. The winery's story serves as a nice example. The Solms-Delta winery's owners have done things like set up a museum in its wine cellar, and establish a trust for the benefit of workers. This is clearly admirable; other South African wineries generally prefer to sweep the past under a rug. But your particular reaction to the story of Solms-Delta is also a good way to delve into your own understanding of the term "Corporate Social Responsibility." Consider: Is highlighting the past as the company is doing an *obligation* owed to the winery's current employees? If so, then Solms-Delta is simply meeting its ethical obligations. But if this is not something owed to current employees, then it seems better cast as a matter of *social responsibility.* Right? To push this theme

further, let's move from the Solms-Delta example and consider a hypothetical company. Here's a litmus test to help you figure out your own views about CSR, and what those views imply. So imagine a company that does all of the following, with reasonable consistency:

- . . . makes a decent product that people feel improves their lives in some small but meaningful way;
- . . . treats employees fairly;
- . . . deals honestly with suppliers;
- . . . tries to do a decent job of building long-term shareholder value;
- . . . cleans up their messes, environmental, or otherwise;
- . . . does its best to follow all applicable laws, and trains and rewards employees suitably;
- . . . pays its taxes, making use of all relevant exemptions but not cynically seeking loopholes.

Next, if you consider yourself a fan of CSR, ask yourself this question: Would such a company count as a *socially responsible* company, in your books? Or is there something more it needs to do in order to garner that designation? Is the company ethically obligated to do something further? If your answer is "Yes, that's a socially responsible company!" then good for you. That's a very reasonable answer. But then you should ask yourself two questions. One, why are you attached to the label "CSR"? Why not just call them a company that does right, or that acts ethically? Why try to shoehorn all the good stuff listed above into a specific little box called "social responsibility"? If your answer is "No, they're still not giving back to the community!" then next you need to ask yourself *what more* and *why.* The company described above is engaging in voluntary, mutually advantageous transactions with customers, making those customers better off (by their own lights). It is doing something good in the world, and being conscientious about how it does it. That seems pretty decent. And whatever your answer is, taking this test should clarify both what your own views are, and perhaps why the term "CSR" is far less useful than it is popular. And whenever two people *think* they agree on the importance of CSR, each of them ought to doubt—or ask—whether they really share the *same understanding* of what social responsibility really means.

Critical Thinking

1. What responsibilities to the broader community do businesses have beyond providing their specific goods and services? Why?

2. As an employee, what, if any, social responsibilities are you obligated to fulfill? Why?

3. Debate with a fellow student/employee that businesses are obligated to give more to communities than their specific goods and services.

Create Central

www.mhhe.com/createcentral

Internet References

Houston Chronicle: Small Business
http://smallbusiness.chron.com/social-responsibility-advertising-52880.html

International Institute for Sustainable Development
https://www.iisd.org/business/issues/sr.aspx

Article

Prepared by: Eric Teoro, *Lincoln Christian University*

Five Steps to Better Ethical Decision Making

Feelings can put a check on rationalizing.

ARTHUR DOBRIN

Learning Outcomes

After reading this article, you will be able to:

- Improve your ethical decision-making.

- Understand several requirements of ethical decision-making.

The **first step** in making an ethical decision is to gather the facts. Try to be as neutral as possible in describing those facts, bearing in mind how inclined we all are to distorting information to benefit ourselves, so you have a tendency to overlook, distort, or stretch the facts to suit ourselves. But if the facts are wrong to begin with, our moral judgment is going to be clouded and lead us down the wrong path.

It is impossible to know all the facts about a situation. Consider how difficult it is to know the subject to which you are closest—yourself. It is amazing how others are able to point out things that you never see about yourself. So, imagine how much more difficult it is to really know another person or an event about which you don't have direct knowledge. Yet, you have to fill in the blanks as best you can when confronted with an ethical problem. You have to rely upon reasonable assumptions. For example, you may not know all the details about conditions in a factory, but you can make an educated guess based upon what we know about factories in general and what you know about the area in which the plant is located.

Facts by themselves mean little; they need interpretation. You want to understand what such facts mean in light of your own values, but you also want to understand what the facts mean to the other people involved. Consider the following situation. Joseph is married to Sabrina, but he is sleeping with Elizabeth. An important value for you may be sexual fidelity, but if Joseph lives in a polygamous society, you need to understand what his sleeping with Elizabeth means to Sabrina. It may mean something quite different from what you first supposed.

Step two is to make a prediction, a guess about the future. A prediction is based on facts that are relevant to the situation at hand: If you do this, you increase your chances of reaching the desired results. You can never know the future for certain, but some things are more probable than others. For example, if you hit someone, you are more likely to get hit back than if you smiled at that person, everything else being equal. Of course, there is always an element of uncertainty. The person you smiled at may be paranoid, for example. Yet, you have to take a guess and select the action that you think is most likely to cause good or most likely to avoid harm.

Step three is to identify your feelings. Some people call it intuition; some call it conscience. When our feelings have been cultivated by compassion, they sometimes highlight what our rational and conscious minds have overlooked. Feelings are one way to check to see whether you are rationalizing.

In **step four** ask whether you could live with yourself if you made that particular choice. Would you be willing to let other people know what you did? Would you feel worse or better about yourself? Would you feel guilty or ashamed? Or would you feel proud and wish that others would do the same under similar circumstances? Would you want everyone to act the way you did?

Finally, in **step five** you should be able to explain your reasons to other people and be willing to engage with others in a moral conversation about your choice. This is similar to the method scientists use as a way of advancing knowledge. They develop a hypothesis, then test it, reach a conclusion, and finally submit it to others in their field for scrutiny. You should be willing to do no less with your ethical judgments. Unlike science, however, the field of morality isn't confined to higher study. Like it or not, you are engaged in many moral situations in business. While scientists advance knowledge about the world by using the scientific method, you advance your moral knowledge by employing a sound process in making ethical judgments.

Critical Thinking

1. What do you think about each step—beneficial or waste of time? Why?

2. Develop an additional step one can take to improve ethical decision-making. Explain and defend your rationale for the step.

3. Provide an example of when you practiced or violated one of the steps. What were the results?

Create Central

www.mhhe.com/createcentral

Internet References

Fast Company
http://www.fastcompany.com/1297926/why-your-gut-more-ethical-your-brain

Global Ethics University
http://www.globalethicsuniversity.com/articles/guilttrip.htm

Good Morning! Your Moral Fiber Is Eroding by the Minute by Drake Bennett

15

Article   Prepared by: Eric Teoro, *Lincoln Christian University*

Good Morning! Your Moral Fiber Is Eroding by the Minute

Drake Bennett

Learning Outcomes

After reading this article, you will be able to:

- Understand how an individual's ethical self-control is depleted throughout the day.

- Recognize the need to recharge one's ability to exercise ethical self-control.

- Structure your day to deal with ethical challenges at the optimal time.

Right now, as I write this, I am at peak integrity, but with every minute that passes, my moral fiber is weakening, like a cereal flake in milk. I don't notice it, but if there are decisions or tasks requiring personal discipline, I should take care of them quickly—by this afternoon, I will be defenseless against my baser instincts.

So say Maryam Kouchaki and Isaac Smith, researchers into organizational behavior, in a new paper in the journal *Psychological Science*. The idea that people can be more or less moral at different times goes back to the earliest recorded stories people told about each other: Achilles is both merciless killer and tender friend, Dr. Jekyll is Mr. Hyde. What's notable about the hypothesis Kouchaki and Smith set out to prove is that a person's moral upstandingness erodes over the course of each day, broken down in a process as regular and as ineluctable as digestion.

The paper sets out to show the effects on moral decision making of a phenomenon called "ego depletion," an influential explanation of human behavior first advanced by the psychologist Roy Baumeister. The basic insight is that a person's store of self-control is finite, and can be depleted. Like a muscle, our self-control weakens when we use it and is restored when we rest it. In one of his best-known studies, Baumeister had subjects sit in a room with a bunch of chocolate cookies. Some

of them got to eat the cookies, others had to eat radishes. The subjects were later given a difficult math problem to solve, and the radish-eaters gave up sooner than the cookie-eaters. Concentration requires willpower, and they had already run down their willpower resisting the sweets.

It isn't just in artificially torturous situations dreamt up by psychologists that we exhaust our willpower, though. It happens all the time in real life. Every decision, no matter how small, uses up some of it—what to wear to work, what to eat for breakfast, whether to tell a white lie about why you're late for a meeting. A person can minimize those decisions in an attempt to husband one's decision-making capacity—President Obama, citing the ego depletion literature, wears only gray or blue suits for this reason—but one can't escape all of them. Moving through one's day, there are inevitably a host of small decisions demanding to be made.

To the extent that acting ethically is a matter of mastering the temptation to do the wrong thing, Baumeister's radish-eaters would also be more likely to cheat or lie than those who hadn't already had to resist gustatory temptation. Or if they had less of a chance to replenish their reserves of self-control: Other research has shown that less sleep is correlated with less-ethical behavior in a workplace.

Kouchaki and Smith's study set out to see whether that steady onslaught of small daily decisions means that people are inevitably more moral in the morning, when their self-regulatory resources haven't yet been taxed, than they are in the afternoon. To a dramatic extent, the researchers found that they were. In one study, test subjects were randomly divided into a morning group and an afternoon group and given a chance to lie to earn more money. The participants in the afternoon group were 50 percent more likely to lie than those in the morning group. Given a math test on which they could easily cheat, subjects in a second study cheated on nearly twice as many questions if they took the test in the afternoon than if they took it in the morning.

Asked on the phone if he has changed anything in his own life because of his finding, Smith said he hasn't. Still, he thinks there are ways to mitigate the effect. He points out that work by Baumeister and others has shown that, just as it does with real muscles, eating—like rest—helps replenish the strength of our decision muscle, so naps and snacks can help slow the transition to afternoon's Mr. Hyde. Also in the paper, he and Kouchaki suggest that "morally relevant tasks should be deliberately ordered throughout the day. Perhaps organizations, for instance, need to be more vigilant about combating the unethical behavior of customers (or employees) in the afternoon than in the morning."

Critical Thinking

1. What do you think of the hypothesis that one's ability to make ethical decisions or to behave ethically can be depleted throughout the day? Defend your position.

2. What steps can you take to recharge your ethical "muscles"? What steps can organizations take to recharge the ethical muscles of their members?

3. Think of ethical challenges you typically face. What specific changes should you make to improve your ethical decision-making and behavior regarding those challenges?

Create Central

www.mhhe.com/createcentral

Internet References

American Psychological Association
https://www.apa.org/helpcenter/willpower-overview.aspx

The New York Times: Magazine
http://www.nytimes.com/2011/08/21/magazine/do-you-suffer-from-decision-fatigue.html?pagewanted=all&_r=2&

Article   Prepared by: Eric Teoro, *Lincoln Christian University*

What's at the Core of Corporate Wrongdoing?

To believe that the people who commit fraud are different from us might make us feel safe. But real safety comes from building an organization that stops these acts before they can take place.

ELEANOR BLOXHAM

Learning Outcomes

After reading this article, you will be able to:

- Understand the importance of corporate governance on the establishment of an ethical culture.

- Recognize personal traits that can lead to unethical behavior.

Fortune—Dennis Levine, who lectured an NYU MBA ethics class as part of his community service many years ago, described the mentality that led to his insider trading conviction as a mentality of having to win the next game, competing with oneself for the next victory, where enough was never enough.

His explanation is applicable to both individuals and entire corporate cultures, such as MF Global (MFGLQ) and Olympus, where losses were allegedly buried from public view on purpose.

But Levine's explanation doesn't address why enough is never enough. What underlies the motivations to hide losses? And why does it often take a very rude awakening for a person (or a company) to change?

What has befallen Olympus has been chalked up to an obedience culture, a management team that was "rotten at the core," and a board "of yes men." MF Global's case has been explained away by Jon Corzine's hubris. But if we examine, rather than impugn, Corzine's motives and those of the board and executives at Olympus, we will realize how these individuals' actions relate to you and me.

As almost any good board member will tell you, the responsibility for corporate culture, or what is commonly referred to as "tone at the top," begins with the board. Good board members monitor the CEO and corporate culture by meeting not only with the CEO but also with other members of a company's management team in social settings, on site visits, in executive sessions without other members of management present, and in regular board and committee meetings. They don't just listen to management speeches: they read body language, observe interactions, and view facilities. They look at the contents of whistle blower and customer hotline call-in logs, employee surveys, performance evaluations, and compensation decisions. They carefully and systematically gauge the level of healthy dissent and openness to discuss troubling situations and imperfect solutions.

This is critical work at the top of a company but necessary throughout it as well. Why? Because there can be many cultures inside one company, a fact that anyone who has considered transferring from one department to another well recognizes.

No matter where in the hierarchy you sit, if you are a member of management, you too should be monitoring the culture of the groups that report to you using the techniques that great boards use. And some insights into individual human personality, including your own, can help you decide what to look for.

Perhaps you are a high achiever who, like many other high achievers, would describe, in private, that some of the influences that originally pushed you have negative undertones. Your upbringing may have caused you to feel your accomplishments were never enough—or you may have excelled to avoid the pain of others' judgments. Your awareness of these pressures is helpful because you can spot them in others, recognizing that, if left unchecked, they can lead to unethical behavior.

Wise-board recruitment requires the selection of thoughtful, high achieving board members who can understand and balance the CEO's natural motivations. These board members recognize the powerful influence of self-preservation when it comes time to publicly admit failure, and the internal battle to fight feelings of inadequacy. Armed with this awareness, savvy board members help less secure CEOs build safe cultures that allow admission of failure, healthy risk-taking, and innovative expression.

The deeper motivations of individuals at Olympus and MF Global are not foreign to students of human nature. To believe that those people are different from us is appealing because such beliefs make us feel safe. But real safety comes from recognizing these traits in others and ourselves and constructing an organization with a culture that can balance rather than ignore these all-too-human tendencies.

Critical Thinking

1. At what level in an organization rests the responsibility for establishing an ethical corporate culture? Why?
2. Using the Internet, find examples of an ethical corporate culture and an unethical corporate culture. What differentiates the two corporate cultures? Why is one firm ethical and the other unethical?
3. Two companies are mentioned in the article—Olympus and MF Global. Outline for class discussion the critical aspects of each firm's corporate culture which may have led to each firm's alleged corporate wrongdoing.
4. If you were a manager, what safeguards would you establish to ensure for an ethical corporate culture?

Create Central

www.mhhe.com/createcentral

Internet References

Corporate Crime Reporter
http://www.corporatecrimereporter.com/news/200/a-recklessness-standard-for-corporate-executive-wrongdoing/

Forbes
http://www.forbes.com/sites/forbesleadershipforum/2012/04/18/how-to-find-and-stop-fraud-within-your-organization/

ELEANOR BLOXHAM is CEO of The Value Alliance and Corporate Governance Alliance (http://thevaluealliance.com), a board advisory firm.

Unit 2

UNIT

Prepared by: Eric Teoro, *Lincoln Christian University*

Ethical Issues and Dilemmas in the Workplace

An ethical issue can be defined as a situation in which a person or group of individuals needs to choose between alternatives, and the need for those alternatives to be assessed as being either morally right or wrong. Typically, ethical issues focus on the conflict between ethical and unethical behavior. An ethical dilemma, on the other hand, refers to a situation in which an individual or group of individuals needs to make a choice between moral requirements. As such, ethical dilemmas pose more complex problems. Regardless of the choice an actor or group of actors makes, they risk violating other ethical principles. Both ethical issues and ethical dilemmas occur within organizational settings. It is imperative, therefore, that managers, employees, and students recognize different courses of action, and determine the ethicality of those courses.

The articles in this unit represent a variety of ethical issues and dilemmas. Should doctors accept gifts from pharmaceutical companies? Does it matter if they provide services to those companies? Should employees blow the whistle when they are aware of corporate wrongdoing? What if that wrongdoing is not illegal? How should such employees navigate the competing claims of loyalty to an employer and the common good? What if blowing the whistle hurts innocent employees? Some of the articles in this unit examine the ethical consistency of businesses.

Can a company be considered ethical if it promotes ethical behavior in one area, but apparently fails to do so in another? Is a company unethical if it does not comply to calls for more stringent employee safety standards when enforcement of current standards could suffice? How should one view a multinational corporation that initiates an internal investigation of corruption within a subsidiary? Which should be given greater weight—the self-initiated investigation or the existent corruption?

Several articles specifically focus on employee behavior. What are the potential long-term effects of apparently minor ethical infractions like stealing a pen at work? How should an employee handle a request from a boss when fulfilling that request would violate the employee's conscience? Other articles discuss an array of topics such as the ethical implications of developing and using intelligent autonomous machines, the nature of executive perks, sexual harassment, and sexual discrimination. They raise questions concerning the rights and responsibilities of employers and employees regarding healthcare costs, the timing of layoffs, and the timing of a generic drug entry into the market. Many of the articles offer advice on creating an ethical workplace, for example instituting safeguards against fraud, lowering the potential of retaliation lawsuits, instilling values throughout an organization, and providing ethical decision-making training.

Article   Prepared by: Eric Teoro, *Lincoln Christian University*

Morals and the Machine

As robots grow more autonomous, society needs to develop rules to manage them.

THE ECONOMIST

Learning Outcomes

After reading this article, you will be able to:

- Describe ethical implications of developing and using intelligent autonomous machines.

- Describe the three laws of robotics: determine responsibility for actions of robotics, ensure embedded ethical systems are widely supported, and improve collaboration among various stakeholders regarding the ethics of robotics.

In the classic science-fiction film *2001*, the ship's computer, HAL, faces a dilemma. His instructions require him both to fulfil the ship's mission (investigating an artifact near Jupiter) and to keep the mission's true purpose secret from the ship's crew. To resolve the contradiction, he tries to kill the crew.

As robots become more autonomous, the notion of computer-controlled machines facing ethical decisions is moving out of the realm of science fiction and into the real world. Society needs to find ways to ensure that they are better equipped to make moral judgments than HAL was.

A Bestiary of Robots

Military technology, unsurprisingly, is at the forefront of the march toward self-determining machines (see Technology Quarterly). Its evolution is producing an extraordinary variety of species. The Sand Flea can leap through a window or onto a roof, filming all the while. It then rolls along on wheels until it needs to jump again. RiSE, a six-legged robo-cockroach, can climb walls. LS3, a dog-like robot, trots behind a human over rough terrain, carrying up to 180 kg of supplies. SUGV, a briefcase-sized robot, can identify a man in a crowd and follow him. There is a flying surveillance drone the weight of a wedding ring, and one that carries 2.7 tons of bombs.

Robots are spreading in the civilian world, too, from the flight deck to the operating theatre. Passenger aircraft have long been able to land themselves. Driverless trains are commonplace. Volvo's new V40 hatchback essentially drives itself in heavy traffic. It can brake when it senses an imminent collision, as can Ford's B-Max minivan. Fully self-driving vehicles are being tested around the world. Google's driverless cars have clocked up more than 250,000 miles in America, and Nevada has become the first state to regulate such trials on public roads. In Barcelona a few days ago, Volvo demonstrated a platoon of autonomous cars on a motorway.

As they become smarter and more widespread, autonomous machines are bound to end up making life-or-death decisions in unpredictable situations, thus assuming—or at least appearing to assume—moral agency. Weapons systems currently have human operators "in the loop," but as they grow more sophisticated, it will be possible to shift to "on the loop" operation, with machines carrying out orders autonomously.

As that happens, they will be presented with ethical dilemmas. Should a drone fire on a house where a target is known to be hiding, which may also be sheltering civilians? Should a driverless car swerve to avoid pedestrians if that means hitting other vehicles or endangering its occupants? Should a robot involved in disaster recovery tell people the truth about what is happening if that risks causing a panic? Such questions have led to the emergence of the field of "machine ethics," which aims to give machines the ability to make such choices appropriately—in other words, to tell right from wrong.

One way of dealing with these difficult questions is to avoid them altogether, by banning autonomous battlefield robots and requiring cars to have the full attention of a human driver at all times. Campaign groups such as the International Committee for Robot Arms Control have been formed in opposition to the growing use of drones. But autonomous robots could do much more good than harm. Robot soldiers would not commit rape, burn down a village in anger or become erratic decision-makers amid the stress of combat. Driverless cars are very likely to be safer than ordinary vehicles, as autopilots have made planes safer. Sebastian Thrun, a pioneer in the field, reckons driverless cars could save 1 m lives a year.

Instead, society needs to develop ways of dealing with the ethics of robotics—and get going fast. In America states have been scrambling to pass laws covering driverless cars, which have been operating in a legal grey area as the technology runs ahead of legislation. It is clear that rules of the road are required in this difficult area, and not just for robots with wheels.

The best-known set of guidelines for robo-ethics are the "three laws of robotics" coined by Isaac Asimov, a science-fiction writer, in 1942. The laws require robots to protect humans, obey orders, and preserve themselves, in that order. Unfortunately, the laws are of little use in the real world. Battlefield robots would be required to violate the first law. And Asimov's robot stories are fun precisely because they highlight the unexpected complications that arise when robots try to follow his apparently sensible rules. Regulating the development and use of autonomous robots will require a rather more elaborate framework. Progress is needed in three areas in particular.

Three Laws for the Laws of Robotics

First, laws are needed to determine whether the designer, the programmer, the manufacturer, or the operator is at fault if an autonomous drone strike goes wrong or a driverless car has an accident. In order to allocate responsibility, autonomous systems must keep detailed logs so that they can explain the reasoning behind their decisions when necessary. This has implications for system design: it may, for instance, rule out the use of artificial neural networks, decision-making systems that learn from example rather than obeying predefined rules.

Second, where ethical systems are embedded into robots, the judgments they make need to be ones that seem right to most people. The techniques of experimental philosophy, which studies how people respond to ethical dilemmas, should be able to help. Last, and most important, more collaboration is required between engineers, ethicists, lawyers, and policy-makers, all of whom would draw up very different types of rules if they were left to their own devices. Both ethicists and engineers stand to benefit from working together: ethicists may gain a greater understanding of their field by trying to teach ethics to machines, and engineers need to reassure society that they are not taking any ethical short cuts.

Technology has driven mankind's progress, but each new advance has posed troubling new questions. Autonomous machines are no different. The sooner the questions of moral agency they raise are answered, the easier it will be for mankind to enjoy the benefits that they will undoubtedly bring.

Critical Thinking

1. What are the three laws of robotics?
2. What are the three laws for the laws of robotics mentioned in the article? Discuss each of the proposed laws and take a pro or con position for each law.
3. Using the Internet, read articles about the emergence of the field of machine ethics. Be prepared to explain to the class the essence of this new field.

Create Central

www.mhhe.com/createcentral

Internet References

New Scientist
   http://www.newscientist.com/article/mg22329863.700-ethical-trap-robot-paralysed-by-choice-of-who-to-save.html#.VCoeGRYzy2x
New Statesman
   http://www.newstatesman.com/future-proof/2014/05/week-un-going-debate-ethics-killer-robots
The New Yorker
   http://www.newyorker.com/news/news-desk/moral-machines

Article Prepared by: Eric Teoro, *Lincoln Christian University*

"Pay-to-delay" Pharmaceutical Deals Smack of Illegal Collusion

EDITORIAL BOARD

Learning Outcomes

After reading this article, you will be able to:

- Understand issues involved in drug patents and competition of generic drugs.

- Understand the nature of "pay-to-delay" practices.

In 2006 Solvay Pharmaceuticals, the maker of the testosterone-therapy drug AndroGel, settled a dispute with a group of generic pharmaceutical companies, agreeing to allow would-be competitors into the market in 2015, 5 years before the AndroGel patent expires. So how is this bad for consumers in search of cheaper drugs?

In fact, the Federal Trade Commission (FTC) will argue Monday before the Supreme Court that this settlement and all others like it are so obviously anticompetitive that they should be presumed illegal. And the FTC has a very good case.

The reason lies in the fact that the generic pharmaceutical companies also agreed to take millions in cash from Solvay as part of the settlement. That arrangement, the FTC argues, stinks of illegal collusion—without which generic versions of the drug might have entered the market even earlier.

If a generic pharmaceutical company wants to introduce its own version of a brand-name drug without waiting for the relevant patent to expire, it can file a claim with the Food and Drug Administration, explaining why the patent is invalid or otherwise shouldn't apply. The brand-name drug firm can then challenge the generic company in court, a proceeding that, if it goes in the generic's direction, would lead to the near-immediate sale of a low-priced, off-brand version of the drug to consumers. But because litigation brings risks to both sides, many of these proceedings end in settlements. These involve an agreement on a date when generics can be introduced. Sometimes, they also involve the brand-name drugmaker paying its would-be competitor immense sums of cash.

What is the brand-name producer paying for? Valuable time, the FTC says. The brand-name company makes huge profit margins when it has no competition. So it's in its interest to pay potential competitors a slice to keep generic firms out of the market longer. Those potential competitors, meanwhile, get enriched simply by delaying their entry. If companies can effectively maintain monopoly pricing for a while longer and split up the profits by way of legal settlements, generics firms are less likely to push for competition to begin at the earliest possible date. Both sides make money in the interim, but consumers pay the price. It's hard to think of a circumstance in which that sort of dealmaking wouldn't indicate a violation of the spirit of the nation's antitrust laws.

The pharmaceutical industry responds that settlements involving big cash payments often still result in the entry of generic competitors years before patents expire. Couldn't taking that option off the table hurt consumers?

Yet there would still be opportunity for settlements, just those in which one side's interests are fully aligned with those of consumers. The brand-name companies would seek to delay the entry of competitors; would-be competitors would seek only to speed it up. The resulting deals would better reflect the merits of their various claims, including the strength of the patents at issue.

The FTC, anyway, isn't saying that the court should ban cash payments entirely, just that the parties involved should have to show that they aren't anticompetitive. That strikes us as a reasonable safeguard against a clear opportunity for collusion.

Critical Thinking

1. Should patent-holding drug companies be allowed to delay the market entrance of generic substitutes by competitors? Why or why not?

2. Is the practice of "pay-to-delay" unethical? Why or why not?

3. Do consumers have a right to generic alternative drugs before associated patents expire? Why or why not?

Create Central

www.mhhe.com/createcentral

Internet References

Competition Policy International

http://www.willkie.com/~/media/Files/Publications/2012/06/Eleventh%20Circuit%20Rejects%20the%20Strength%20of%20a%20Paten/Files/EleventhCircuitRejectsTheStrengthpdf/FileAttachment/Eleventh_Circuit_Rejects_The_Strength

Forbes

http://www.forbes.com/sites/matthewherper/2013/08/11/how-the-staggering-cost-of-inventing-new-drugs-is-shaping-the-future-of-medicine/

SheppardMullin

http://www.intellectualpropertylawblog.com/archives/supreme-court-confirms-that-generic-drug-manufacturers-can-challenge-brand-name-use-code-descriptions-in-patent-litigation.html

Article   Prepared by: Eric Teoro, *Lincoln Christian University*

Unfair Business Practices

Are Perks Dividing Your Company?

VADIM LIBERMAN

Learning Outcomes

After reading this article, you will be able to:

- Describe the nature of perks and their impact on employees.

- Recognize the role perceptions play in employee satisfaction.

- Describe the concepts of fairness and inequality within organizational contexts.

It Begins with a Cup of Coffee.
Suppose your company were to restrict access to the corporate coffee machine to senior executives only. Why? Because busy bigwigs shouldn't have to wait with plebeians for caffeine jolts. Sure, assistants to assistants also battle endless to-do lists, but let's be blunt: Regardless of who prizes whose time more, a senior leader's minutes are certainly more valuable to the organization. Thus, for everyone else, there's a Starbucks around the corner.

An executive coffee policy—absurd, right? But replace coffee with a company jet, and the ridiculous suddenly appears sensible. Maybe.

What might start with coffee and end with air travel bursts with a cornucopia of corporate perquisites: car allowances, country-club memberships, home security, financial-planning assistance, corner offices, telecommuting, reserved parking, reserved restrooms, and reserved dining rooms. Reserved— that is, nonmonetary compensation restricted to individuals or groups based on any number of criteria.

Perks are unlike benefits, which employers offer to *all* workers: medical insurance, a communal cafeteria, on-site dry cleaning, a foosball table, several colorful items that pop up when you Google "Google benefits," and, thankfully, coffee. Whereas benefits can distinguish your company from others, perks mainly differentiate workers *within* your organization. And because the list of possible perks stretches wide, so can the gulf between your firm's haves and have-nots.

Who Gets and Who Doesn't

What does it mean to treat people fairly? Ultimately, that's the central question here. While protestors pose it to Wall Street from the outside, it's worth asking it of corporations from the inside. Perks are ideal conduits to get at an answer because they're the most visible manifestations of how your organization sets people apart. (You may not know others' salaries, but you're painfully aware that the company isn't paying for you to tee off at the club this weekend.)

How do—how ought—you draw lines between who will have and who will have not? A common reply: Distribute perks that jibe with your company's culture. Obviously.

Not. Accepting this illogic legitimizes corporate-cultural relativism, whereby your company's approach is best because your organization says it is.

"Companies should ask, 'Which perks would align best with the culture we're trying to create?'" says Gaye Lindfors, a Minnesota-based consultant and former HR director at Northwest Airlines. Put differently, apportioning perks is not a *consequence* of but how you *create* corporate culture. "Actually, perks deserve more attention than other business decisions when defining culture because they are so personal," adds Jennifer Robin, a research fellow at the Great Place to Work Institute, a research, consulting, and training firm.

What do people deserve? When do they deserve it? Why do they deserve it? What does it mean to *deserve* anything? Your answers will shape your culture.

Yes, this is more philosophy than it is HR strategy. There's scarce research on corporate perks that pushes beyond describing to prescribing, which means that an HR director who wants to get perks right must aim to turn philosophy into practice.

What do people deserve? When do they deserve it? Why do they deserve it? What does it mean to deserve anything? Your answers will shape your culture.

Here's how to ponder who flies in first class, who's in economy; who'll play golf, who'll watch it on TV; who gets an office with a window, and who gets an office with a window working from home. Who gets and who doesn't.

Diminished Expectations

If only it were as simple as coffee. As the competition dangles more, and more valuable, shiny things to recruit and retain, you're perpetually forced to play a Darwinian game of Keeping Up With the Googles. Don't want to play? You'll still lose. You won't make best-places-to-work lists; talent will head elsewhere.

You've witnessed this with skyrocketing executive compensation. To an extent, similar criticisms apply regarding perquisites. "Just ten years ago, executive perks were based on competitive practices almost exclusively," explains Don Lindner, executive-compensation practice leader at World at Work, a provider of HR education, conferences, and research. "They would get out of hand." It took only one CEO down the street to get a new car to compel other corporate boards to channel Oprah: And *you* get a car, and *you* get a car, and *you* get a car. And you, Karen Kozlowski, get a Tyco-sponsored $2 million birthday party. And you, Jack Welch, get an $11 million GE apartment. Legalities aside, the dotcom era produced a golden age of perks.

Today, it's more of a copper age. Businesses began seriously slashing perks 5 years ago, after the SEC mandated disclosure of perks and personal benefits with an aggregate value of more than $10,000, down from $50,000. "Other compensation," the proxy-statement pay category that includes perks, fell from $338,815 to $228,929 between 2005 and 2010 for the top 100 CEOs, according to compensation-analysis firm Equilar.

A bigger factor than the prospect of having to publicly defend the indefensible: the economy. Now that just having a job feels like a perk, it's unsurprising that the number of companies granting perks to CEOs has slipped, from 90 percent of organizations in 2009 to 78 percent in 2010 to just 62 percent in 2011, according to compensation trackers at Compdata Surveys. "The nature of perks is nowhere near what we've seen in

the past," says Brett Good, senior district president at Robert Half International, a consulting and staffing firm. Good predicts that even when the economy gathers steam, no one should expect companies to start picking up birthday-party tabs. Instead, anticipate a continued rise in things you won't see on proxies: hoteling, flex workweeks, job-sharing, and other work/life perks that, for many workers, aren't perks at all.

Everyone Deserves (to Desire) a Trophy

So what does a CEO perk look like these days? In 2010, the most prevalent were supplemental life insurance (offered to 29 percent of CEOs), company cars (24 percent), and club memberships (22 percent), according to Compdata. There is, after all, cachet attached to perks perceived to have high monetary value—which begs another question: Does value reside in the perk or its status?

Decades ago, where you peed signified who you were. An executive-restroom key unlocked far more than a physical door. Where you urinate today typically holds less exclusivity, but some perks, like a company car, still carry trophy value. Except: Don't title and salary (known or perceived) already sufficiently convey status?

In a 2006 paper, "Are Perks Purely Managerial Excess?," University of Chicago B-school professor Raghuram Rajan and Harvard Business School's Julie Wulf write: "There are only so many corner offices or so many places on the corporate jet, and who gets them can signal the recipient's place in the pecking order better than cash compensation can." Does a leader also need a corporate Mercedes to flaunt feathers?

Rajan and Wulf speculate that "the CEO needs to be offered perks (in fact, the most perks) so as to legitimize the status attached to the perk: a prestigious country club membership would not convey as much status for other executives if the CEO did not belong to it." However, this fails to address perks that accrue only to the CEO, and it doesn't justify something like club memberships overall.

Interestingly, the authors reference the military, where medals confer status. They ask, "[W]hy can corporations not invent their own medals or ribbons, which will cost them virtually nothing, instead of paying with perks?"

Good question. Employers invented their own ribbons long ago—plaques and certificates. They don't convey status—you can't park a framed certificate in front of the HQ building, in a space emblazoned with your title—so much as reward performance. Rewards, like plaques, gift certificates, and other recognition tools, don't typically stoke feelings of injustice the way perks do because they seem more meritocratic. You do something well: You get something good. Perks, by contrast, accrue regardless of job performance.

Of course, when asked, corporations invariably insist that they link most perks to performance. Of those that actually mean it, some may even believe it. But what do they believe?

If—*if!*—considering performance at all, companies don't grant top officers perks such as subsidized apartments and business-class plane tickets with the goal of motivating low-level daydreamers. That's not to say a mailroom clerk isn't fantasizing right now about reclining, Prada-clad feet perched atop a big desk twenty floors up, but that's a mere side effect of executive perks. Rather, we think of perks more as components of compensation packages that aim to optimize the work of leaders.

Truthfully, Rajan and Wulf's question about perks versus rewards is a nonstarter. Companies can—and should—use each differently. One may lead to better performance, the other recognizes it, and it probably makes little difference which you offer first to improve performance. "It's management's job to start the chicken-and-egg cycle," recommends Jennifer Robin.

The more relevant issue: If a car, or any perk, were turned into a reward instead—that is, something you got as a consequence of rather than a precursor to doing a good job—would that impact performance? It's a tough question to answer because most companies don't dangle such extravagant rewards in front of anyone outside of the sales department. (Then, too, all this assumes that a link between perks and performance actually exists. For more on making—or not—the business case for perks.)

The Price of Perks

None of us works for a corporation just for the fun of it. We're all paid salaries. Some of us get bonuses. A few of us enjoy stock options. We're all acutely aware of the numbers on our pay stubs—and what those numbers can buy. So why view perks differently than cash?

Because perks have a different perception value than cash. We emotionally connect to perks in ways we don't to dollars because we think of them less as standards and more as extras, and who doesn't like a little—or a lot of—extra? It's as though we're getting something for free—even if it's preposterous to stick a "free" tag on something over which companies and individuals haggle.

We emotionally connect to perks in ways we don't to dollars because we think of them less as standards and more as extras, and who doesn't like a little—or a lot of—extra?

It's often easier for companies, particularly those strapped for cash—as well as candidates and employees—to negotiate perquisites rather than salary. "You can't replace big chunks of

pay with perks," points out Don Lindner, "but if you're paying an executive at the median instead of the sixtieth percentile, then offering perks may be a way to keep that person."

Then again, because the greater currency of perks lies in perception, some corporations hesitate to offer them in lieu of cash. A country-club membership costs pennies next to a $20 million pay package, but on a proxy statement, those can be some contentious coins. For example, in 2008, General Motors CEO Rick Wagoner flew to Washington to ask Congress for a bailout aboard the company's $36 million jet. Twenty grand, the trip's approximate cost, pales in comparison to the $12 billion Wagoner asked from Uncle Sam, but it's probably a salary for someone's uncle Sam.

"If you're getting paid $2 million and the proxy reveals that you're also getting a $5,000 financial-planning allowance, it gives the impression that you're piggish," argues Steve Gross, a senior partner at HR consultancy Mercer. To fend off criticism, he recommends, the company should just increase salary by the perk's pecuniary cost.

And yet, the more firms pay execs, the more perks they give them. This indicates not only the obvious—some companies boast deeper pockets than others—but another explanation posited by Rajan and Wulf: "A senior executive may not be willing to pay out of his own pocket for executive jet travel if it were not offered as a perk since his private value for it may be far smaller than the benefit to the company."

Even so, not everyone is convinced that a person joins or leaves an organization based on first-class rides in planes, trains, and automobiles. "Perks make up only 5 to 8 percent of an executive-compensation package," Lindner explains. "They're not going to make the difference in recruiting or retention."

Agrees Gaye Lindfors: "People don't go to organizations and stay because of perks. What keeps them there is a feeling of engagement."

Because You're Worth It?

Till now, an 800-pound gorilla has been lurking in this article—the entitled executive. Though no enterprise will cop to basing actions on entitlement, "it's probably the main basis on which companies continue to make decisions about perks," reveals Laura Sejen, global practice leader for rewards at Towers Watson. The problem isn't that people feel entitled to perks, it's that—

Actually, that *is* part of the problem. Steve Gross recalls working with an executive who demanded matching corporate sedans for him and his wife. The employee explained that should his car need repairs, his wife's would be a backup. "He was obviously a pig," Gross says.

"People begin to assume that perks are like benefits," adds Jennifer Rosenzweig, research director at The Forum, an HR consultancy affiliated with Northwestern University.

"Companies have to be careful about getting into patterns of people expecting them."

"Hey," you might be thinking, "I worked hard to get to where I am, so damn it, I deserve a club membership." But you'd be confusing perks for position with perks for performance, which aren't perks but rewards. Also, you'd have to be high to think a high title accompanies high performance. A glance around your company should confirm the two are hardly synonymous. "But hold on again—I earn more money than others, meaning the company values me more, so give me my friggin' club membership too!" That argument would hold if cash and perks traded in equivalent currency, but since they don't, entitlement by any other name is still greed.

So: If employees who feel entitled are just part of the problem, the other part are the companies that inflate their egos. In the end, it's not someone who thinks the "C" in his title warrants entitlement but the organization that deserves an "F" for perpetuating it. The problem, of course, is that the "C" people run the company. It's a lot to ask the entitled to put down the Kool-Aid.

But that doesn't mean we shouldn't ask. "You face a challenge then," Sejen cautions. "If perks are not about hierarchy, you'll have a hard time defending why you've decided to make Person X eligible and Person Y ineligible." It is not, however, impossible. "As long as there are development opportunities and encouragement to get into higher positions, then differential perks based on one's position are less important," explains Jennifer Robin. Here's another way to look at it: If you give a perk to someone who feels entitled, that's OK—as long you don't grant the perk *because* someone feels entitled. Otherwise, adds Robin, "you create an environment of haves and have-nots, which can be damaging because that kind of mentality will work against you in the long run."

Entitlement by any other name is still greed.

Fairness Through Inequality

Let's be real: No workplace ever could be completely egalitarian.

No workplace ever *should* be completely egalitarian.

Many of us assume the fact of the former to justify the latter, but even if total egalitarianism were impossible, shouldn't we at least earnestly push toward it and not let perfect stand in the way of good? And isn't workplace egalitarianism, you know, *good*?

"You don't want to create perceptions and resentment that top people are getting more at the expense of everyone else," says Steve Gross. "It's like asking me to go from an office to a

---

The Proof is in the Perk

Businesses aren't as eager today to offer perks simply because the competition does. Instead, there must be a "business case," says practically every observer. But doesn't vying for talent serve a business purpose? You probably hear the business-case imperative so often that you nod approvingly without pausing to ponder the term's meaning or relevance. *Because you know it.* A perk must aid performance, engagement, productivity, *business*.

Indeed, "companies are now being more thoughtful about what's appropriate," says World at Work's Don Lindner. "Today, most companies are asking, 'Do we really need to offer a country-club membership?' They can't answer that, so we're seeing a lot of perks go away because they can't be shown to support attraction or retention."

Yet one in four organizations still offer CEOs club memberships. Do they have a business case? Yes, no, and maybe. It's no secret that a company can rationalize anything—everything—with a business purpose. Perhaps club memberships allow CEOs unique opportunities to broker deals. Perhaps not. Maybe the perk really does attract and keep talent. Maybe not. The point is, dig deep enough and you'll always unearth a business case for a perk. The real question is whether you can *prove* it. "If you can't show how perks support business strategy, you shouldn't be using them," Lindner suggests.

The "proof," however, tends to be anecdotal and correlative, at best. That doesn't mean you should dismiss such data or trash your perks. Rather, an absence of harder evidence likely reinforces what Albert Einstein knew: "Not everything that counts can be counted."

—V.L.

---

cubicle while my boss keeps his giant office. 'If I'm making a sacrifice, where's yours?' The more perception of unfairness, the less likely you'll have engaged workers."

You don't want to create perceptions and resentment that top people are getting more at the expense of everyone else.

Sure, pay and other factors already buttress office classism, but this article isn't *The Communist Manifesto*, and just because divisions exist in the workplace doesn't imply we shouldn't strive to minimize—or at least not maximize—them via perks.

While some organizations have eschewed perks in the spirit of fairness (see "The End of the Perk?"), others use them to promote fair treatment. But what does that mean? It does *not* mean that everyone is equal, or even equally valuable. After all, each of us has different strengths and weaknesses. So when your CEO claims he values every employee, he's not lying. He's simply failing to add "just not equally."

Instead, think of fairness as equal consideration of workers' interests, or needs. For example, Google's benefits-and-perks priority is "to offer a customizable program that can be tailored to the specific needs of each individual."

"Too many times, organizations assume that fairness means equal treatment, but we have people performing different roles at different levels, so their needs will be different," explains Jennifer Robin. By matching perks to individual needs, she continues, "companies can send a signal: 'We understand you, and here are things that will make your job and life easier and that will also help the organization.' " You'll end up distributing perks unevenly, not unfairly.

Having Needs

Sometimes needs pertain to the job. For example, only staffers who must be on call get to make calls from company cell phones. Or only a few leaders get private security due to their high-profile positions. "It's declassifying and re-crafting what have traditionally been status symbols into more functional perks," explains Jennifer Rosenzweig. In other words, providing people with the tools they need to do their jobs. But if something is necessary, not just nice, are we really still talking about perks?

Yes, because anything an organization gives to you and not me is technically a perk. Yet a nagging feeling remains: It's weird to regard necessities as perks. And that's OK. When employees cease to view perks as perks, class divisions erode, supporting teamwork, and engagement.

Perks catering to personal needs are thornier. Often, these are work/life perks, such as telecommuting or Google's reimbursement of up to $500 for takeout meals to new parents during a newborn's first 3 months so employees can concentrate more on work. When a perk doesn't directly relate to a job, some may grumble, "Why don't I get that too?"

For instance, "I don't have, nor want, children, but I'm also crunched for time. Give me $500 for food so I can be more productive!" Jennifer Benz, a San Francisco-based HR consultant, parallels this example to tuition reimbursement. Imagine a staffer insisting, "I don't want to go to school, but give me the tuition money anyway." As if. "There's no need to justify every perk just because 100 percent of the workforce can't take advantage of it," Benz explains. "The important thing is to meet as many needs as possible." Indeed, employees eligible for other perks will rarely protest, as complaints usually arise in

The End of the Perk?

To promote greater egalitarianism, or at least the perception thereof, some companies seek to shun perks. "Intel does not have programs for providing personal benefit perquisites to executive officers, such as permanent lodging or defraying the cost of personal entertainment or family travel," reads the company's 2011 proxy statement. The company also boasts a goal "to maintain an egalitarian culture in its facilities and operations." In fact, former CEO Andy Grove, who said he despised "mahogany-paneled corner offices," famously worked out of an 8 ft. by 9 ft. cubicle, as does current chief Paul Otellini.

"[W]e do not normally provide perquisites or other benefits to our named executive officers that are not generally available to all eligible employees," reads the current proxy for JDS Uniphase, a communications-products manufacturer. The company adds that "executive officers are not entitled to operate under different standards than other employees"—meaning they don't get subsidized financial and legal advice, personal entertainment, recreational club memberships or family travel, reserved parking spaces, and separate dining facilities.

But might abolishing perks in the spirit of equality beget anything but? Does it merely spread unfairness equally?

Other firms that tout egalitarian environments include Nvidia, Dell, and Hewlett-Packard. Not surprising that they are giants in the tech industry, where massages, dry cleaning, photo-processing services, catered meals, monthly wine tastings, and foosball tables continue to define workplaces. A true egalitarian enterprise, it seems, provides benefits to all, not perks to some.

But might abolishing perks in the spirit of equality beget anything but? Does it merely spread unfairness equally? "I've seen companies that have said they won't do anything unless it's equal across the board," reveals Jennifer Robin, co-author of *The Great Workplace: How to Build It, How to Keep It, and Why It Matters*, "so even if it makes sense for you to work from home, you're not allowed because another group of workers can't. Even if it makes sense to have a laptop because you travel, 'You can't have one because we can't give everyone a laptop.' You end up with an over-structured organization." Impressive intentions with oppressive outcomes.

Ultimately, it's impossible and impractical to treat everyone identically—*someone* has to sit in the corner office, or corner cubicle. Someone will always get something that someone else does not. Some people need laptops, some need to telecommute, some need (depending on how you define the word) to fly on the corporate jet. "Intel's company-operated aircraft hold approximately 40 passengers and are used in regularly scheduled routes between Intel's major United States facility locations, and Intel's use of non-commercial aircraft on a time-share or rental basis is limited to appropriate business-only travel," the company's proxy continues. JDS's proxy also points out: "[CEO] Mr. Heard received a total of $95,125 to assist with his relocation to Germantown, Maryland. Additionally, Mr. Heard received a commuter allowance of $20,000 for the period from October 2010 through May 2011."

Intel and JDS—and, no doubt, other businesses—don't have true zero-perks policies. Thus, JDS's statement that it does "not normally provide perquisites or other benefits to our named executive officers" is true only so long as the emphasis is on *normally*.

—V.L.

cultures of perceived disenfranchisement. At Google, you'd be hard-pressed to point to a neglected group.

Nevertheless, timesaving perks are hardest to defend. We're all squeezing ninety into 60 minutes of work, so why should CEOs fly aboard a corporate plane while you languish in baggage check? "The CEO has to spend most of his time and energy on the job. This isn't as much the case lower down," explains Don Lindner. "This perk will do the most good at the highest level." In other words, your CEO values every employee, just not equally—*and he (and the board) values himself most.*

Subsequently, the perk becomes not the plane but, rather, time itself. It makes sense for an enterprise to give more to those who have less of it. Overall, though, time-related perks are perhaps the only ones for which you become increasingly ineligible the higher up you go. It's easier to grant flextime to an accountant than to the CFO.

True Value

Because people have different needs, they predictably value perks differently. "What is important to you may be unimportant to me," says Steve Gross, who cites a Mercer executive who worked his way up to a senior level but turned down a larger office. "He couldn't care less," recalls Gross.

Not everyone wants to work in pajamas, park near the entrance, or fly Air Your-Company-Name-Here. Suppose a company were to extend corporate-aircraft access to everyone (about as likely as restricting coffee to the C-suite). If 99 percent

of workers have no business need to fly, what good is access without usage? The organization would be boasting nothing but lip service to egalitarianism based on a worthless perk to most employees. Take note: Individuals, not the company, determine the subjective values of perks.

Now, some people—get ready for this—desire status. Should the company satisfy that need too?

Equal consideration of interests is just that—consideration. It is not equal fulfillment. All needs are not of equal value, so the best, if imperfect, approach is to carefully weigh different interests when deciding on perks, including one's need for status versus everyone's perceptions of fairness. "I worked with a company that offered reserved parking to directors and above. It was clearly a status thing," recounts Laura Sejen. "The company consistently talked about valuing teamwork. There was a disconnect for lots of employees, who saw who the company thought was really important." Everyone already *knew* who was important; there was no need for parking spots to reinforce that.

Of course, you can argue that a director's time is more valuable so he should get to park upfront, but you can make the my-time-is-more-important-than-your-time case for almost every perk. That doesn't mean you should, especially when balancing it against perceptions of injustice and possible disengagement. At Google, for example, special parking spots go only to pregnant women, the handicapped, and people needing outlets to plug in electric cars.

Similarly, you could argue that financial-planning services for top leaders save them (their more valuable) time, but "it's probably not your senior executives but your lower-paid individuals who need help with financial planning most," says Jennifer Benz. "Why not offer it to everyone?"

Why not? Silicon Valley has been transforming perks into benefits for years. Whether tech companies such as Google offer endless lists of benefits to recruit and retain, allow employees to do their jobs better, or simply keep workers tethered to the office, the search giant is inching closer to an egalitarian environment and engaging people. "Slanting things that can support the whole workforce toward senior executives is not the best use of resources," Benz says. "A lot of companies are still very shortsighted and have traditional views of their workforce and are hesitant to implement programs that we know help people do their jobs better."

Other times, you may have to remove perks because revenues are down or they don't seem to impact performance positively. Taking them away can feel like a breach of an emotional contract for employees. "It's like ripping off a bandage; it's going to hurt," says Jennifer Rosenzweig. "But being forthright and transparent will go a long way to keeping employees' trust."

Ultimately, you'll need to develop a fair system of perks to compete in the marketplace and function well. Whether you add or subtract perks or turn them into benefits, you may still never purge your organization of entitlement or meet everyone's job and personal needs. But isn't it worth trying?

Critical Thinking

1. What happens when some employees receive perks, those employees most likely being in senior-level positions, and lower-ranking employees do not receive perks?

2. Are there questions of ethics and fairness in such situations?

3. What is meant by the concept of fairness through inequality?

4. Assume you are a consultant advising management about perks and their distribution. What would be your advice to management and why?

5. The article concludes with a statement, ". . . you may still never purge your organization of entitlement or meet everyone's job and personal needs." Do you agree with this statement? Why or why not?

Create Central

www.mhhe.com/createcentral

Internet References

Forbes
http://www.forbes.com/sites/jeffreydorfman/2013/07/18/the-wrong-people-care-about-ceo-pay-and-they-care-for-the-wrong-reasons/

The Conference Board Review
http://tcbreview.com/tcbr-business-environment/unfair-business-practices.html

Liberman, Vadim. From *The Conference Board Review*, Winter 2012, pp. 42–51. Copyright © 2012 by Vadim Liberman. Reprinted by permission of the author.

Article   Prepared by: Eric Teoro, *Lincoln Christian University*

D.C. Principal Slammed for Reporting Cheating

Jay Mathews

Learning Outcomes

After reading this article, you will be able to:

- Understand the difficulty inherent in changing an unethical organizational culture.

- The personal costs that can attend whistleblowing.

If you were waiting as I was for a firsthand account of test tampering at a D.C. public school, it came this week. A 42-year-old former principal says she was reduced to tears and hounded out of her job after she reported cheating at her Northeast Washington campus.

Adell Cothorne was hired in 2010 by then-D.C. schools chancellor Michelle A. Rhee to run the Crosby S. Noyes Education Campus. She had been an administrator in Baltimore and Montgomery counties. She was warmly welcomed by Wayne Ryan, the award-winning principal she replaced at Noyes. He was promoted to instructional superintendent and became her boss.

Cothorne was thrilled to land the Noyes job. Its test scores were among the best in the District, and it had been named a Blue Ribbon School of Excellence by the US Education Department. But just weeks into the school year, she couldn't square those high test scores with what she says she saw in classrooms: mediocre teaching and faltering student performance. She began to worry that the scores were fraudulent.

On Nov. 3, 2010, just hours after her students took the DC-BAS test, a practice exam, she discovered three staffers with pencil erasers poised above test answer sheets, in the midst of what looked to her like changing answers, she told me. That night, she says, she called two D.C. school officials she trusted to report what she had found. She assumed they would report the matter to their boss, then-acting schools chancellor Kaya Henderson.

Cothorne said she doesn't know whether Henderson was ever informed. But on Nov. 19, according to Cothorne and documents she filed in federal court, Ryan ordered her to his office and said: "I heard that you don't respect the legacy that has been built at Noyes."

Ryan did not respond to requests for comment, and a man who answered a phone listed in his name declined to comment.

Cothorne first told her story to education correspondent John Merrow in a PBS "Frontline" documentary scheduled to air again Thursday. She also gave a detailed account in a two-hour telephone interview with me and my wife, Linda Mathews, who conceived and edited a March 2011 series in USA Today that revealed widespread wrong-to-right erasures at several D.C. schools, particularly at Noyes.

Cothorne also filed a federal complaint against the D.C. government in May 2011, alleging that the awards Noyes and the school system had won had been obtained fraudulently by faking test scores. That lawsuit, in the US District Court for the District of Columbia, was unsealed in December and was publicly reported this week, after the US Education Department and the US Justice Department decided against joining it.

D.C. Schools Chancellor Kaya Henderson, in a statement, said Cothorne's lawsuit was based on "fictitious claims." She said "there is no widespread cheating at DCPS."

What is most striking about Cothorne's account, which fits with testing data and previous reports about Ryan's methods, is that no D.C. official with the power to investigate her complaints ever bothered to interview her about them. In the federal complaint, she identifies Josh Edelman and Hilary Darilek, then both prominent D.C. school officials, as the persons she called on Nov. 3 after accidentally discovering the apparent erasures.

D.C. schools spokeswoman Melissa Salmanowitz said Edelman and Darilek said they "never heard from Ms. Cothorne about these specific cheating allegations." They said they were in frequent conversation with her but that she never told them about the erasing incident.

While what happened at Noyes could be seen as a he said, she said incident—and it is certainly possible that Cothorne misinterpreted what she saw—Henderson's rejection of Cothorne's account is in tune with her dismissal of other evidence of cheating at Noyes.

The school had 75 percent of its classrooms flagged by the testing company CTB/McGraw-Hill for unusual numbers of wrong-to-right erasures in 2008, followed by 81 percent in 2009 and 80 percent in 2010. At least five Noyes classrooms had wrong-to-right erasure rates of more than 10 per child, while the D.C. average was fewer than two.

University of North Carolina at Chapel Hill testing expert Gregory Cizek, who worked on the investigation of similar erasures in Atlanta, said only test tampering could produce so many changes from wrong answers to right ones.

At a time when test security was tightened system-wide, Cothorne changed the locks on the Noyes room where answer sheets were kept for tests in April 2011. The result: Scores dropped dramatically. The portion of Noyes students proficient in reading fell from 61 to 32 percent, and in math from 54 to 28 percent.

By the end of the 2010–11 school year, Ryan had left the district. D.C. officials never made clear whether the most highly touted principal in the district was fired or resigned. Despite the decline in scores at Noyes, Cothorne was asked to stay. But, in the summer of 2011, she quit to start a cupcake shop in Ellicott City and recover from what she said was her worst year in education.

No one in power ever explained to her what happened. The subject of cheating was toxic. Cothorne's next supervisor told her to focus on "moving forward."

Isn't anyone in the D.C. government curious about what happened at Noyes, and why? Don't they want to know why scores so quickly peaked, then immediately plummeted? Perhaps, the D.C. Council or a congressional committee can find a way to take testimony from all involved, under oath, and get to the truth.

Cothorne, who wants to return to education, said she still thinks of how much more she could have done if the test scores had accurately reflected her students' achievement levels, or if headquarters had exposed the lying and cheating she says she saw at Noyes. "The kids did not get the caliber of instruction that they needed"—remedial work, extra tutoring, perhaps counseling, she told me.

Cothorne was trying to protect the students and the system, while it appears the system is just trying to protect itself.

Critical Thinking

1. What do you think about how Cothorne handled what she perceived? What, if anything, would you have done differently?

2. How would you handle apparent unethical behavior by your coworkers? By your boss?

3. How can companies prevent the alleged types of behavior recounted in the article?

Create Central

www.mhhe.com/createcentral

Internet References

Huffington Post
http://www.huffingtonpost.com/2011/03/29/dcs-noyes-school-joins_n_842276.html
Michigan Live
http://www.mlive.com/news/muskegon/index.ssf/2014/08/fremont_teacher_files_whistleb.html
Washington Post
http://www.washingtonpost.com/local/education/e-mails-show-dc-schools-officials-were-alerted-to-cheating/2014/01/30/26cbc592-89ec-11e3-916e-e01534b1e132_story.html

JAY MATHEWS is an education columnist for The Washington Post. You can contact him at mathewsj@washpost.com.

Article   Prepared by: Eric Teoro, *Lincoln Christian University*

Gap's Inconsistent Corporate Ethics

The retailer should join an accord to protect Bangladeshi garment workers.

GREG RANDOLPH

Learning Outcomes

After reading this article, you will be able to:

- Understand how actions can lead to perceptions of inconsistency.

- Think more deeply about an organization's responsibility toward employees.

- Think more critically about what inclusion entails.

The liberal social media bloc was abuzz recently with praise for Gap, the ubiquitous apparel company known for its khaki, clean-cut sense of style and—most recently—an advertisement that featured a visibly Sikh male model, sporting a pagdi (turban), and a full beard. The ad achieved nationwide fame when the company produced a swift and emphatic response to racist graffiti scribbled over it in a New York subway station.

But another of Gap's recent decisions—its refusal to join a groundbreaking accord to protect Bangladeshi garment workers—calls into question whether the corporate ethic of inclusion extends beyond marketing campaigns.

By selecting Waris Ahluwalia to model in its "Make Love" campaign, and immediately denouncing the act of an intolerant graffiti artist who changed that slogan to "Make Bombs," Gap sent an important message of inclusion to 280,000 Sikhs living in the United States, telling them that Gap believes their faces and lived experiences are part of the American story.

Socially minded consumers might find it surprising then, that on another issue of justice and inclusion, Gap's response has been anemic. After the death of nearly 1,200 apparel workers in the horrific collapse of Rana Plaza—a dilapidated building housing several garment factories on the outskirts of Dhaka—retailers around the world sought channels for improving working conditions in the country. A landmark agreement emerged, aimed at strengthening worker protections in Bangladesh's massive apparel industry, but Gap has refused to sign on.

The Accord on Fire and Building Safety in Bangladesh goes beyond traditional corporate social responsibility. First of all, a broad coalition of corporations, trade unions and workers' rights organizations negotiated jointly and endorse the agreement. Second, its signatories are legally obligated to fund independent inspection of facilities, plus structural repairs and renovations of existing factories. Over 100 international brands—including Gap competitors like Abercrombie & Fitch, American Eagle Outfitters and H&M—have already signed on.

The accord is about basic human rights. Bangladeshi workers possess the right to safe working conditions, the right to fair wages and the right to life.

It's also about inclusion. Mirroring the globalization story in many countries, economic growth in Bangladesh has been rapid, but its rewards have not been shared broadly. Rather than creating an economic culture of shared prosperity, Bangladesh has engaged in a "race to the bottom"—maintaining substandard wages and working conditions in order to make production costs attractively, and artificially, low. The accord is a first step toward transforming those marginalized by globalization into its beneficiaries.

If it joined the accord, Gap would send another powerful message of inclusion to 4 million Bangladeshi garment workers: your economic opportunity, your ability to obtain a just job, and your right to share in the fruits of economic growth, matter to us. Further, it could demonstrate to its new Tweeting extollers that the company's progressive attitudes inform its supply chain management, not only its advertising.

Arsalan Iftikhar, the social commentator and online personality who made the Gap ad famous, wrote last month: "I want to live in an America where a fashion model can be a handsome, bearded brown dude in a turban who is considered as beautiful as a busty blonde-haired white girl in see-through lingerie."

That America does sound nice. But a fashion industry committed to diversity and inclusion stands on hollow ground if the products it markets are founded in economic exclusion. With the power of its brand and the size of its supply chain, Gap can and should do more to create just jobs in the apparel sector. Signing the accord is a necessary step.

Critical Thinking

1. Debate with a fellow student/colleague Gap's decision to not sign the Bangladesh accord, one defending Gap and one accusing Gap of an ethical lapse.

2. Do you think that Gap's unwillingness to sign the Bangladesh accord is conclusive evidence of a lack of concern toward employees? Why or why not?

3. Do you think Gap behaved unethically in not signing the Bangladesh accord? Why or why not?

Create Central

www.mhhe.com/createcentral

Internet References

CBC News
http://www.cbc.ca/news/business/bangladeshi-garment-workers-protest-66-a-month-offer-1.2422470

Gap Inc.
http://gapinc.com/content/gapinc/html/media/pressrelease/2014/med_pr_Most_Ethical_Companies.html

Rabble.CA
http://rabble.ca/news/2013/11/how-gap-and-wal-mart-are-dodging-worker-safety-bangladesh

---

GREG RANDOLPH is the manager of strategy and outreach at JustJobs Network.

Article   Prepared by: Eric Teoro, *Lincoln Christian University*

When You're Most Vulnerable to Fraud

In the best of times, entrepreneurs tend to take their eye off the ball.

ROB JOHNSON

Learning Outcomes

After reading this article, you will be able to:

- Describe situations in which entrepreneurs are susceptible to fraud.

- Establish safeguards to prevent fraudulent behavior by employees.

F ive years ago, Ed Couvrette was on top of the world. The manufacturing company he founded, E.F. Couvrette Co., was ringing up sales of $10 million a year and was negotiating contracts for triple that amount. On employees' birthdays, he routinely gave out bonus checks—a week's pay for every year they'd been at the company.

"Now I can hardly afford birthday cards," he laments.

His revenue is down more than half, customers have abandoned him in droves, and he has been forced to severely slash jobs. He can't line up credit, and some weeks there's not enough money in the bank to cover payroll at his Salem, VA, operation, which does business as Couvrette Building Systems.

Mr. Couvrette didn't get trapped by the collapsing economy or a shrinking industry. Instead, he says he was the victim of massive fraud by his chief operating officer—who, among other things, pocketed over $300,000 he was supposed to send to the Internal Revenue Service to cover payroll taxes. The former officer is now in prison; his attorney, Tony Anderson of Roanoke, VA, declined to comment on the case.

Mr. Couvrette's case offers a hard lesson for small businesses: When times are great—watch out. Because that's when you're most vulnerable to fraud. Sales are soaring, and the biggest problem seems to be where to fit all the new equipment and employees. But those heady days can be perilous, since success can distract the founder from such mundane financial duties as collecting payroll taxes and verifying the accuracy of bills.

"It's often when things are going well in a small business that betrayal strikes," says Walter Jones, a fraud examiner and retired IRS agent who's now a consultant to Mr. Couvrette. "In an atmosphere where sales and profits are increasing, the diversion of funds is masked by success."

"Small on Administration"

For some entrepreneurs, another factor makes them prime targets for fraud: Overseeing finances doesn't come naturally. That was the case with Mr. Couvrette, who has an engineering background. He was most comfortable on the factory floor at his company, which makes kiosks to house drive-up automated teller machines at banks; he enjoyed supervising everything from the welding of the steel housings to painting them with banks' logos.

"I was big on production, small on administration," says Mr. Couvrette, now 58.

Mr. Couvrette had also long taken his books for granted, thanks in large part to a series of dependable company controllers, including his father, a certified public accountant. Further, Mr. Couvrette says he couldn't imagine his company getting victimized—given that its mission involved *preventing* crime. "We got into the drive-up ATMs at a time when banks were becoming more security conscious about customers being robbed while walking up to the machines," Mr. Couvrette says. "More banks were interested in ATM facilities where the customers could stay in their cars and leave quickly if they felt threatened."

He admits his guard was down in 2001 when he hired Roy Dickinson, an accountant with a sound track record, as the growing company's chief operating officer.

How to Steer Clear of Fraud? The Experts Weigh In

Small businesses are victimized by embezzlement far more often than bigger companies, according to a survey this year by the Association of Certified Fraud Examiners, a trade group based in Austin, Texas.

In fact, 31 percent of all business frauds nationally were in companies with fewer than 100 employees, according to the study, and an additional 23% were suffered by those with under 999 workers. Only 21% were committed in companies with more than 10,000 employees.

What's more, small businesses in the U.S. typically suffer larger losses than big companies do. The median loss for companies with fewer than 100 employees was about $150,000–compared with $84,000 in businesses with payrolls exceeding 10,000.

Andi McNeal, director of research at the ACFE, says small businesses are relatively easy targets for internal fraud "because there are usually less formal financial controls. There's usually a lot of trust put in one person, which may be necessary for these businesses to run, but it can come back to haunt."

So, how to protect your company from fraud? Here are some tips from the association.

- If you're delegating responsibility for accounts receivable and the company's disbursements, don't put the same person in charge of both, even if it means you have to hire an additional employee.
- Bring in an outside accountant at least once a year to review your business financial records. Typical fees are $100 to $150 an hour, depending on how organized your records are. Consider retaining different outside accountants occasionally to have a fresh eye involved in the review.
- Be aware of employees who are involved with your company's finances and never take time off. Embezzlers rarely take vacations for fear their theft will be discovered by someone filling in.

- Embezzlers usually spend the money they steal very quickly. Tip-offs include changes in lifestyle such as spending on expensive cars and vacations.
- One common internal fraud is kickbacks involving vendors, so stay alert to unusually close relationships between employees responsible for finances and suppliers and customers.
- Be the first person to open your monthly business bank statements. Even if you don't have time to examine them closely, your attention sends a message to any potential fraudster.
- When perusing your bank statements, don't just look at the numbers; examine the actual images of canceled checks. Otherwise you can't confirm where the money really went.
- Remember that some internal theft doesn't leave an audit trail.

For example, skimming involves stealing a company's cash before the receipts are entered into the accounting ledger. In a sales skim, the fraudster collects a customer's payment at the point of sale and simply pockets the money without recording it. The loss may come to light only via clues such as inventory shortages or lower-than-expected cash flow.

- Look at receipts for deposits of both federal and state taxes.
- Remember that liabilities can double the amount of taxes due, including penalties and interest, within a year, so don't take more than a few months between your informal audits.
- Maintain an open-door policy that encourages employees who have suspicions about misappropriations or questionable spending to tell you in confidence.

—Rob Johnson

After hiring Mr. Dickinson, Mr. Couvrette says he made a mistake in judgment that is common in small-business embezzlement cases: He put the same employee—Mr. Dickinson—in charge of both receipts and disbursements. While entrusting both ends of the money-moving chores to one employee may seem to streamline paperwork, it's just too risky, says Mr. Jones, the fraud expert. "I believe in what Reagan said about nuclear-missile treaties: Trust but verify."

In February 2005, Mr. Couvrette says he noticed that a high-profile new area of his business being run by Mr. Dickinson—making software and hardware adjustments on dozens of ATMs

around the country—wasn't producing a profit. "I kept waiting for our cash flow and margins to get where they should be with expenses, and they didn't," says Mr. Couvrette.

In March 2005, Mr. Couvrette scheduled a meeting with his chief operating officer, calling him back to Salem from a New York business trip. "He didn't show, so I fired him," says Mr. Couvrette.

That confrontation led to the hiring of an outside auditor, Mr. Jones. The examination revealed myriad financial problems, including payroll taxes that had been collected but not forwarded to the IRS, according to Mr. Jones. Mr. Couvrette was ultimately responsible for paying the IRS; the agency agreed to a settlement of about $320,000, according to Mr. Jones, who was Mr. Couvrette's intermediary with the government. "Stealing payroll taxes is a form of misappropriation that small-business owners don't catch because the money isn't going for company expenses anyway," says Mr. Jones.

In February of last year, meanwhile, Mr. Dickinson pleaded guilty in the US District Court in Roanoke to conspiracy to commit mail and wire fraud, and attempting to interfere with IRS laws. He was sentenced to 3 years in prison—a term he's currently serving—and ordered to pay restitution of more than $300,000.

Beyond pocketing the money intended for the IRS, Mr. Dickinson pleaded guilty to several acts of fraud. He used company money to cover remodeling costs for his home, for instance, and covered his tracks by altering company records, according to his plea. And he used his company American Express card to purchase items such as a $6,850 Rolex watch and altered the bills to show those transactions as business expenses, according to his plea.

In 2005, word that the IRS had issued tax liens against Couvrette Building Systems spread to the company's creditors and customers, according to Mr. Jones. Both categories consisted largely of banks, and "tax problems are the kiss of death when you're dealing with banks," says Mr. Jones. "So, Ed's credit quickly dried up and he lost millions of dollars in contracts."

Now Mr. Couvrette's annual revenue has been slashed by 60 percent and so has his production line—to about 30 workers, down from 150 five years ago. The hulking gray manufacturing plant on his company's 10-acre site contains pockets of workers, but most of the production line is quiet. Many of his former bank customers have found other suppliers. And Mr. Couvrette's credit is shot.

"I have zero elasticity of funds right now," he says. "I need loans to rebuild my delivery trucks and pay vendors," and of course meet payroll.

A Death in the Family

Sometimes it isn't just success that distracts entrepreneurs. Personal issues can also take owners' focus off the business and leave them vulnerable to fraud. Consider **Interactive Solutions** Inc. in Memphis, TN. In 2002, the videoconferencing company achieved its then-highest annual sales, about $6 million, and was recording double-digit profit margins.

"Things were going so well I bought a brand-new BMW 525 for my company car, and paid cash for it," says Jay Myers, the 53-year-old founder and chief executive.

Amid the success, Mr. Myers suffered a personal loss: His brother, John, died at age 50. The two had been close, and

Mr. Myers started taking occasional days off while in mourning. His attention wandered from the company's finances, and he began relying more heavily on Linda Merritt, a bookkeeper who had come on board a month before John's death, to keep things straight.

"I wasn't paying the attention I should have to the business," says Mr. Myers, adding that his trust in Ms. Merritt was based on her solid job references, which he says included "a lawyer and someone who sang with her in the church choir."

"It was dumb luck," he says, that finally caused him to become suspicious in May 2003, after he read a magazine article detailing a case of internal fraud at a small machinery supplier in Illinois. "Something clicked as I read the story: That could happen to me."

Although he vowed to have his books checked by an outside auditor, Mr. Myers feared what might be found—a common reaction that fraud investigators say sometimes delays the uncovering of embezzlement. After all, says Mr. Myers, "this was humiliating—a potential disaster if my employees found out. It might sink the company. What about my clients and vendors?"

The thefts—in the form of bogus bonuses and commissions by the dozens, according to evidence later presented in court—weren't difficult to verify. When the outside auditor showed Mr. Myers some of the checks for such payments, he says, "Some of them were to a receptionist. I thought, 'A receptionist doesn't get commissions, she answers the phone.' I felt like such a fool for not knowing this was going on."

In November 2005, Ms. Merritt pleaded guilty to misappropriating funds in federal district court in Memphis, and is now serving an 8-year term in a Texas federal prison. According to the sentencing document in the case, she was ordered to repay more than $260,000, to Mr. Myers and an insurance company and bank involved in Interactive Solutions' finances.

Ms. Merritt's attorney, Stephen Shankman, a federal public defender in Memphis, declined to comment on the case.

New Vigilance

Mr. Myers was able to recover $80,000 via a "dishonest employee liability" rider on his insurance policy. Such clauses can be written to cover everything from credit-card fraud to embezzlement.

Today, Mr. Myers says, he's insured for about $240,000 in losses due to employee dishonesty. He also made an arrangement for partial restitution from an accounting firm that had failed to uncover the embezzlement in a routine examination of Interactive Solutions' books a few months before it was discovered.

Since the fraud episode, Interactive Solutions is riding high. Sales have more than doubled to about $14 million annually. In part, that's thanks to timing; the videoconferencing business is surging as companies look to cut travel costs during the recession. The company has also branched into new areas that are proving popular, such as telemedicine, in which doctors and patients can huddle over long distances.

Mr. Myers is being careful not to get taken unawares again. In fact, he credits part of his recent success to better hiring and employee-retention practices. He takes more time to get to know prospective workers and to check out their backgrounds. These days, Mr. Myers has separate employees who are responsible for handling accounts receivable and paying the company's bills. What's more, he says, he's much more vigilant personally. "When those monthly bank statements come in, nobody opens them now before me."

Mr. Myers now makes it a point to let employees know that if they betray his trust, they could risk jail time. In a recent meeting he warned his 40 workers: "I said if you steal a dollar or a thousand dollars, and I catch you, I will prosecute."

Meanwhile, at Couvrette Building Systems, the employees soldier on. Matt Musselman, a Couvrette design engineer, works at his computer screen on a recent afternoon with an eye to the future. Hoping innovation can win more orders, Mr. Musselman, a member of Couvrette's research-and-development team, diagrams a solar-powered ATM for one of the company's longtime bank customers that has remained loyal, Wells Fargo & Co.

"We're going into green technology," Mr. Musselman says.

Ross Campbell, a painter, sticks around even though he occasionally isn't paid for weeks at a time. He says, "Ed Couvrette is a good guy. I have a lot of faith in him."

Critical Thinking

1. Why are entrepreneurs vulnerable to fraud?
2. What can they do to protect themselves?

Create Central

www.mhhe.com/createcentral

Internet References

About

http://sbinformation.about.com/cs/insurance/a/ucfraud.htm

Bank Info Security

http://www.bankinfosecurity.com/interviews/small-business-at-greater-fraud-risk-i-2068

Time

http://business.time.com/2013/05/17/arresting-small-business-fraud/

MR. JOHNSON is a writer in Roanoke County, Va. He can be reached at reports@wsj.com.

Article   Prepared by: Eric Teoro, *Lincoln Christian University*

Doctors Face New Scrutiny Over Gifts

New Health Law Calls for Increased Disclosures

Peter Loftus

Learning Outcomes

After reading this article, you will be able to:

- Understand how public perceptions can impact personal behavior.

- Describe the potential benefits and pitfalls of gifts and related income between pharmaceutical companies and physicians.

- Understand some of the nuances of transparency and their effects.

U.S. doctors are bracing for increased public scrutiny of the payments and gifts they receive from pharmaceutical and medical-device companies as a result of the new health law.

Starting this month, companies must record nearly every transaction with doctors—from sales reps bearing pizza to compensation for expert advice on research—to comply with the so-called Sunshine Act provision of the US health-care overhaul. The companies must report data on individual doctors and how much they received to a federal health agency, which will post it on a searchable, public website beginning September 2014.

Many doctors say the increased disclosures are making them rethink their relationships with industry, citing concerns about privacy and accuracy, and worry that the public will misinterpret the information. Some fear patients will view the payments as tainting their medical decisions, and will lump together compensation for research-related services with payments of a more promotional nature.

Drug companies collectively pay hundreds of millions of dollars in fees and gifts to doctors every year. In 2012, Pfizer

Inc., PFE –0.59 percent, the biggest drug maker by sales, paid $173.2 million to US health-care professionals. Some companies including Pfizer have decreased these payments in recent years; Pfizer's total was $195.4 million for 2011.

Consulting and speaking fees are an important source of income for some physicians, who can be paid tens of thousands of dollars a year for such services. But now physicians say they will be much more selective about the work they do and what they will accept from industry representatives. Some are even restricting access to their offices by sales reps, or requiring forms that document the value of anything brought to the office, according to medical societies.

John Mandrola, a cardiologist in Louisville, KY, said he has been paid a total of $1,500 to $2,000 this year by medical-device makers for speaking engagements. Knowing that such transactions will become public has caused him to be more cautious about what fees to accept, he said. He avoids industry reps visiting his office, believing he can get information on new drugs elsewhere.

"I'll continue to weigh the benefits and the negatives, and I think the Sunshine Act and the public reporting of all this stuff makes us think about that," said Dr. Mandrola. "And I think that's a good thing."

A benefit of transparency, Dr. Mandrola said, is that it will help doctors evaluate medical research from peers if they know whether the researchers receive payments from certain companies. Still, he worries that the disclosures could squelch legitimate interactions—for example, when doctors receive consulting fees to help companies develop drugs and determine their best use.

"I don't think all physician-industry interaction is bad," he said.

The push for greater transparency was driven by concerns that doctors' prescribing decisions are tainted by the payments and gifts, as well as allegations that drug companies have used payments to induce doctors to prescribe drugs for unapproved, "off-label" uses. Several drug companies have paid large penalties to settle government allegations of off-label marketing, and were required to disclose physician-payment data as conditions of the settlements.

"The idea is that transparency will encourage doctors to evaluate whether these are appropriate relationships with companies or not," said Daniel Carlat, a psychiatrist and director of the prescription project at the Pew Charitable Trusts, which supported the Sunshine Act. He expects patients won't have much of a problem if their doctors receive $200 worth of company-provided lunches, but may question doctors who receive tens or hundreds of thousands of dollars from the industry annually.

Several drug and device makers—including Pfizer and Eli Lilly, LLY −1.65%& Co.,—have been posting physician-payment data online for the past few years. Some US states already require companies to report such information. But the Sunshine Act will significantly widen the scope because it applies to most companies—any company whose products are covered by Medicare—and the government's launch of the database could draw greater public attention.

Richard B. Aguilar, a diabetes-care specialist, received a total of $42,339 from Lilly for the first 3 months of 2013, according to Lilly's online payment database. Dr. Aguilar, who has a private practice in Downey, CA, said he speaks about Lilly drugs at programs to teach other doctors, and the information is consistent with the FDA-approved prescribing labels. He says the payments are fair compensation for his expertise and travel.

Dr. Aguilar plans to continue serving as a paid speaker, but he says other doctors are increasingly opting out of attending or speaking at such programs for fear of what the public will think about the payment disclosures.

Dr. Aguilar said he hopes the public would see the value of physicians learning new information about drugs from an expert at speaker programs, rather than having to rely upon their own educational resources to keep current. "This, in essence, is reducing the number of valuable expert educational speakers who might otherwise have provided teaching and experience to many health-care providers," he said.

Some doctors fear the payment data will be inaccurate and could mislead the public about the nature of their relationships with the industry. Gary M. Cowan, an ophthalmologist in Fort Worth, Texas, said he has occasionally attended company-sponsored dinners to hear a lecture from an expert in his field. He plans to monitor the payments that companies report in his name.

"I think it behooves every physician to look and see what's said about him," he said.

Drug makers said they've been preparing for the new reporting requirements and have implemented technology systems to collect the data, but they will continue to work with physicians because the interactions improve science and medicine.

The Centers for Medicare & Medicaid Services, which is implementing the Sunshine Act, is advising doctors to keep records of all payments and transfers of value received from industry. Once the agency receives payment data from manufacturers, it will give doctors about 2 months to review the data and work with companies to make any corrections before it is made public.

CMS also will break down the payment data into more than a dozen categories—such as meals, travel, research, or speaking fees—to give a clearer idea of the nature of a doctor's relationship with industry.

One key exemption: Companies won't have to report compensation to doctors who speak at certain accredited events where physicians receive continuing medical education—as long the sponsoring company doesn't select or directly pay the speaker, but rather delegates those duties to a third-party organization. CMS initially proposed to require that such payments be reported, but granted the exemption in its final rule issued earlier this year, saying industry support for accredited or certified continuing medical education is a "unique relationship." Continuing-medical education providers pushed for the exemption, arguing that industry support would dwindle if the payments had to be reported.

Stefanie A. Doebler, an attorney with Covington & Burling LLP who represents health-care companies, said the exemption for indirect payments to speakers at continuing-medical education events could help sustain industry support for such programs. However, companies will be required to report certain other expenses for these programs, such as meals provided to physician attendees if the cost of each meal is separately identifiable. Some companies have decided not to fund such meals, she said, which could cause program providers to charge attendees for the meals.

To ensure accuracy, CMS is required to conduct audits of the data submitted and levy civil monetary penalties against companies for failing to submit data, or for submitting inaccurate data. Companies that fail to report information in a timely, accurate or complete manner face penalties of at least $1,000 per transaction, with a total maximum annual penalty of up to $1.15 million per company, according to CMS.

CMS plans to publish the data each year on a public website starting in the Fall of 2014. CMS says patients will be able to look up their doctors and see if they have any financial relationships with companies, which types of payments they receive and how much.

Some companies are taking steps to prepare the doctors with whom they do business. Later this year, Roche AG's, RHHBY -0.79 percent Genentech unit, which sells the cancer drug Avastin, will launch an online portal called "Sunshine

Track," which will allow doctors to review payment data before it is reported to CMS. "We have implemented extensive processes to validate all payment information we collect," said a spokeswoman.

Genentech also allows physicians to opt out of receiving meals from the company at speaker programs or during office visits by sales reps. Doctors opting out of meals at speaker programs must certify this on a sign-in sheet and can either pay for the meal themselves or not partake, the spokeswoman said.

Critical Thinking

1. What are the benefits and pitfalls of doctors receiving gifts from pharmaceutical companies?
2. Is suspicion warranted whenever a doctor receives a gift from a pharmaceutical company? Why or why not?
3. What guidelines would you implement to guide the relationship between pharmaceutical companies and doctors?

Create Central

www.mhhe.com/createcentral

Internet References

American College of Emergency Physicians
http://www.acep.org/Clinical—Practice-Management/Gifts-to-Emergency-Physicians-from-Industry/

American Medical Association
http://www.ama-assn.org/ama/pub/physician-resources/medical-ethics/code-medical-ethics/opinion8061.page?

BusinessWeek
http://www.businessweek.com/debateroom/archives/2008/04/doctors_stop_taking_pharma_gifts.html

Article   Prepared by: Eric Teoro, *Lincoln Christian University*

Wal-Mart Inquiry Reflects Alarm on Corruption

STEPHANIE CLIFFORD AND DAVID BARSTOW

Learning Outcomes

After reading this article, you will be able to:

- Describe Wal-Mart's challenges with bribery and compliance issues in international markets.

- Describe Wal-Mart's response to bribery allegations and the extent of the company's internal investigation.

- Recognize the difficulty large companies have in sustaining consistent ethical practices.

Wal-Mart on Thursday reported that its investigation into violations of a federal antibribery law had extended beyond Mexico to China, India, and Brazil, some of the retailer's most important international markets.

The disclosure, made in a regulatory filing, suggests Wal-Mart has uncovered evidence into potential violations of the Foreign Corrupt Practices Act, as the fallout continues from a bribery scheme involving the opening of stores in Mexico that was the subject of a *New York Times* investigation in April.

The announcement underscores the degree to which Wal-Mart recognizes that corruption may have infected its international operations, and reflects a growing alarm among the company's internal investigators. People with knowledge of the matter described how a relatively routine compliance audit rapidly transformed into a full-blown investigation late last year—involving hundreds of lawyers and three former federal prosecutors—when the company learned that *The Times* was examining problems with its operations in Mexico.

A person with direct knowledge of the company's internal investigation cautioned that Thursday's disclosure did not mean Wal-Mart had concluded it had paid bribes in China, India, and Brazil. But it did indicate that the company had found enough evidence to justify concern about its business practices in the three countries—concerns that go beyond initial inquiries and that are serious enough that shareholders needed to be told.

Wal-Mart issued a statement confirming the new disclosures, and said it would be inappropriate to comment further on the new allegations until it had concluded the investigations.

The Justice Department and the Securities and Exchange Commission, with Wal-Mart's cooperation, are also looking into the company's compliance with the antibribery law.

The Times reported in April that 7 years ago, Wal-Mart had found credible evidence that its Mexican subsidiary had paid bribes in its effort to build more stores, a violation of the corrupt practices act, and that an internal investigation had been suppressed by executives at the company's Arkansas headquarters.

Wal-Mart has so far spent $35 million on a compliance program that began in spring 2011, and has more than 300 outside lawyers and accountants working on it, the company said. It has spent $99 million in 9 months on the current investigation.

Consequences of the expanding investigation could include slower expansion overseas and the identification of even more problems. The company said in the filing on Thursday that new inquiries had begun in countries "including but not limited to" China, India, and Brazil.

While the disclosure did not specify the nature of the possible bribery problems in the three countries, it "clearly will cause more scrutiny on every real estate project being considered, and one would think at the minimum it will slow down the process as more controls need to be passed through," said Colin McGranahan, an analyst with Sanford C. Bernstein.

International growth is critical to Wal-Mart, the world's largest retailer, and Brazil, India, China, and Mexico together make up the largest portion of the company's foreign locations.

Wal-Mart's international division had been on a growth binge, though that has been slowing lately. In third-quarter results reported Thursday, the company said international sales rose 2.4 percent to $33.2 billion, making up about 29 percent of the company's overall sales.

More than half of Wal-Mart's 10,524 stores are international. Mexico has 2,230 stores. Brazil has 534, China, 384.

C. Douglas McMillon, chief executive of Walmart International, said in June that he did not expect the investigation to hinder international growth. "Only time will tell," he said.

Wal-Mart's expanding investigation began in spring 2011 as a relatively routine audit of how well its foreign subsidiaries were complying with its anticorruption policies. It is keeping the Justice Department and the S.E.C. apprised of the investigation.

The review was initiated by Jeffrey J. Gearhart, Wal-Mart's general counsel, who had seen news reports about how Tyson Foods had been charged with relatively minor violations of the Foreign Corrupt Practices Act. He decided it made sense to test Wal-Mart's internal defenses against corruption.

The audit began in Mexico, China, and Brazil, the countries Wal-Mart executives considered the most likely source of problems. Wal-Mart hired the accounting firm KPMG and the law firm Greenberg Traurig to conduct the audit. The firms conducted interviews and spot checks of record systems to check whether Wal-Mart's subsidiaries were carrying out required compliance procedures.

For example, Wal-Mart's anticorruption policy requires background checks on all third-party agents—lawyers, lobbyists—who represent the company before government agencies. The firms checked whether background checks were in fact being done. By July 2011, the firms had identified significant weaknesses in all three subsidiaries.

"It was clear they were not executing," a Wal-Mart official with knowledge of the audits said.

The problems were enough to persuade Wal-Mart to expand the audit to all 26 of its foreign subsidiaries. This work began in Autumn 2011. The outside firms dispatched "compliance teams" of lawyers and accountants all over the world. The teams attributed many of the problems they identified to a lack of training.

Senior Wal-Mart executives were concerned by the findings, but not overly alarmed. The audit was uncovering the kinds of problems and oversights that plague many global corporations.

But in late 2011, Wal-Mart learned that *The Times* was examining Wal-Mart's response in 2005 to serious and specific accusations of widespread bribery by Wal-Mart de Mexico, the company's largest foreign subsidiary.

In October 2005, a former lawyer for Wal-Mart de Mexico had spent hours telling company investigators how Wal-Mart de

Mexico's leadership had orchestrated a vast campaign of bribery to accelerate expansion. Hundreds of bribes, he said, were paid to obtain construction permits and other licenses needed to open new stores. The lawyer's accusations were especially powerful because he had been in charge of getting permits for Wal-Mart de Mexico's new stores.

Wal-Mart rapidly escalated its internal investigation. It hired new outside lawyers, this time from the firm Jones Day. They began to investigate whether top executives had quashed the company's investigation into the lawyer's claims. In December 2011, Wal-Mart sent Jones Day lawyers to Mexico to interview the lawyer and other crucial players. The company began to look into other specific accusations of wrongdoing, both in Mexico and it its other subsidiaries.

It effectively created two lines of inquiry—the first being the global compliance review begun by Greenberg Traurig and KPMG. The second was the internal inquiry into specific accusations of bribery and corruption.

Some changes at Wal-Mart have already resulted. General counsels for each country used to report in to the chief executives of that country—which could create conflicts of interest if the chief executive was involved in corruption—and now they report to the general counsel of Walmart International. The company recently hired several compliance executives, and a vice president for global investigations who had previously worked at the F.B.I. It has also changed its protocol on investigations, including asking international subsidiaries to alert the global ethics office in Bentonville before any inquiry into wrongdoing begins.

The new disclosure by Wal-Mart on Thursday "does support their effort to be transparent," said Matthew J. Feeley, a lawyer with Buchanan Ingersoll & Rooney who focuses on foreign bribery cases. In cases like these, a company will regularly update the S.E.C. and the Justice Department with "very detailed presentations about the results of the internal investigation" in the hope of receiving lesser punishment from the agencies.

Though the government issued new compliance guidelines for the law on Wednesday, largely aimed at lawyers handling such cases, the Wal-Mart disclosure was not a result of those new guidelines. It was included in the company's third-quarter earnings announcement.

It was not clear Thursday whether authorities in China, India, and Brazil were conducting investigations of their own into Wal-Mart's practices, as the authorities in Mexico have done in response to the bribery accusations in that country.

Last month, Indian regulators started looking into whether Wal-Mart violated an Indian foreign investment rule.

Charlie Savage, Vikas Bajaj and Andrew Downie contributed reporting.

This article has been revised to reflect the following correction:

Correction: November 17, 2012

An article on Friday about Wal-Mart's broadening of an internal investigation into possible violations of a federal antibribery law described incorrectly, in some editions, a foreign investment rule that the company may have violated in India. The initialism F.D.I. stands for "foreign direct investment," but the Indian rule is not "known as" F.D.I.

Critical Thinking

1. Do you think Wal-Mart's response to the bribery allegations is commendable? Why or why not?
2. What practices could Wal-Mart implement to lower the probability of continued bribery in international markets?

3. How can multinational companies develop consistent compliance to ethical standards?

Create Central

www.mhhe.com/createcentral

Internet References

Business Insider
   http://www.businessinsider.com/new-details-in-walmart-bribery-scandal-2012-12

The New York Times
   http://www.nytimes.com/2014/06/05/business/after-walmart-bribery-scandals-a-pattern-of-quiet-departures.html

Article   Prepared by: Eric Teoro, *Lincoln Christian University*

American Apparel and the Ethics of a Sexually Charged Workplace

Gael O'Brien

Learning Outcomes

After reading this article, you will be able to:

- Describe the nature of sexual harassment and a hostile work environment.

- Understand the need for congruent values within a work environment.

- Understand the role of organizational culture on employee behavior.

American Apparel finds itself once again in a familiar place—sued again for sexual harassment and creating a hostile work environment, because of the vulnerability its CEO's philosophy of sexual freedom in the workplace creates for the publicly held company.

In discussing a 2006 sexual harassment suit, founder, chairman, and CEO Dov Charney expressed the belief that consensual sexual relationships in the workplace were appropriate: "I think it's a First Amendment right to pursue one's affection for another human being."

Recently, Irene Morales, 20, sued Charney, 42, American Apparel, and its directors for about $250 million, alleging Charney forced her into sex acts when she was 18 and an employee. The company has accused Morales of extortion. A lawyer for the company dismissed the allegations, saying when Morales left the company and accepted severance, she signed a statement saying she had no claims against the company and agreed that any future claims would be addressed by confidential arbitration. A judge has halted Morales' suit until March 25, pending a decision on whether it should go to arbitration or trial.

Notwithstanding the distinction of being dubbed "American Apparel's chief lawsuit officer," Charney is a complex figure.

His website, filled with photos of him and provocative shots he took of the company's young models, tells the story of his immigrant family, religion, creating the company as a teenager, philosophy on sexual freedom, and politics. Passionate about immigration reform, proud his clothing is "made in America," he pays his 10,000 workers well above garment industry rate.

Charney owns 51.8 percent of the company and the board has thus far apparently gone along with his philosophy of sexual freedom. However, the company is no longer on solid financial footing. Blame the recession or other factors, but it appears that sexy marketing isn't selling American Apparel the way it did several years ago; stock prices have been dropping.

Among the questions Dov Charney's philosophy raises is whether there really can be consensual sex in a workplace if both parties aren't equal in status, salary, and intention?

Is the term a delusion if one of the parties is the CEO? For example, how can both parties freely accept responsibility for the consequences of a relationship when one party has power over the other's salary, promotion, or keeping the job?

If tone at the top encourages workplace sexual expression, what are the constraints to protect employees? American Apparels' ethics policy talks about "promoting ethical conduct, including the handling of actual or apparent conflicts of interest between personal and professional relationships."

So who decides if a conflict of interest has occurred between personal and professional relationships and if harm was done in a fleeting or more sustained expression of sexual interest? What about harm to bystanders who just want to do their job and are made uncomfortable by sexual innuendo and graphic language?

If you were doing a cost/benefit analysis of sexual drama (which is an inevitable byproduct of a sexually charged workplace), would the benefits come out ahead if everyone affected got to weigh in?

In interviews, Charney has tied the importance of sexual energy to creative energy on which he says the fashion industry depends. No argument about the value of released endorphins.

Interesting to note that many leaders have championed endorphin highs to stimulate creativity. Among dozens of examples, they set aside areas for ping pong, volleyball, or fitness equipment, or hold events recognizing employee achievements—few, if any, of which, have resulted in litigation and loss of company and CEO reputation.

Every leader gets to figure out if what she or he is doing is working and what to change (before a board answers that question for them). Charney enjoyed the reputation as a wunderkind. Now the company is in a different phase facing financial and strategic challenges, as well as another lawsuit about its culture.

The irony of sexual freedom in the workplace is that it is about power, not romance. It often ends up exploiting those most vulnerable—the way, for example, immigrants have often been treated in some workplaces; it also gives ammunition to those who, seeing where a company has made itself most vulnerable, move in for their own kill.

Update–March 28, 2011: Justice Bernadette Bayne held a hearing March 25, 2011 with counsel from both sides in the sexual harassment suit, Morales v. American Apparel. Judge Bayne initially indicated the case should go to arbitration and later said she'd review the additional documents. She gave no indication when she'd rule if the case can go to trial. On March 23, Apparel chairman and CEO Dov Charney was hit with the second sexual harassment suit this month. Kimbra Lo, 19, a former sales associate, alleges she was sexually assaulted when she went to Charney's LA home seeking to be rehired as a model and photographer. Both Lo and Morales went on the Today Show to talk about their lawsuits. The company contends the relationships were consensual.

Critical Thinking

1. What is meant by the allegations of a sexually charged workplace and a hostile work environment?

2. How are the allegations related to ethics and ethical behavior?

3. What lessons for management might be drawn from the article?

4. Identify one lesson for management and defend its importance.

Create Central

www.mhhe.com/createcentral

Internet References

Bloomberg Businessweek
   http://www.businessweek.com/stories/2005-06-26/living-on-the-edge-at-american-apparel

Business Ethics: The Magazine of Corporate Responsibility
   http://business-ethics.com/2010/08/07/4535-mark-hurds-leadership-failure/

Los Angeles Times
   http://articles.latimes.com/2011/mar/10/business/la-fi-charney-lawsuit-20110310

GAEL O'BRIEN is a Business Ethics Magazine columnist. Gael is a thought leader on building leadership, trust, and reputation and writes The Week in Ethics, a weekly column where this article was first published.

Article Prepared by: Eric Teoro, *Lincoln Christian University*

What the Wal-Mart Ruling Means for Big Business

The Supreme Court ruling in favor of Wal-Mart in a closely watched sex discrimination class action suit will have a far-reaching impact on businesses—and on female workers.

ROGER PARLOFF

Learning Outcomes

After reading this article, you will be able to:

- Describe the sexual discrimination case filed against Wal-Mart and the Court's decision.

- Understand the difficulty in substantiating allegations of wrongdoing.

- Recognize the potential diversity of interpretations of managerial behavior.

Fortune—Today's ruling in the *Dukes v. Wal-Mart* sex discrimination class action—the largest such suit ever and the most important case on the US Supreme Court's business docket this term—is a powerful, multipronged victory for business, though not necessarily for businesswomen.

One key ruling—that most class actions seeking monetary compensation cannot be brought under lenient procedures that were originally designed for suits seeking only injunctive relief—was unanimous, sending a sharp rebuke to the US Court of Appeals for the Ninth Circuit, which had held otherwise by a 6–5 margin.

At the same time, the more far-reaching rulings in the case, which relate to the more fundamental question of just how much in common a million and a half women must have before than can sue as a class for gender discrimination, were decided along narrow, familiar ideological lines, 5–4.

Justice Antonin Scalia wrote the opinion of the Court, and Justice Ruth Bader Ginsburg wrote the partial dissent.

Here are the headlines:

Unconscious Discrimination

The majority drove a stake—multiple stakes, really—through the heart of a very common, powerful genre of employment discrimination class action that revolves around the claim that a company gives its managers excessive discretion in making pay and promotion decisions, allowing those managers to engage in *unconscious* discrimination. In the past, similar suits have been brought against the likes of Costco (COST), Home Depot (HD), and FedEx (FDX), and a group of other large corporations, including Altria (MO), Bank of America (BAC), and Hewlett-Packard (HPQ), had filed amicus briefs in which they admitted feeling vulnerable to suits brought on the Wal-Mart (WMT) template.

Category of Class Action

The Court unanimously agreed that this case—and possibly any class action seeking monetary compensation—*cannot* be brought (as this one was) using the lenient and minimal procedural safeguards that the Federal Rules of Civil Procedure require of suits seeking only injunctive or declaratory relief. This is a ruling of broad significance, *not* confined to the employment discrimination context.

Commonality

The majority decided that for plaintiffs to win the right to proceed as a class, they must demonstrate a relatively high degree of "commonality" between their claims. "Commonality requires the plaintiff to demonstrate that the class members have suffered the same injury," Justice Scalia wrote. "This does not mean merely that they have all suffered a violation of the same provision of law. . . . What matters . . . is not the raising of common *'questions'* . . . but rather the capacity of a classwide proceeding to generate common *answers* apt to drive the resolution of the litigation."

Individual Hearings

The Court unanimously agreed that the lower courts' attempts to streamline the adjudication process in this case to accommodate the litigation of more than a million claims at once deprived litigants—not just Wal-Mart, but also absent class members—of needed statutory safeguards. The lower court had let the case to go forward on the theory that it could be decided based on elaborate computer models, but without hearings ever being held to determine whether individual class members were entitled to relief. The Court unanimously rejected such a "Trial by Formula," as Justice Scalia dubbed it.

The Judge's Fact-Finding Role

The majority said that in performing its gatekeeping function in ensuring that classes are composed of plaintiffs whose legal situations share a sufficient minimum degree of "commonality," judges are permitted to make some findings about disputed questions of fact—a role that many judges had thought had to be reserved for later resolution by a jury. In addition, the majority suggested that judges at the class certification stage can probably also make gatekeeping decisions about whether expert witnesses are engaging in junk science.

Victimization Ratio

The majority noted in passing that while the Court had, in a previous case, permitted plaintiffs to allege a "pattern and practice" of discrimination by an employer where one in eight class members claimed victimization, in the *Dukes* case the plaintiffs had only demonstrated that one in 12,500 class members had complained of wrongdoing. The court implied that such a sparse showing was insufficient. Though the majority insisted that it was not setting up any new statistical threshold for making "pattern and practice" claims, the Court's citation of these ratios clearly invites such inferences in the future by lower court judges, who crave brightline rules of thumb of this type.

To recap the basics, in 2004 a San Francisco federal judge allowed six female Wal-Mart employees to sue on behalf of every one of the nearly 1.5 million female employees who then worked, or had worked, at any of Wal-Mart's 3,400-plus stores nationwide since December 26, 1998. The suit alleged gender discrimination with respect to promotions and pay. (Had the case been allowed to proceed, it would actually have been much bigger than what the Court described—Wal-Mart now has more than 4,300 stores nationwide, for instance—but the Court cites statistics that were accurate when the lower court record on class certification was created in 2004.) In April 2010, the Ninth Circuit pared the class very slightly, but generally approved the lower court's ruling.

The plaintiffs alleged that Wal-Mart allowed individual store managers to make pay and promotion decisions based on excessively subjective criteria. As a consequence, these store managers (who are more often than not men) *unconsciously* tended to choose people like themselves (i.e., other men) to receive career advancements, it was claimed. Over time, Wal-Mart's failure to curb store-manager discretion in the face of continuing statistical gender disparities in pay and promotion rates was then said to amount to intentional discrimination by the company.

Since individual store managers made most promotion and pay decisions at Wal-Mart, one obvious question was whether the alleged abuse of discretion by certain store managers at a small percentage of stores could be extrapolated to establish abuse of discretion at all Wal-Mart stores. In response, the plaintiffs argued that Wal-Mart's strong corporate culture led store managers to unconsciously abuse the discretion they were granted in uniform ways.

At oral argument in March, Justice Scalia had protested that he felt whipsawed by that argument, commenting: "On the one hand, you say the problem is that [the decisions] were utterly subjective, and on the other hand you say there is a strong corporate culture that guides all of this. Well, which is it?"

In today's ruling he rejected almost every aspect of this theory, including the core notion that excessive subjectivity in personnel decisions could amount to a "general policy of discrimination" susceptible to a class-action remedy. Scalia stressed that while Wal-Mart's expert on organizational sociology, William Bielby, said he believed Wal-Mart's procedures were "vulnerable" to discrimination, Bielby admitted that he could not say whether 0.5 percent or 95 percent of store manager employment decisions were actually motivated by improperly stereotyped thinking. "Whether 0.5 percent or 95 percent of the employment decisions at Wal-Mart might be determined by stereotyped thinking is the essential question on which respondents' theory of commonality depends," Scalia wrote. "If Bielby admitted he has no answer to that question, we can safely disregard what he has to say."

Though some will interpret today's majority ruling as reflecting the conservative majority's pro-business tilt, an alternative explanation is more likely. There was always a thermonuclear issue lurking just beneath the surface of this case, though it was not one of the specific technical issues the Court asked the parties to brief.

Conservatives view lawsuits like this one as coming very close to permitting gender (or race) discrimination to be proven on the basis of little more than statistical disparities in the workforce that are extremely widespread in our society and which might simply result from a stew of complex, innocent, cultural causes. Many conservatives fear that if employers have to avoid statistical disparities to avoid getting sued, they will feel pressured to adopt secret quotas, which are illegal.

Critical Thinking

1. What allegations of workplace sex discrimination are identified in the article?

2. How might a code of ethics have prevented the alleged sex discrimination discussed in the article?

3. What lessons for management might be drawn from the article? Identify one lesson for management and defend its importance.

Create Central

www.mhhe.com/createcentral

Internet References

Huffington Post
http://www.huffingtonpost.com/2012/06/06/walmart-sex-discrimination-women-_n_1575859.html

Wal-Mart Class Website
http://www.walmartclass.com/public_home.html

Article   Prepared by: Eric Teoro, *Lincoln Christian University*

When Your Boss Makes You Pay for Being Fat

LESLIE KWOH

Learning Outcomes

After reading this article, you will be able to:

- Describe differing opinions regarding the rights and responsibilities of companies regarding employee healthcare coverage.

- Describe the effectiveness of various approaches to influencing employee behavior regarding healthcare coverage.

- Think more critically regarding employee rights and responsibilities.

A re you a man with a waist measuring 40 inches or more? If you want to work at Michelin North America Inc., that spare tire could cost you.

Employees at the tire maker who have high blood pressure or certain size waistlines may have to pay as much as $1,000 more for health-care coverage starting next year.

As they fight rising health-care costs and poor results from voluntary wellness programs, companies across America are penalizing workers for a range of conditions, including high blood pressure and thick waistlines. They are also demanding that employees share personal-health information, such as body-mass index, weight and blood-sugar level, or face higher premiums or deductibles.

Corporate leaders say they can't lower health-care costs without changing workers' habits, and they cite the findings of behavioral economists showing that people respond more effectively to potential losses, such as penalties, than expected gains, such as rewards. With corporate spending on health care expected to reach an average of $12,136 per employee this year, according to a study by the consulting firm Towers Watson, penalties may soon be the new norm.

Employers may argue that tough-love measures, such as punishing workers who evade health screenings, benefit their staff and lower health-care costs. But such steps also portend a murky future in which a chronic condition, such as hypertension, could cost workers jobs or promotions—or prevent them from being hired in the first place.

Until recently, Michelin awarded workers automatic $600 credits toward deductibles, along with extra money for completing health-assessment surveys or participating in a non-binding "action plan" for wellness. It adopted its stricter policy after its health costs spiked in 2012.

Now, the company will reward only those workers who meet healthy standards for blood pressure, glucose, cholesterol, triglycerides, and waist size—under 35 inches for women and 40 inches for men. Employees who hit baseline requirements in three or more categories will receive up to $1,000 to reduce their annual deductibles. Those who don't qualify must sign up for a health-coaching program in order to earn a smaller credit.

Employee-rights advocates say the penalties are akin to "legal discrimination." While companies are calling them wellness incentives, the penalties are essentially salary cuts by a different name, says Lew Maltby, president of Princeton, NJ-based National Workrights Institute, a nonprofit advocacy group for employee rights in the workplace. "No one ever calls a bad thing what it really is," he says. "It means millions of people are getting their pay cut for no legitimate reason."

Companies may say they have tried softer approaches, but many haven't exhausted their options, like putting healthier food in their cafeterias, building a fitness center or subsidizing gym memberships, he adds. "At best, these programs are giving employers an enormous amount of control over our private lives."

Michelin denies any discrimination and says the policy is voluntary. Not participating means employees won't get the incentives. Wayne Culbertson, Michelin's chief human resources officer, says the old incentive programs didn't lead to meaningful change. For example, an employee could pledge to start walking daily, he says, but never have to prove it. "It was sort of free, you know? You got $600 just for being a good employee."

Six in 10 employers say they plan to impose penalties in the next few years on employees who don't take action to improve their health, according to a recent study of 800 mid- to large-size firms by human-resources consultancy Aon Hewitt. A separate study by the National Business Group on Health and Towers Watson found that the share of employers who plan to impose penalties is likely to double to 36 percent in 2014.

Current law permits companies to use health-related rewards or penalties as long as the amount doesn't exceed 20 percent of the cost of the employee's health coverage. John Hancock, a veteran labor and employment attorney at Butzel Long, a Detroit-based law firm, says that while companies can't legally dock a worker's pay for a health issue, they can tie an employee's health-care bill to whether the worker meets or misses health goals. As long as employers offer exemptions for workers with conditions that prevent them from meeting health goals, the firms are in the clear.

The situation is less clear if, for example, a company ends up singling out obese employees by charging them more for health coverage. If the obesity is linked to an underlying condition, the employer may be liable for discrimination, Mr. Hancock says.

Currently, most companies tie between 5 percent and 10 percent of employee premium costs to incentives, but that will likely go up, says Charlie Smith, chief medical officer for national accounts at insurer Cigna Corp.

Pharmacy chain CVS Caremark sparked outrage among employees and workers-rights advocates last month by asking staff members to report personal health metrics, including their body fat, blood sugar, blood pressure, and cholesterol levels, to the company's insurer by May or pay a $600 penalty.

Health Costs

How your shape can weigh on your wallet.

- **$652** Additional amount that General Electric employees who self-identify as smokers must pay for health care each year.
- **$1,000** Penalty that Honeywell is adding for workers who get certain types of surgery without seeking more input.
- **$600** Annual penalty CVS employees must pay if they fail to report their weight, body fat and cholesterol levels to the company's benefits firm.

- **$100** Monthly penalty that Mohawk Industries charges employees who don't participate in a health-risk assessment.
- **$1,000** Maximum additional amount Michelin employees with high blood pressure or large waistlines could pay for health care.

Few workers can afford to refuse, but some aren't happy. "It opens a Pandora's box," says a full-time CVS employee who works at a distribution center in Florida. "It's none of their business." While the 26-year-old describes himself as healthy, he says he is worried about disclosing health information that could be shared without his knowledge. He says he plans to cancel his health plan, which also covers his wife and child, and will start looking for work elsewhere.

CVS, which maintains that the change is intended to make workers aware of their health risks, says it doesn't have access to workers' screening results.

Mohawk Industries, a Calhoun, Ga.-based flooring company, says participation in its company's health-risk assessment process shot up to 97% after the company imposed a $100 monthly penalty on nonparticipants. The company had previously offered rewards for participating in the assessment, but enrollment rates were low, says Phil Brown, senior vice president of human resources.

Honeywell International Inc. recently introduced a $1,000 penalty—deducted from health-savings accounts—for workers who elect to get certain procedures such as knee and hip replacement and back surgery without seeking more input. The company had offered $500 for participating in a program that provides access to data and additional opinions for workers considering surgery, but less than 20% of the staff joined up. Since it flipped the incentive to a penalty, the company says, enrollment has been above 90%.

There are no new data on surgeries, but the change is projected to save at least $3 million annually, says Brian Marcotte, Honeywell's vice president of compensation and benefits, who presented the plan at the Conference Board's Employee Health Care Conference last month.

Typically, 20% of a company's workforce drives 80% of health-care costs, according to Cigna's Mr. Smith, and roughly 70% of health-care costs are related to chronic conditions brought on by lifestyle choices, such as overeating or sedentary behavior. But when employers target those conditions, employees themselves may feel targeted, especially when it comes to their weight. While companies can't say it outright, many of their measures—such as high cholesterol and high blood pressure—are proxies for obesity.

A 2011 Gallup survey estimated obese or overweight full-time U.S. workers miss an additional 450 million days of work each year, compared with healthy workers, resulting in more than $153 billion in lost productivity.

Worse, chronic conditions could someday harm workers' chances of getting hired, says Deborah Peel, a psychiatrist and founder of the Austin, Texas-based nonprofit Patient Privacy Rights. Patient information sometimes gets leaked, sold or stolen, she warns, noting that she has fielded complaints from job seekers claiming that employers requested health records before extending an offer. "It's incredibly unfair," she says. "It should be about our track record" doing our jobs.

For now, employers are trying to balance the carrot and the stick. Plenty of companies will be watching to see if inflicting a little financial pain leads to change in the long run. "What are the right pain points?" asks Paul Keckley, executive director of Deloitte LLP's health-care research arm, the Center for Health Solutions. "Ultimately, you have to make behavior change automatic. We've got to make this like brushing your teeth."

Critical Thinking

1. Are the companies covered in the article behaving unethically toward employees? Defend your answer.

2. What responsibilities do companies have toward employees regarding healthcare coverage? What rights do companies have toward employees regarding healthcare coverage?

3. Design a healthcare coverage system that you consider ethically sound. Provide rationale for the various components of your system.

Create Central

www.mhhe.com/createcentral

Internet References

Fox Business
http://www.foxbusiness.com/personal-finance/2013/01/15/why-some-employers-are-paying-employees-to-lose-weight/

Gallup Well-Being
http://www.gallup.com/poll/150026/unhealthy-workers-absenteeism-costs-153-billion.aspx

Health Affairs
http://content.healthaffairs.org/content/28/1/46.full

Article   Prepared by: Eric Teoro, *Lincoln Christian University*

Fighting the High Cost of "Getting Even" at Work

Employee retaliation lawsuits are at a record high, and they're hard for companies to win. So what can companies do?

ANNE FISHER

Learning Outcomes

After reading this article, you will be able to:

- Recognize the difficulty employers have in defending against retaliation lawsuits.

- Understand how retaliation is practically defined.

- Employ steps that could prevent or decrease the potential of losing retaliation lawsuits.

For many years, race discrimination charges were the most common complaint against employers, but that has changed. The new no. 1, reports the US Equal Opportunity Commission, is retaliation, meaning alleged actions by employers aimed at getting even with workers who have made other complaints.

In 2010, these cases—36,258 of them—cost companies $404 million, the highest annual total the EEOC has ever obliged private-sector employers to pay. Not only that, but "each one costs six figures to fight in court, regardless of the outcome," notes Kelly Kolb, an employment lawyer at Fowler White Boggs. "They're expensive even if the company wins."

Not that the company is likely to win, for a couple of reasons. First, the definition of retaliation is a bit slippery. Until a few years ago, an employee who filed a retaliation charge had to show some financial loss, such as a firing or demotion, that a boss meted out as punishment for complaining about, say, sexual harassment in the workplace.

Then, in 2006, the Supreme Court decided that definition was too narrow. The upshot of a landmark case, *Burlington*

Northern Santa Fe v. White, is that plaintiffs no longer need to have suffered a monetary setback in order to make a charge of retaliation stick.

"Now, anything that would discourage someone from complaining about unfair practices at work can be considered retaliation," notes Kolb. "It could range from passing you over for a promotion to refusing to let you leave early for your kid's softball game."

A second reason why employers usually lose retaliation lawsuits: Juries don't trust them. Says Kolb, "Jurors are predisposed to believe that employers retaliate."

So what can companies do? One tactic: If you're planning to fire someone, don't telegraph the fact in advance. Kolb says that plaintiffs' attorneys often engineer "a set-up": "If you say to an employee, 'Be in my office tomorrow at 2:00 to discuss whether you're going to be let go or quit,' that person can call a lawyer who will instruct him or her to email you a barrage of complaints before 2:00 so they can claim that the firing was 'retaliatory.'"

As a broader matter of policy, Kolb says many retaliation complaints could be avoided if managers took "a more structured approach than in the past. Everything having to do with a person's performance needs to be documented, so that you have a clear paper trail showing the exact reasons for whatever actions someone's boss may have taken."

Just as important, human resources staffers need to be kept apprised of everything that happens, Kolb adds: "In court, you need to be able to show that there was an objective third party involved, so that any personal animus between a boss and a subordinate was not the motivation behind the company's actions."

Of course, HR departments decimated by outsourcing and layoffs may find such painstaking prevention a tall order and that, Kolb, says, may be a big part of the problem.

"So many HR functions now are so shrunken that managers may be tempted to say, 'Instead of bothering HR with this, we can just handle it ourselves,'" he says. "But letting individual managers make [these] decisions all on their own can be a very costly way to go."

Critical Thinking

1. Why are more allegations of retaliation at work lawsuits being filed now than in previous years?

2. What reasons are given in the article why employers often lose retaliation at work lawsuits?

3. What is the importance of an employer establishing a "paper trail" about an employee's performance?

4. What is the role of a Human Resource department in employee retaliation situations?

5. What statement concerning retaliation at work should be in a code of ethics? Write a statement and defend it. If you do not believe such a statement belongs in a code of ethics, explain your reasoning why such a statement should not be included in a code of ethics.

Create Central

www.mhhe.com/createcentral

Internet References

Ethics Resource Center
http://www.ethics.org/news/fear-backlash-reporting-misconduct-sure-sign-ethically-challenged-workplace

The State Journal: West Virginia's Only Business Newspaper
http://www.statejournal.com/story/24776557/tit-for-tat-how-retaliation-is-causing-costly-workplace-lawsuits

Workforce
http://www.workforce.com/articles/walking-on-eggshells-avoiding-retaliation-claims-when-an-employee-who-files-a-discrimination-complaint-doesnt-leave

Article   Prepared by: Eric Teoro, *Lincoln Christian University*

People Have to Come Before Profits, Even in a Crisis

The Fukushima Daiichi power plant disaster has become a textbook example of what not to do in an emergency.

ALISTAIR NICHOLAS

Learning Outcomes

After reading this article, you will be able to:

- Understand the difference between talking and communicating; communication requires relevant understanding on the part of listeners.

- Recognize the need for training on ethical decision-making so individuals will be more likely to make ethical decisions during a crisis.

After a gigantic earthquake and a devastating tsunami, Japan now has a nuclear crisis which is becoming a case study in bad crisis management. The Fukushima Daiichi nuclear power plant disaster may overshadow the 1984 Union Carbide Bhopal chemical leak, the 1989 Exxon Valdez oil spill or last year's BP oil spill in the Gulf of Mexico as a textbook example of what not to do.

This is not just Japan's problem. A cloud now hangs over the future of nuclear power throughout the "Pacific Ring of Fire" earthquake zone as locals stage traditional and online protests against nuclear energy.

A few organizations will need to adopt new ways of operating after this situation is brought under control. The regulatory authority responsible for nuclear power plants in Japan needs to reassess how to build plants in an earthquake zone. (It appears that the design and location of the Fukushima Daiichi plant was just plain wrong.)

The Tokyo Electric Power Company (TEPCO), which runs the plant, and the Japanese government need to change the way they release critical information in a crisis. (The New York Times has documented the failure of communications.) The flow of information has been slow and vague. In the West we'd describe it as stonewalling. Possibly for the first time in Japanese history, people started seriously questioning those in positions of authority. They felt they had a right to get accurate and truthful updates in a timely manner and that it was not forthcoming.

Japanese authorities also need to assess how they make decisions in a crisis. It appears that much of the decision-making, at least at first, placed a higher value on profit than it did on human life. For example, the Wall Street Journal claims that TEPCO delayed using sea water to cool the reactors because it was concerned about the damage salt water would do to its assets. At least 80 people's lives (those working in the plant at the time of the accident) are at risk because of this decision, plus others involved in the response later on.

This points to a bigger problem in crisis management, worldwide, and not just in Japan: lack of training in ethical decision-making in emergencies. Crisis-preparedness training normally focuses on technical details of how to fix problems and how to communicate with the media.

But executives are poorly prepared for making ethical decisions under pressure. When lives are at stake—particularly as they are in a potential nuclear meltdown—you can't stage an escalated response. You must have an ethical response. You should be throwing everything you have at the situation from the beginning.

Japan is not facing a Chernobyl-style full meltdown. All the reactors at Fukushima have been successfully shut down and the focus has been on cooling the plant. The worst case scenario for Fukushima Daiichi is probably the Three Mile Island nuclear accident of 1979. This may mean a contaminated area of 30 kilometres around the plant. This is not great news—but it is not bad for a serious nuclear accident.

Could the outcome have been better? Possibly—if sea water had been used at the outset of the crisis. But we'll have to wait for the final report following the inevitable investigation.

What does this mean for the future of nuclear energy, especially in earthquake-prone regions? China, which is part of the Pacific Rim of Fire and has experienced its own devastating earthquakes (Tangshan in 1976 and Sichuan in 2008), plans to build a staggering 40 new nuclear power plants by 2015. Since the incident in Japan Beijing has halted approvals for these pending an investigation into its own safety standards. But the plants will almost certainly proceed. Asia and the rest of the world need energy to sustain economic growth and development. Nuclear power is the best source because, accidents like this notwithstanding, it is much cleaner than oil and coal which contribute substantially to global warming.

Abandoning nuclear energy would be like refusing to cross roads because you might be run over. If you know the risks you can manage them. The nuclear energy industry now has a better understanding of the risks as a result of this unfortunate accident. (Here's a stock tip: buy uranium mining and nuclear energy shares now. While prices have fallen close to 30 percent since the tsunami, they will surely rise again. The future is in nuclear energy.)

Lessons will be learned about the design and location of power plants. To start with, they won't be placed too close to the coast or major rivers. It wasn't the earthquake itself that created the problems, but the flooding from the tsunami.

Lessons also will be learned about communications during an Asian crisis. The basic principles are: communicate often, communicate clearly, communicate truthfully, and communicate transparently. This may be more difficult in Japan. Japanese, like Chinese, is not a direct language; it is much more nuanced and intuitive than European languages. (At one point a Japanese official dealing with the crisis apologized publicly for causing "bother." In the context of normal Japanese interaction this might have made sense; in a nuclear crisis it seemed out of touch

with reality.) Japan's agony may teach other Asian nations how to convey information quickly and accurately.

As I tell my clients in crisis situations: stop talking and start communicating. What the public expects—and has a right to expect—is the truth. But the most important lesson of the last ten days should be to incorporate training on ethical decision making into crisis preparedness training. People must come before profits—always and unconditionally.

Critical Thinking

1. Why does it allegedly appear that the Tokyo Electric Power Company (TEPCO) placed a higher value on profit than on human life in the early period after the Fukushima Daiichi nuclear power plant disaster?

2. How might training in ethical decision making as part of crisis preparedness training ensure that people come before profits?

Create Central

www.mhhe.com/createcentral

Internet References

Huffington Post
http://www.huffingtonpost.com/2013/08/26/japan-fukushima-plant_n_3816038.html

New York Times
http://www.nytimes.com/2011/06/13/world/asia/13japan.html?pagewanted=all

Wall Street Journal
http://online.wsj.com/news/articles/SB10001424052748704608504576207912642629904?mod=WSJAsia__LEFTTopStories&mg=reno64-wsj&url=http%3A%2F%2Fonline.wsj.com%2Farticle%2FSB100014240527487046085045762079126426299904.html%3Fmod%3DWSJAsia__LEFTTopStories

ALISTAIR NICHOLAS is Executive Vice President, Asia Pacific, with public relations firm Weber Shandwick and its public affairs arm Powell Tate. He is also a member of the Advisory Board of the China Global Risk Council. The views expressed herein are entirely those of the author and do not necessarily reflect those of his employers or their clients, or of any other organizations with which he is associated. Alistair Nicholas has represented nuclear energy companies and companies involved in the nuclear energy supply chain. He blogs about China, reputation management, and everything else at Off The Record.

Article   Prepared by: Eric Teoro, *Lincoln Christian University*

New Rules Would Cut Silica Dust Exposure

STEVEN GREENHOUSE

Learning Outcomes

After reading this article, you will be able to:

- Describe the conflicting claims regarding silica dust exposure and employee safety.

- Describe the difference between stricter adherence to current guidelines and the call for stricter guidelines.

- Discuss company responsibility toward employee safety.

The Occupational Safety and Health Administration proposed long-awaited rules on Friday to limit crystalline silica, a move it said would prevent nearly 700 deaths a year by reducing exposure to these very small particles that can cause lung cancer and other diseases.

OSHA faced heavy pressure from labor leaders, who argued that the current exposure limits, adopted four decades ago, were lax and should be strengthened to prevent silicosis, an irreversible respiratory disease that can be fatal. But business groups lobbied against the proposal, questioning whether it would be feasible to carry out and noting that silicosis deaths were declining.

"Exposure to silica can be deadly, and limiting that exposure is essential," said David Michaels, the assistant secretary of labor in charge of OSHA. He estimated that the proposed rule would prevent 1,600 new cases of silicosis each year.

Dr. Michaels said the rules—issued after 2.5 years of delay—would affect 534,000 businesses, 90 percent of them in construction. He said it would cost industry $640 million to comply with the new rules, averaging $1,242 a company—but he estimated that the total benefits would exceed $4 billion.

Crystalline silica—tiny particles no more than one-hundredth the size of grains of sand—is created during work with stone, concrete, brick or mortar. It can occur during sawing, grinding and drilling and is common in glass manufacturing and sand blasting. One government study found that many workers in hydraulic fracturing, known as fracking, were exposed to 10 times the permissible level of silica.

Dr. Michaels said, "Every year, exposed workers not only lose their ability to work but also to breathe. This proposal is expected to prevent thousands of deaths from silicosis—an incurable and progressive disease—as well as lung cancer."

He said the public would have 90 days to submit written comments before public hearings would be held.

Marc Freedman, executive director of labor law policy at the United States Chamber of Commerce, questioned the need for the rules. For general industry and maritime, the proposed permissible exposure levels will be cut to 50 micrograms a cubic meter of air from 100 micrograms. The construction industry's exposure levels will be cut 80 percent, to 50 micrograms from 250 in a cubic meter of air.

Mr. Freedman said many businesses thought rigorous enforcement of current standards would be sufficient. "I'm not saying employers don't want to spend the money on safety—the question is, Is this doable?" he said.

Tighter restrictions, he said, would affect the fracking industry. "This could have a big impact on fracking, when that industry has been doing a lot of good things for the economy," he said.

OSHA officials said that fracking executives had assured them that they were working to reduce silica exposure.

Peg Seminario, director of safety and health for the A.F.L.-C.I.O., applauded OSHA's move. "It's a very important rule—there are over 2 million workers exposed to silica," she said.

"It's long recognized as a hazard. The current standard was adopted more than 40 years ago, and it doesn't protect workers."

She said the proposal would require businesses to measure periodically for silica and to offer medical testing every 3 years, including chest X-rays and lung function tests, for workers exposed to permissible limits 30 days or more a year.

Ms. Seminario noted that many Canadian provinces already had the tighter exposure limits. She acknowledged, however, that there might not be enough certified laboratories to test whether businesses' air quality met the new standards.

Dr. Michaels said it would cost an average of $550 for firms with fewer than 20 employees to comply with the proposed rules. Among the steps companies could take to reduce silica particles, Dr. Michaels said, would be to use a vacuum or water hose with saws that produce such dust. For businesses that do extensive grinding, the grinding apparatus could be inside an airtight housing with a vacuum that draws away the particles.

Labor unions and other worker advocacy groups had criticized the Obama administration for the delays, saying the Office of Management and Budget—known for insisting on thorough cost-benefit analyses—sat on the proposal for more than 2 years. Dr. Michaels said the main reason for the delay was that his agency needed to analyze the new rules for 130 industries. He predicted that industries would find cheaper ways than OSHA foresees to tighten exposure limits.

"The proposed rule uses common-sense measures that will protect workers' lives and lungs—like keeping the material wet so dust doesn't become airborne," he said. "It is designed to give employers flexibility in selecting ways to meet the standard."

The American Chemistry Council, an industry group, issued a statement, saying the current exposure limit was "appropriate to protect against silica-related disease, provided it is adhered to strictly." Noting that the mortality rate from silicosis has dropped more than 90 percent over the last 45 years, the council said, "The cases of silicosis that still occur result from noncompliance with the current" limit.

But the American Public Health Association, a nationwide group of public health professionals, applauded OSHA's move. Georges C. Benjamin, the association's executive director, said, "The proposal marks an important step in addressing a serious health hazard for workers."

Critical Thinking

1. Which position do you think is ethically required—creating stricter guidelines or enforcing stricter adherence to current guidelines? Why?

2. To what degree are companies ethically responsible for employee safety on the job?

3. What role should government play regarding employee safety?

Create Central

www.mhhe.com/createcentral

Internet References

American Chemistry Council
  http://www.americanchemistry.com/Media/PressReleasesTranscripts/ACC-news-releases/Crystalline-Silica-Panel-Statement-on-New-OSHA-Silica-Regulation.html

New York Times
  http://www.nytimes.com/2013/08/24/business/new-rules-would-cut-silica-dust-exposure.html

Article   Prepared by: Eric Teoro, *Lincoln Christian University*

Opting to Blow the Whistle or Choosing to Walk Away

ALINA TUGEND

Learning Outcomes

After reading this article, you will be able to:

- Describe challenges involved in reporting unethical behavior on the part of managers.

- Discern motives behind whistleblowing.

- Determine when to refrain from making managerial behavior public.

Whistle-blowers have been big news lately—from Chelsea Manning, formerly known as Pfc. Bradley Manning, to Edward J. Snowden. Yet, for most people, the question of whether to expose unethical or illegal activities at work doesn't make headlines or involve state secrets.

But that doesn't make the problem less of a quandary. The question of when to remain quiet and when to speak out—and how to do it—can be extraordinarily difficult no matter what the situation.

And while many think of ethics violations as confined to obviously illegal acts, like financial fraud or safety violations, the line often can be much blurrier and, therefore, more difficult to navigate.

According to the Ethics Resource Center, a nonprofit research organization, the No. 1 misconduct observed—by a third of 4,800 respondents—was misuse of company time. That was closely followed by abusive behavior and lying to employees.

The findings were published in the organization's 2011 National Business Ethics Survey, which interviewed, on the phone or online, employees in the commercial sector who were employed at least 20 hours a week. It has been conducted biannually since 1994.

But offensive behavior that creates a hostile work environment, although often not thought of as unethical behavior, is the leading reason people leave their jobs, said Patricia J. Harned, president of the center. "Abusive and intimidating behavior by supervisors and managers creates a toxic work environment."

So does lying to employees. Lester, who asked that I use only his first name to avoid possible legal issues, worked at a global consulting company for about 3 years, earning high performance ratings. At one point, he said, he accidentally learned that his manager had deliberately lied to deny him a promotion opportunity. Lester spoke to the hiring manager to no avail, and because the company had a strong ethics program—including a specific "no retaliation policy" and a hot line to report ethics complaints—he reported the situation.

An investigation found no wrongdoing, and although Lester appealed the findings, no action was taken against the manager. That is when he says the retaliation began.

"All my direct reports were taken away from me and I was given the most difficult projects with the least resources," he said. "A whole series of things happened, which were unlikely to be a coincidence."

After about 8 months of this, he decided to leave.

Lester's experience may be the reason the misconduct most often seen is not the one most often reported. According to the Ethics Resources Center report, which is sponsored by major corporations like Wal-Mart and Northrop Grumman, less than half of those who observed a boss lying to employees reported it.

On the other hand, while only 12 percent said they had witnessed someone stealing from the company, almost 70 percent of those who saw such activity reported it.

One of the difficulties in cases like Lester's is that no law has been broken. True whistleblowing, according to Stephen M. Kohn, a lawyer and executive director of the National Whistleblowers Center, is when people report seeing or experiencing something at their company that is against the law, rather than cases in which employees feel mistreated, but nothing illegal has occurred.

It appears, however, that an increasing number of employees are willing to come forward in both types of cases. More people are using their companies' ethics procedures to report misconduct, and more people are filing whistle-blower claims.

Mr. Kohn, whose organization refers potential whistle-blowers to lawyers, said there had been a 30 percent increase in the number of people requesting referrals over the last 18 months, which comes to about 1,500 requests a year.

He also said the quality of complaints—with more documentation and from higher-level employees—had increased.

Some of this is because of legislation rewarding whistle-blowers for coming forth and protecting them against retaliation. The most prominent of those is the Dodd-Frank Act, which passed in 2010. Under that act, the Securities and Exchange Commission oversees the Office of the Whistleblower, which in 2012 alone received 3,001 tips.

It may seem counterintuitive that reporting bad behavior would go up during the recession and afterward, when people fear for their jobs. Ms. Harned said, however, that one explanation was that employees were less able to change jobs, so they might be more willing to try to change a negative work culture.

"Historically, when the economy is good, companies take more risks and focus more on the bottom line," Ms. Harned said. "They're not talking about ethics as much."

But, just as reporting is on the rise, so is retaliation. More than one in five employees interviewed said they experienced some sort of reprisal when they reported misconduct, ranging from being excluded from decision-making activities and getting the cold shoulder from other employees to being passed over for promotion.

That is almost double the number who said they were retaliated against in the 2007 study.

Even more alarming, in 2009, 4 percent of those who said they experienced reprisals for reporting wrongdoing cited physical threats to themselves or their property. In 2011, that rose to 31 percent.

"Whistle-blowing does threaten cultures and individuals, even when companies say they want it and think they want it,"

said Kirk O. Hanson, executive director of the Markkula Center for Applied Ethics at Santa Clara University.

And, he said, it's very easy to rationalize that an action—say, denying a promotion—is not actually payback for reporting misconduct, but because the worker isn't a team player.

So, while it's important to expose unethical behavior, it's also necessary to be very clear why you're doing it—and how to do it right.

"A good thing to ask yourself is, 'Why am I doing this? Am I trying to help the company or just get someone in trouble?'" said Stuart Sidle, director of the Industrial-Organizational Psychology program at the University of New Haven.

You need to ensure that you're not talking yourself out of taking an ethical stand, nor talking yourself into reporting something for the wrong reason, Professor Hanson said.

"Have someone you can bounce dilemmas off who has similar values," he said. "To make sure you're not rationalizing not doing anything, and to make sure there's a genuine problem—someone to help you be strong but also to test your realities."

In general, employees should follow the proper channels, like addressing the issue with the person directly supervising the supposed culprit, said John M. Thornton, a professor of accounting ethics at Azusa Pacific University.

Along the same lines, think very hard before going public.

"I question someone trying to report externally before reporting internally," Mr. Sidle said. It's too easy, now, he said, to put up a video of bad behavior on YouTube or lash out on Facebook without ever speaking with the people who might be willing to resolve the problems.

On the other hand, don't shy away from reporting bad behavior because you don't want to be seen as that worst elementary school insult—a tattletale.

"You don't want a culture of tattling, but you do want a culture of telling if something is harming the company and the community," Professor Sidle said.

And companies need to be specific in how they talk about ethics, he added.

"It's useless just to talk about unethical behavior," he said. "Everyone is against fraud. Everyone is against disrespectful behavior, but how is it defined? Leadership has to give examples. If someone asks you to backdate something because the client asked, it's unethical, even if it's commonly done."

And, finally, whistle-blowers should know that most cases are not settled in their favor. "This may be attributable to injustices in the system, or lack of merit or proof of the alleged wrongdoing," Professor Thornton said.

For good or for bad, most of us will never face the decisions that Mr. Manning and Mr. Snowden have. But that doesn't mean our choices—to confront or to ignore—aren't important.

"Some will always cheat on their expense reports," Professor Hanson said. "Some will never cheat. Most of us are in the middle. It's a constant struggle to do the right thing."

Critical Thinking

1. Is reporting unethical behavior ever an unethical act? Why or why not?
2. What are the challenges inherent in whistleblowing?
3. What advice would you give to someone who is considering whistleblowing?

Create Central

www.mhhe.com/createcentral

Internet References

U.S. Department of Labor
   http://www.whistleblowers.gov/

U.S. Equal Employment Opportunity Commission
   http://www.eeoc.gov/laws/types/facts-retal.cfm

U.S. Securities and Exchange Commission
   http://www.sec.gov/whistleblower

Article   Prepared by: Eric Teoro, *Lincoln Christian University*

Two Years After Dodd-Frank, Has Wall Street Changed?

16 Percent on Wall Street would engage in insider trading if they knew they could get away with it.

MEG HANDLEY

Learning Outcomes

After reading this article, you will be able to:

- Recognize the need for greater transparency if increased ethical behavior is desired.

- Understand the limits of rules and enforcement in securing ethical behavior.

- Describe challenges faced within the financial industry regarding ethical behavior.

Ever since the bigwigs heading Wall Street's biggest financial firms helped bring the global economy to its knees back in 2008, the government has been instituting all sorts of regulations to make sure behind-closed-door dealings don't blow up the economy again.

But on the eve of the second anniversary of the Dodd-Frank Wall Street Reform and Consumer Protection Act, are all these new rules designed to keep Wall Street on the straight-and-narrow working?

It would appear not, at least according to a report released this month that shows shady ethics remain rampant and widespread in the industry.

To be sure, Wall Street certainly isn't known for a squeaky clean image when it comes to ethics. Still, almost a quarter of executives see bending and breaking the rules as a key to success, according to a survey released this month by whistleblower law firm Labaton Sucharow, an "alarming" figure according to the firm.

The survey, which polled 500 senior executives in the United States and the United Kingdom, also found that 26 percent had observed or had firsthand knowledge of wrongdoing in their workplace.

Perhaps most shocking, almost a third of respondents felt pressured to break the law or compromise ethics based on compensation plans and the prospect of bonuses. About 16 percent would actually commit a crime—insider trading, for instance—if they knew they could get away with it.

"The financial services industry, its moral compass is broken," says Jordan Thomas, partner and chair of Labaton Sucharow's whistleblower representation practice. "Until these organizations re-establish a culture of integrity and stewardship, investors are at great risk."

But Wall Street isn't likely to do so without a stronger nudge from regulators, Thomas says.

"The heart of it is within the organization, but law enforcement authorities—with additional resources—have the ability to drive change," he says. "[Regulators] need to police the beat more aggressively until the organizations re-establish that culture of integrity and stewardship."

Still, regulators and law enforcement can only do so much in the face of a "culture of silence" that encourages employees to keep mum about dodgy dealings at their firm. Despite the fact that 94 percent of those surveyed said they would report wrongdoing given the protections offered by the Securities and Exchange Commission and other financial regulators, fewer than half knew of the programs or how to report misdeeds. But their help is key, Thomas says.

"They aren't mind readers. They can't predict the future. They can't see into every organization," he says of regulators. "The heart of the solution is within the organization."

Transparency has long been an issue in the financial services industry, which has invented increasingly complex financial products in recent years. Some of those same products—including subprime mortgages and derivatives—were blamed in part for the near-collapse of the world's financial system.

But not everyone thinks just tacking on more and increasingly restrictive rules is the way to fix Wall Street's conscience problem. Making trades, open positions, and other financial dealings part of the public record would go a long way in ensuring that financial services execs are a little more scrupulous, according to some.

"We believe that transparency is a real alternative to regulation and it can be much more effective and much less costly," says Michael Borland, compliance officer and general counsel at financial services firm OANDA. "If one of the objectives [of Dodd-Frank] is to instill a higher level of business ethics, of trust, honesty, and transparency, rules can only go so far."

To that end, OANDA, an Internet-based forex trading and currency information firm, publishes all of its open positions online, minus the client's name.

Critical Thinking

1. What concrete steps could a Wall Street CEO take to promote ethical behavior on the part of the firm's employees?

2. What role should external entities play in promoting ethical behavior on Wall Street?

3. What are your thoughts about individuals stating they would engage in illegal behavior if they could get away with it?

Create Central

www.mhhe.com/createcentral

Internet References

CNBC
  http://www.cnbc.com/id/47075854

Forbes
  http://www.forbes.com/sites/franksorrentino/2014/07/24/after-four-years-of-dodd-frank-bank-regulation-is-still-a-guessing-game/

Labaton Sucharow
  http://www.labaton.com/en/about/press/upload/US-UK-Financial-Services-Industry-Survey.pdf

Article   Prepared by: Eric Teoro, *Lincoln Christian University*

The Unexpected Cost of Staying Silent

Not blowing the whistle may seem like the easy way out, but those who choose silence pay a price.

AMY FREDIN

Learning Outcomes

After reading this article, you will be able to:

- Recognize that individuals who remain silent about wrongdoing in organizations often regret doing so.

- Recognize various deterrents to whistleblowing, enabling possible reporting improvements.

". . . and another massive fraud was just uncovered today thanks to a whistleblower who came forward with critical information. . ." We've all heard these reports on the news and read about them in the newspapers, but this type of activity wouldn't happen in *my* organization, right? And even if it did, certainly *my* employees would quickly take corrective action, right? Let's take a look at the current landscape for organizational wrongdoing, including fraud, as well as the prevalence of whistleblowing in response to these activities. The findings alone may be surprising.

To bring these topics a little closer to home, additional analysis outlines the situations of wrongdoing some of our fellow IMA members encountered. Many individuals in the survey did blow the whistle in these wrongdoing cases, but others chose not to report the situations. This article looks further at their reasons for staying silent and their subsequent feelings of regret associated with that decision.

What Do the Surveys Say?

PricewaterhouseCoopers (PwC) has conducted several global studies of economic crime over the past decade. Most recently,

its 2011 study reports data from nearly 4,000 companies worldwide, including 156 from the United States. (See www.pwc.com/gx/en/economiccrime-survey/index.jhtml for PwC's 2011, 2009, and 2007 Global Economic Crime Surveys.)

Data from the 2011 study indicates that 34 percent of all companies (45 percent of US companies) reported having uncovered a significant economic crime during the previous 12-month period. The term "significant" means the crime had a definite impact on the business, either from direct, tangible damage or from collateral or psychological damage. These crimes occurred in companies of all sizes and industries. The noted wrongdoings included such instances as cybercrime, bribery and corruption, accounting fraud, and, most frequently, asset misappropriation.

Just 2 years earlier, more than 3,000 companies worldwide (71 US companies) responded to PwC's 2009 survey where 30 percent of companies (35 percent of US companies) reported experiencing a significant economic crime over the previous 12-month period. Considering both of these recent surveys, the prevalence of these crimes is disturbing, to say the least. The loss amounts are staggering as well. In 2011 (and 2009), 54 percent (44 percent) of US companies estimated their fraud losses to be between $100,000 and $5 million, with another 10 percent (8 percent) reporting that their losses amounted to more than $5 million.

PwC also identified detection sources for these crimes. In 2009, 34 percent of the incidences worldwide were initially found because of internal or external "tips," but the largest source of detection during that time frame came from companies' own internal controls, which accounted for 46 percent. In 2011, the global survey reported similar rankings but an even larger disparity between these two detection methods, with only 23 percent of frauds being detected by "tips," while 50 percent were detected from a variety of internal control procedures. Kalaithasan Kuppusamy and David Yong Gun Fie reported similar rankings in their October 2004 article, "Developing Whistleblowing Policies: An Aid to Internal Auditors," in *Accountants Today*. They reported global survey results where auditors ranked first and whistleblowers ranked second in terms of detection sources for economic crime.

Though detail for US detection sources in 2011 wasn't reported, the sources of detection in the US in 2009 looked very different from the global results. "The single most common way that fraud was detected among US survey respondents was through tip-offs," the report notes, where whistleblowers alerted officials to 48 percent of the crimes; internal controls initially detected 28 percent of the crimes during this time period.

With the prevalence of crime and the importance of whistleblowing well documented, it might lead you to believe that more and more individuals are coming forward to report organizational wrongdoing. But what percentage of individuals who either know about or suspect wrongdoing come forward? Going back to 1992, a US federal government survey of its own employees reported that as many as 50 percent of individuals who were aware of a crime chose to remain silent.

A slightly later study, "Whistle-Blower Disclosures and Management Retaliation" by Joyce Rothschild and Terance Miethe, published in the February 1999 issue of *Work and Occupations,* reported a similar level of nonreporting, but does that level still apply today? As we head into a new era where whistleblowers have the potential to be rewarded financially for their information because of the recently instituted Dodd-Frank Wall Street Reform and Consumer Protection Act, it seems appropriate to take an even more current look at the landscape around those who observe organizational wrongdoing.

The IMA Study

In an effort to understand this issue from an insider's perspective, I surveyed attendees at IMA's Annual Conference & Exposition in 2007. Attendees could complete an anonymous survey, which included questions predominantly related to whistleblowing and internal controls, in exchange for a chance to win one of 10 $50 cash prizes. Of the 75 individuals who completed the survey, 45 reported having observed wrongdoing within their organizations, and 27 of these 45 individuals stated that they reported this information to the appropriate authorized party, suggesting a 60 percent report rate.

The 60 percent rate suggests we may be making strides in encouraging whistleblowers to come forward. Yet five of the 27 individuals who blew the whistle on one situation admitted to staying silent on at least one other. The remaining 18 of the 45 individuals who had observed one or more incidences of wrongdoing didn't report any of them. If this last group of 18 nonreporters is analyzed on its own, it suggests that the nonreporter rate is 40 percent. But if the five individuals who both reported and stayed silent on different issues are allowed to be included in both groups, then the nonreporter rate goes up to 51 percent (23 out of 45). At this level, we're back to where we started-the 50 percent range of reporting and nonreporting that previous studies have documented.

In order to better understand the situations behind these reports (and nonreports), the survey asked respondents to describe incidence(s) of wrongdoing that they observed. Table 1

Table 1   Instances of Reported Wrongdoing

Type of Activity Observed	No. of Reports	Examples Noted
Theft of Company Property/Cash	2	Theft of company computer
		Mishandling of petty cash
Unauthorized/Inappropriate Use of Company Assets	5	Unauthorized use of company vehicle
		Misappropriation of funds
		Inappropriate use of grant money
		Purchase misuse
		Irrelevant advertising expenditures that weren't approved
Financial Statement Manipulation	5	Misstated product line P&L
		Aggressive estimates affecting income
		Income statement misrepresentation
		Financial statement misstatements
		Overstatement of inventory value

(conitnued)

Table 1   Instances of Reported Wrongdoing *(continued)*

Type of Activity Observed	No. of Reports	Examples Noted
Claiming Personal Expenses for Reimbursement	4	Airfare for spouse purchased with company credit card
		Inappropriate personal spending on company credit card
		Improper expense submission
		Questionable expense receipts/charges
Sexual Harassment	2	Sexual harassment of a coworker
		Sexual harassment
Inappropriate Human Resources/Payroll Practices	4	Fraud in the selection process
		Hiring spouse of executive
		Back pay being withheld inappropriately
		Inappropriate untaxed bonuses
Other	5	Kickbacks
		Overbilling client
		Employee using counterfeit money in vending machine
		Inappropriate use of cash-basis accounting
		Violation of corporate risk management policy
TOTAL	**27**	

outlines the situations on which individuals blew the whistle. These reported wrongdoing activities varied greatly from mishandling petty cash to misrepresenting the company's income statement to sexual harassment.

Table 2 describes the other situations—the ones on which individuals remained silent. These unreported situations of wrongdoing also varied greatly—from an employee stealing company supplies to manipulating revenues and expenses to claiming personal expenses for reimbursement. When comparing the situations in Tables 1 and 2, the uncanny crossovers are hard to dismiss. The situations described in both tables are very similar, suggesting that it isn't just the event's nature or the significance that drives an individual to report-or not report-wrongdoing.

Table 3 provides a closer look at the survey respondents to see if there are any key demographic differences between those who reported wrongdoing and those who didn't. This information is provided for the entire group of survey respondents along with comparison detail for the two different reporter groups (reporters, the 27 who reported at least one situation of wrongdoing; nonreporters, the 23 who stayed silent on at least one instance of wrongdoing). There doesn't appear to be much difference in the ages and length of time at current companies of those who blew the whistle as opposed to those who stayed silent. The average age across the board was approximately 47, and average time with their current company was also quite steady at approximately 8 or 9 years.

But there are some gender differences between the groups. Though 55 percent of the entire sample was male, only 48 percent of those blowing the whistle were male. Further, of the individuals who remained silent, 70 percent were male. A meta-analysis by Jessica Mesmer-Magnus and Chockalingam Viswesvaran, "Whistleblowing in Organizations: An Examination of Correlates of Whistleblowing Intentions, Actions, and Retliation," in the Spring 2005 issue of the *Journal of Business Ethics,* looked at four specific studies on actual whistleblowers and noted a similar gender difference across those studies: Women blew the whistle more often than men did.

In addition to a gender difference in my study's respondents, the remainder of the data shows that these individuals come from businesses of all types and sizes and that the whistleblowing reports are spread fairly evenly among all such companies. Further, both the reporter and nonreporter groups appear to be composed of similar individuals in regard to their certifications held and degrees completed: The vast majority are either a CMA® (Certified Management Accountant) or CPA (Certified Public Accountant) or both, and the majority in both groups also have a master's degree. In other words, even these highly educated individuals with valued credentials and experience find it difficult to deal with wrongdoing in the workplace.

Although this detail portrays the background information of all respondents as well as the wrongdoing situations that they observed, the survey asked more probing questions of the silent

Table 2 Instances of Unreported Wrongdoing . . . and Regret Associated with Staying Silent

Type of Activity Observed	No. of Similar Reports	Examples Notes	Level of Regret Experienced*
Theft of Company Property/Cash	2	Employee stealing supplies from the company	no regret
		Unauthorized purchases; incorrect recording of cash	some regret
Inappropriate Use of Company Assets	1	Accessing pornography on work computer	little regret
Financial Statement Manipulation	5	Inappropriate month-end adjustments	great regret
		Accounting estimate adjustments for bad debt	no regret
		Manipulating revenue and expenses	some regret
		Earnings manipulation	some regret
		Income smoothing using accrual manipulation	little regret
Claiming Personal Expenses for Reimbursement	4	Personal travel of children	great regret
		Misclassifying expense reports	little regret
		Personal assets purchased by company	no regret
		Personal expenses purchased on corporate card	little regret
Sexual Harassment	1	Sexist comments	little regret
Inappropriate HR/Payroll Practices	3	Inappropriate time-sheet reporting	little regret
		Profit-sharing calculations unverifiable	little regret
		Reporting payments to employees as travel vs. wages to avoid payroll taxes	little regret
Other	7	Collusion within upper management; sharing inside information	great regret
		Executive cover-up	some regret
		Violation of federal manufacturing law	great regret
		Fraudulent information reported on tax returns	little regret
		Controller cover-up on missing equipment	great regret
		Noncompetitive supplier selected	no regret
		Sabotage of a new process change	great regret
TOTAL	23		

* Subjects were asked if they were currently experiencing (or had in the past experienced) any regret associated with their decision to stay silent. They were asked to respond in one of the following ways: no regret, little regret, some regret, and great regret.

observers. Since the rate of whistleblowing has remained constant at around 50 percent for at least the past 18 years, there must be something more that we can learn from these nonreporters-something that can help us "break through" to future observers that may give them the courage to come forward with their information.

One such survey question asked these individuals to explain why they chose to remain silent. Table 4 reports the reasons they gave. Not surprisingly, the most common reason for not blowing the whistle was fear of retaliation in one form or another, including job loss and difficult working conditions.

Others noted reasons such as the wrongdoing wasn't serious enough to worry about; they didn't feel they had enough proof to bring the allegation forward; and/or they felt somebody else would report the situation. Two individuals further noted that they voluntarily left the company because of what was going on.

. . . the most common reason for not blowing the whistle was fear of retaliation in one form or another . . .

Table 3   Survey Respondents

	All		Reporters		Nonreporters	
Age (in years)						
Mean	47.5		46.7		49.1	
Range	27 to 71		29 to 67		30 to 71	
Tenure with Organization (in years)						
Mean	8.6		9		8.3	
Range	0.25 to 31		2 to 20		0.75 to 30	
	N	**Percentage**	**N**	**Percentage**	**N**	**Percentage**
Gender						
Male	41	55 percent	13	48 percent	16	70 percent
Female	33	44 percent	14	52 percent	7	30 percent
Missing Data	1	1 percent	0		0	
Total	**75**		**27**		**23**	
Industry Membership						
Manufacturing	27	36 percent	10	37 percent	7	30 percent
Professional Services	17	23 percent	7	26 percent	6	26 percent
Education	7	9 percent	2	7 percent	5	22 percent
Government	5	7 percent	1	4 percent	1	4 percent
Pharmaceuticals/Healthcare	4	5 percent	1	4 percent	0	0 percent
Other/Missing	15	20 percent	6	22 percent	4	17 percent
Total	**75**		**27**		**23**	
# of Employees in Company						
Less than 100	20	27 percent	11	41 percent	6	26 percent
101 to 500	19	25 percent	5	19 percent	6	26 percent
501 to 2,000	10	13 percent	5	19 percent	5	22 percent
2,001 to 10,000	11	15 percent	1	4 percent	3	13 percent
More than 10,000	13	17 percent	4	15 percent	3	13 percent
Missing	2	3 percent	1	4 percent	0	0 percent
Total	**75**		**27**		**23**	
Certifications Held						
CMA (w/o CPA)	22	29 percent	8	30 percent	7	30 percent
CPA (w/o CMA)	16	21 percent	6	22 percent	3	13 percent
CMA & CPA	20	27 percent	8	30 percent	5	22 percent
Others (no CMA or CPA)	3	4 percent	1	4 percent	1	4 percent
None/Missing	14	19 percent	4	15 percent	7	30 percent
Total	**75**		**27**		**23**	
Highest Degree Completed						
Associate's	1	1 percent	1	4 percent	1	4 percent
Bachelor's	29	39 percent	10	37 percent	7	30 percent
Master's	41	55 percent	16	59 percent	14	61 percent
Doctorate	3	4 percent	0	0 percent	1	4 percent
Missing	1	1 percent	0	0 percent	0	0 percent
Total	**75**		**27**		**23**	

Table 4 Reasons for Not Reporting the Wrongdoing

Reason Given	Number of Similar Reports
Fear of job loss and/or other retaliation	10
Not that big of a deal	4
Didn't have enough proof	3
Thought somebody else would report it	2
Chose to leave the company instead	2
Other	5
Total*	**26**

* Three individuals each gave two reasons for staying silent, thus the total adds up to 23 + 3 = 26.

Regret from Not Blowing the Whistle

But what have these individuals experienced since their decision to remain silent? Did they avoid the retaliation they were hoping to avoid, or were there other negative consequences associated with staying silent, too? One question asked these silent observers whether they were currently experiencing (or had in the past) any regret associated with their decision to remain silent. This data speaks for itself. Presented alongside the unreported situations in the last column of Table 2, the vast majority of silent observers, 19 of the 23 individuals who chose not to report the wrongdoings, acknowledge having experienced at least some regret (rated as either little, some, or great) associated with their decision to remain silent.

It further appears that these individuals have experienced regret-to varying degrees-for many different types of wrongdoing situations. Not only did some experience regret for the "bigger" issues, such as "fixing" the numbers or theft of property, but individuals also experienced regret for letting "smaller" issues go unreported, including such things as bypassing proper procedures in order to justify a purchase or letting some personal expenses count for reimbursement.

Tone at the Top

It's clear that there's no easy way to deal with wrongdoing in the workplace. Once an individual becomes aware of illegal and/or unethical activity, there are ramifications for reporting and not reporting it. Unfortunately, organizational wrongdoing occurs in companies of all sizes and in all industries. Further,

Once an individual becomes aware of illegal and/or unethical activity, there are ramifications for reporting and not reporting it.

given that many businesses today find themselves in fragile financial positions with lower-than-desired headcounts, there are fewer resources to allocate toward enhanced internal controls and ethics training.

But there's still something companies can do, at relatively no cost to them, to combat and prevent fraud and wrongdoing. Businesses can espouse an ethical culture, one that truly is motivated from the top tiers of the organizational chart, to show their employees that they mean business. The importance of a company's "tone at the top" certainly it isn't a new phenomenon (see "Tone at the Top: Insights from Section 404" by Dana Hermanson, Daniel Ivancevich, and Susan Ivancevich in the November 2008 *Strategic Finance*). And this is getting even more pronounced attention as a fraud prevention factor in today's fast-paced, risk-laden marketplace. PwC captured this message loud and clear when it concluded its 2011 global economic crime survey with the following statement: "Establishing the right 'tone at the top' is key in the fight against economic crime."

No Easy Way Out

The data in this article suggests that the level of whistleblowing has stayed relatively constant over the past two decades at around 50 percent and gives reasons as to why the remaining 50 percent chose to remain silent on these issues. Yet through this analysis it becomes clear that these silent observers don't come out unscathed because they have to live with their decision, knowing that some individuals are benefitting at the expense of others. They have to live with their regret-knowing that their silence may be perpetuating fraud, harassment, law violations, and the like, within that company. The stress associated with this regret may be a cost that they didn't anticipate, but it's a cost nonetheless. Perhaps the potential for financial rewards will now give some of these otherwise silent observers enough incentive to come forward with their information. And perhaps these and other reward opportunities will eventually give all whistleblowers the compensation they desire and deserve to help offset the personal costs that come with whistleblowing.

One thing is certain, though. We can all learn something from the survey respondents. Blowing the whistle on organizational wrongdoing isn't an easy thing to do, but staying silent on these issues may not be an easy way out, either.

Critical Thinking

1. Comment on the methodology used in the IMA Study reported in the article. Are the results of the study generalizable given its methodology? Why or why not?

2. Examine Table 4 in the article. Of the reasons given for not reporting wrongdoing (i.e., not blowing the whistle), which of the reasons do you find most compelling? Why? Which the least compelling? Why?

3. Examine Table 2 in the article. What might be the reasons for a finding of great regret versus a finding of no regret? Make a list of possible reasons for feeling or not feeling of regret for use in class discussion.

4. Examine Table 1—Instance of Reported Wrongdoing. Develop a table or a chart in which you analyze the seriousness of the reported wrongdoing. Then, relate your analysis of Table 1 to the results reported in Table 2. What conclusion might you draw from Tables 1 and 2?

Create Central

www.mhhe.com/createcentral

Internet References

New York Times
    http://www.nytimes.com/1987/02/22/us/survey-of-whistle-blowers-finds-retaliation-but-few-regrets.html

Reuters
    http://www.reuters.com/article/2012/02/17/us-citigroup-whistleblower-idUSTRE81G06Y20120217

The Guardian
    http://www.theguardian.com/money/2014/sep/23/whistleblower-bank-personal-cost-sec

---

AMY FREDIN, PhD, is an assistant professor of accounting at St. Cloud State University in St. Cloud, Minn. She also is a member of IMA's Central Minnesota Chapter. You can reach her at (320) 308-3287 or ajfredin@stcloudstate.edu.

Article   Prepared by: Eric Teoro, *Lincoln Christian University*

Stealing a Pen at Work Could Turn You On to Much Bigger Crimes

EMILY COHN

Learning Outcomes

After reading this article, you will be able to:

- Recognize the personal effects of minor ethical breaches.
- Recognize the danger of justifying unethical behavior.

Steal a pen from your office and you could find yourself on a path toward becoming the next Bernie Madoff.

That's the warning of a new study, called "The Slippery Slope: How Small Ethical Transgressions Pave The Way For Larger Future Transgressions," by David Welsh of the University of Washington, Lisa Ordóñez of the University of Arizona, Deirdre Snyder of Providence College, and Michael Christian of the University of North Carolina at Chapel Hill. According to the study, which was published in the *Journal of Applied Psychology*, minor unethical behavior at work, if undetected, puts workers on a "slippery slope" that could lead to worse behavior over time.

To most of us, fairly innocuous sins like taking a pen from work or neglecting to refill the office coffee pot are much easier to justify than, say, racking up $2 billion in trading losses. But over time, the researchers found, those minor misdeeds make it easier to justify more and bigger evils in the long run.

"People rationalize their behavior to justify it," Ordóñez, one of the study's authors, said in a press release. "They might think 'No one got hurt,' or 'Everyone does it.' . . . they feel fine about doing something a little bit worse the next time and then commit more severe unethical actions."

The researchers tested this theory by watching subjects in a number of different situations. One interesting experiment found that subjects who were given 25 cents for doing a minor unethical thing were much more likely to take $2.50 to do something more egregious later on than those who were offered $2.50 to do a big no-no at the start. According to the researchers, this shows that people are less likely to commit what they call "abrupt and large dilemmas" when they haven't already committed gradual, small transgressions.

The study cites Madoff, who was sentenced to 150 years in prison for orchestrating the largest Ponzi scheme in history and spoke of this phenomenon to his longtime secretary, according to Vanity Fair: "Well, you know what happens is, it starts out with you taking a little bit, maybe a few hundred, a few thousand. You get comfortable with that, and before you know it, it snowballs into something big."

So what can you do to prevent yourself from becoming the next Jeff Skilling? The researchers offer a number of tips to discourage the minor stuff, like putting in place a firm set of ethical guidelines and calling workers out for the small things, like taking home too many office supplies.

"The ideal is for employees to recognize when they've committed a minor transgression and check themselves," Michael S. Christian, one of the paper's coauthors, wrote.

Critical Thinking

1. Do you think minor ethical breaches are serious enough to warrant attention? Why or why not?

2. Provide examples of minor ethical breaches that occur in the workplace.

3. How would you respond to someone who is trying to justify a minor ethical breach?

Create Central

www.mhhe.com/createcentral

Internet References

European Molecular Biology Labrotory

http://www.embl.de/aboutus/science_society/discussion/discussion_2004/ref14may04.pdf

Houston Chronicle

http://smallbusiness.chron.com/catch-thief-workplace-19098.html

University of North Carolina—Chapel Hill: Kenan-Flagler Business School

http://www.kenan-flagler.unc.edu/news/2014/06/Slippery-Slope

Unit 3

UNIT

Prepared by: Eric Teoro, *Lincoln Christian University*

Business and Society: Contemporary Ethical, Social, and Environmental Issues

Contemporary businesses face several significant challenges in today's global marketplace. World trends are changing the expectations that individuals and whole societies have of business. No longer is the traditional product or service value proposition considered sufficient; today's company must also demonstrate ethical values and a commitment to social good if it is to engender trust.

One area in which trust can easily be compromised is privacy. Several of the articles in this unit explore the nature of privacy in the digital age. A tension often exists between employee and customer rights, raising the question of what forms, if any, of employer monitoring are acceptable. Would it depend upon the nature of the industry under discussion? How should companies handle private data collected as part of safety initiatives? Automotive black boxes, for example, provide valuable information regarding vehicle safety while recording personal driving behaviors. Should companies be allowed to track customer computer use? What if such practices resulted in better customer service or desired advertisements? Other articles look at different uses of the Internet and associated ethical issues. What protections should be in place regarding what minors post on the Net? Should a service provider be allowed to shame online, a client, who refuses to pay for services rendered?

Several articles in this unit examine ethical challenges faced by companies doing business abroad. How should managers respond when their goods are held up in port and will continue to be so unless they pay bribes or facilitation payments? Would it matter if the goods were needed medical supplies or luxury items? What steps can businesses take to prevent such situations? What difficulties arise when a company tries to institute ethical practices in a host country when that country's culture is significantly different from the home country's culture? Different authors provide guidance for developing global business ethics and choosing appropriate governance systems. Businesses today face another challenge regarding their role in sustainability. While some articles present cases for corporate social responsibility and sustainable business practices, such as promoting water conservation, another article describes how the market and private property rights are the keys to safeguarding the environment.

Article   Prepared by: Eric Teoro, *Lincoln Christian University*

Wall Street vs. Its Employees' Privacy

JEAN EAGLESHAM AND MICHAEL ROTHFELD

Learning Outcomes

After reading this article, you will be able to:

- Understand the nature of unintended consequences.

- Describe the pros and cons of employee monitoring in the financial industry.

- Understand the potential tension between employee and customer rights or interests.

State efforts to block companies from monitoring employees' personal Facebook and Twitter accounts are under fire from a new front—securities regulators.

An unlikely alliance of regulators and industry groups is seeking to carve out exemptions in state laws that would allow certain financial firms to sidestep bans on looking at the personal social-media accounts of employees.

Wall Street's self-regulator, the Financial Industry Regulatory Authority, says financial firms need a way to follow up on "red flags" suggesting misuse of a personal account, according to a spokesman. Finra has asked lawmakers in about 10 states to make changes to proposed legislation, the spokesman said.

Securities regulators worry that the raft of new laws aimed at protecting employees' privacy puts investors at risk. They say the fast spread of financial advice on social networks such as Facebook Inc. and Twitter Inc. could create new channels for Ponzi schemes and other frauds, and that fighting those frauds will be harder if state lawmakers snarl efforts by companies to monitor what employees are pitching to investors.

California, Illinois, Maryland, and Michigan adopted social-media privacy laws last year, and a similar new law in Utah takes effect in May. Social-media privacy legislation has been introduced or is under way in 35 states since the start of 2013, according to the National Conference of State Legislatures.

Supporters of the new laws say they are needed to protect employees, even when their employer may be the subject of tweets or other messages made using an employee's personal account on a social-networking website.

"We'd balk if an employer said, 'I want to look at your photo albums once a week or listen in on your dinner party conversation,'" said Allie Bohm, an advocacy and policy strategist at the American Civil Liberties Union. "By allowing them to monitor your social-media presence, that's what they might be doing."

The split shows how financial firms and regulators are struggling to change their ways in the Facebook era. Earlier this month, the SEC issued new guidance that lets companies use social media to disseminate market-moving news. Companies must tell investors which ways they intend to communicate, such as by tweets or Facebook posts.

California's social-media privacy law went into effect Jan. 1. Before that, the Securities Industry and Financial Markets Association, a trade group, made a request to California Gov. Jerry Brown to veto the bill. Sifma says some employee-privacy provisions are at odds with existing rules that brokerage firms police investment advice tweeted and posted by their employees. California's employee-privacy protections would place firms in the "untenable position of having to violate either state law or their Finra obligations," the group wrote in a letter to Mr. Brown.

California lawmakers rebuffed requests by Finra and securities-industry groups for a carve-out clause in the state's new law.

A spokesman for Mr. Brown, a Democrat, referred to a comment he made after signing the bill. California's move will "protect all Californians from unwarranted invasions of their personal social-media accounts," Mr. Brown said.

Legislation often includes narrow language that allows employers to conduct legitimate checks, such as during a formal investigation into alleged misconduct by an employee.

Sifma said such a change in the California law is "helpful," but fails to address the legitimate need for general monitoring and recording of any business-related tweets and postings. The new law "puts customers at risk, as it will be much harder for firms to detect serious problems," the trade group added.

The Financial Services Institute, which represents independent broker-dealer operations, believes the state laws and pending legislation could place "investors at risk, as well as creating a significant headache for brokerage firms," according to David Bellaire, the group's general counsel. Most financial firms use specialized software to keep track of what their employees are tweeting and posting on business issues, a spokesman added.

A Securities and Exchange Commission spokesman said the US agency is "monitoring developments" in states. More than 65 social-media privacy bills have been introduced so far this year, according to Sifma. Much of the proposed legislation will die if it isn't passed by lawmakers before their current sessions end in late May or June, according to the National Conference of State Legislatures.

Financial advisers are keen about the potential of social networks to interact with investors and lure new business. More than one-third of financial advisers use social media for business purposes several times a week, according to an April survey by American Century Investments, a fund firm.

For several years, criminal authorities have wrestled with challenges caused by communication about illicit activities, from securities fraud to drug dealing to terrorism, through messaging tools in social networks, videogame systems, and other digital platforms.

Providers of such services generally aren't required to build capabilities for law-enforcement surveillance into their systems. Telephone companies must do so under a 1994 federal law.

The Federal Bureau of Investigation and other agencies have approached some technology companies to request that they erect monitoring systems or let the US government use its own systems, people familiar with the efforts say. The tools can be complicated and costly, though the government sometimes reimburses companies.

Some companies comply with the government's requests, but other firms have refused. "These negotiations can take a long time. They can take years," said Michael Sussmann, a former Justice Department official who now is a lawyer at Perkins Coie LLP and has represented companies that got such requests.

Finra has taken some action to crack down on rogue tweets. Jenny Quyen Ta, founder of Titan Securities, a broker-dealer in Dallas, was disciplined in 2010 for alleged misconduct that included using her Twitter account to tout stock in Advanced Micro Devices Inc.

Examples of allegedly "unbalanced" and "overwhelmingly positive" tweets included one from September 2009 that said, "Keep an i on AMD ppl!" and predicted its share price would double.

Ms. Ta agreed to pay a $10,000 fine to settle the case, without admitting or denying the allegations. A spokeswoman for Titan declined to comment.

Courts haven't ruled on whether the state laws or Finra rules should take precedence on employee privacy. "It may be that the Finra rules will preempt the state ban, but that's not been tested," said Scott Rahn, a lawyer at Greenberg Traurig LLP.

Brian Rubin, a partner at law firm Sutherland Asbill & Brennan LLP, said the continuing uncertainty "can become serious" because "firms can be caught between a rock and a hard place."

Critical Thinking

1. When is monitoring employee personal social-media accounts acceptable?
2. Debate with a colleague or fellow student the acceptability of monitoring personal social-media accounts.
3. Should employees ever be reprimanded or held accountable for content they post to personal social-media accounts? If so, how?

Create Central

www.mhhe.com/createcentral

Internet References

Computerworld

http://www.computerworld.com/article/2497492/data-privacy/state-social-media-privacy-laws-a-mixed-bag-for-businesses.html

National Conference of State Legislatures

http://www.ncsl.org/research/telecommunications-and-information-technology/employer-access-to-social-media-passwords-2013.aspx

Article   Prepared by: Eric Teoro, *Lincoln Christian University*

Automotive "Black Boxes" Raise Privacy Issues

G. Chambers Williams III

Learning Outcomes

After reading this article, you will be able to:

- Understand the nature of conflicting interests, for example, privacy versus valuable safety-related information.

- Describe the use of automotive black boxes.

- Think more critically about the nature of permission regarding private information.

If you're involved in a traffic accident with no witnesses except you and the other driver, it's just your word against his, right?

Wrong.

Your own car just might tattle on you if you're at fault.

So-called event data recorders that function much like the "black boxes" on airplanes, and which are now installed on virtually all new vehicles, can give investigators incriminating details about your driving behavior in the final seconds before a crash.

Some motorists—fearful of what they see as an invasion of privacy—aren't too happy about that.

"I didn't think my '98 Saturn was new enough to have the data recorder, but apparently it does, and I think it should be up to me to decide how and when I share that information with someone else," said Bob McClellan Jr., 35, of Antioch.

"If I were given the opportunity to agree to have this on the vehicle when I buy it, then that probably would be OK," McClellan said. "But if I own the car, it's my business what's on the recorder, and no one should be able to access it unless I say so."

Details that can be scrutinized include how fast the vehicle was going, as well as whether the brakes or accelerator were being pressed, which way the car was being steered, and—yes—even whether the occupants were wearing their seatbelts. The data is always being recorded, but it's only saved to the device's memory if an air bag deploys, automakers say.

Critics argue that the system is a snoop and unfair to consumers.

"It's in the cars, it can't be turned off, and the information is available to anyone with a court order," said Gary Biller, executive director of the National Motorists Association, a group that advocates on behalf of drivers in instances of unfair traffic enforcement.

"Our members ask whether these devices can be disabled, but they can't, because they are integral to the computer systems that control modern cars," Biller said.

Laws have been implemented in 13 states to limit access to the information in the recorders, but there are no such regulations on the books in Tennessee and many other states to prevent someone from uploading the data without permission.

Getting that data is easier on some vehicles than others, but a Nashville company, VCE Inc., has been at the forefront of using information from the recorders to reconstruct traffic accidents since the introduction of the devices in the mid-1990s.

"We have been involved from the start and were among the first ones to begin downloading the data from these recorders for the accident reconstructions we do for attorneys and insurance companies," VCI Vice President Todd Hutchison said.

"We typically get permission from the owner of the vehicle, but that's not necessarily who owned it at the time of the accident," he pointed out. "If the insurance company has bought the salvaged vehicle, they can give us permission."

Data Easy to Collect (AT)

Collecting the data is simple. VCE investigators merely connect to the vehicle's diagnostic system using a cord that attaches to a laptop computer, and special software then reads the data, Hutchison said.

Both Metro police and the Tennessee Highway Patrol have the equipment to capture the information after an accident, he said.

It doesn't always take a wired connection to access the data. Beginning with the 2011 Chevrolet Cruze, General Motors will be able to upload the information from the recorders wirelessly through the OnStar system included on most of the automaker's vehicles.

And Biller said his organization has heard of possible transponder-style readers that could upload the data just by coming close to a vehicle that is equipped with special technology similar to that used by automated toll-collection systems.

"It's a valuable tool for insurance companies," said Buddy Oakes, a Columbia-based insurance claims adjuster. "If there is no way to tell right away what happened in an accident, sometimes we request permission from the vehicle owner or through the court to extract the data, which gives us the last 15 seconds of activity before the impact."

"It shows how fast the car was going, how hard it was being braked, what evasive moves were made. We've had people say they were sitting still at a stoplight and got hit, when the data recorder shows they were doing 30 mph through the intersection."

Data Used to Calculate Rates

Some insurance companies also are using the data to help rate customers' driving habits to determine how much their premiums should be, but that would be only with the customers' cooperation, Oakes said.

As for the expectation of privacy, "that pretty much went out the door for most things a long time ago," he said. "I don't know that there's privacy on anything anymore. Every phone call you make can be tracked, and just about anything that becomes a legal matter becomes public information." Automakers defend the development and use of the data recorders as a great research tool to help make vehicles safer.

"For us, the whole purpose was safety research," said GM safety spokeswoman Sharon Basel.

The devices were first installed in conjunction with the introduction of air bags in cars nearly two decades ago to show what forces were involved in activating the bags and to help automakers improve them, automakers say.

"We have them in all of our vehicles, and have had since the mid-'90s," Basel said.

Nissan, Ford, Toyota, and most other automakers have been using the technology in their new vehicles since at least the mid-2000s.

There are no requirements for them to put the devices in cars, but beginning with the 2011 model year, the National Highway Traffic Safety Administration requires that automakers state in the vehicle owner's manual whether a recorder is installed and where it is located. Locations vary by make, model, and year.

"We feel that, overall, it is a benefit for auto safety, but we also go to great lengths to protect our customers' privacy," said Ford Motor Co. spokesman Wes Sherwood. "If anyone wants access to the data, they will need the owner's consent or the proper legal authority to do so. But the devices are included on all Ford vehicles now, and we have a supplier that provides a tool for reading the information. It's widely available to law enforcement or anyone else with the authority to download the data."

Dealership service departments can download the data from the recorders, which also store reports about vehicle malfunctions to help pinpoint maintenance problems, said Nelson Andrews, general manager of Nelson Cadillac and Land Rover Nashville. He said the devices go "a long way toward helping us fix" whatever is wrong.

"There's really nothing people can do about it," Andrews adds. "But my cellphone collects more data than these devices do."

Nissan is among automakers that provide dealers with software to collect and analyze data from the recorders, said spokesman Steve Yaeger.

"We have event data recorders on all of our vehicles, and we have software called Consult that can be used by qualified people to read that data," Yaeger said. "All of our dealers have it. But it's protected by a code, and is not available to just everybody."

"If it's requested by law enforcement or court order, though, we can provide the information for that."

Critical Thinking

1. Should a person's driving behavior be recorded if he/she has not given explicit permission for such recording? Why or why not?
2. Does the act of purchasing a new car implicitly give permission to record driving behavior? Why or why not?
3. Why is recording of driving behavior a privacy issue?
4. From an ethical view, what are positive and negative aspects of such recordings?

Create Central

www.mhhe.com/createcentral

Internet References

Consumer Reports

http://www.consumerreports.org/cro/news/2012/08/new-black-box-standards-advance-auto-safety/index.htm

National Conference of State Legislatures

http://www.ncsl.org/research/telecommunications-and-information-technology/privacy-of-data-from-event-data-recorders.aspx

National Public Radio

http://www.npr.org/blogs/alltechconsidered/2013/03/20/174827589/yes-your-new-car-has-a-black-box-wheres-the-off-switch

Article   Prepared by: Eric Teoro, *Lincoln Christian University*

Digital-Privacy Rules Taking Shape

Julia Angwin

Learning Outcomes

After reading this article, you will be able to:

- Describe do-not-track policies and the difficulties inherent in them.
- Recognize privacy issues related to computer use.

Frustrated by a flood of privacy violations, the Federal Trade Commission on Monday issued a strong call for commercial-data collectors to adopt better privacy practices and called for Congress to pass comprehensive privacy legislation.

In a starkly written 73-page report on privacy in the digital age, the agency called on United States commercial data collectors to implement a "Do Not Track" button in Web browsers by the end of the year or to face legislation from Congress forcing the issue.

"Simply put, your computer is your property. No one has the right to put anything on [your computer] that you don't want," said Jon Leibowitz, chairman of the FTC, at a news conference Monday.

The agency also for the first time turned its attention to offline data brokers—which buy and sell names, addresses, and other personal information—calling on them to create a centralized website providing consumers with better access to their data. The agency also wants legislation requiring data brokers to give consumers the right to see and make corrections to their information.

Linda Woolley, executive vice president of the Direct Marketing Association, which represents data brokers, said the group opposes giving consumers access to marketing information because it would be expensive, difficult to keep secure and the type of data used by marketers doesn't harm consumers.

The agency wants internet firms to . . .

- Store data securely, limit collection and retention, and promote data accuracy.
- Include a "Do Not Track" mechanism in Web browsers by the end of the year.
- Provide consumers access to data collected about them by data brokers that buy and sell names, addresses, and other personal information.

"We are very wary about taking the information out of the information economy," Ms. Woolley said.

The FTC doesn't have the authority to write new rules for privacy. Instead, it hopes its report will spur the industry to agree to abide by its voluntary guidelines.

The FTC can then use its authority to prosecute "deceptive" behavior if companies that agree to the guidelines don't live up to their promises.

Last month, the FTC notched a win for its guideline approach when the online-advertising industry voluntarily agreed to one of the main privacy recommendations: the development of a "Do Not Track" mechanism that would let users limit Web tracking using a single setting in Web browsing software.

Previously, the industry had urged consumers to individually "opt out" of more than a hundred different companies that track Web browsing behavior.

However, the agreement—which was announced at the White House last month—has been mired in debate about what "Do Not Track" means. The online-ad industry has agreed to what amounts to a "Do Not Target" definition, which would still allow data to be collected for purposes such as market research and product development. Privacy advocates are pushing for it to mean that data won't be collected. An international standards body is working to develop a consensus agreement on the definition of Do Not Track by June.

The Digital Advertising Association, which represents more than 400 companies, said it is pushing ahead to implement its definition of Do Not Track. "We're not at the finish line, but we're pretty close," said the trade group's counsel Stuart P. Ingis.

FTC Commissioner J. Thomas Rosch dissented from the vote approving the report, in part because he said "it is not clear that all the interested players in the Do Not Track arena" will be able to agree on a definition.

Critical Thinking

1. Do you believe that the FTC should require commercial data collectors to implement digital-privacy safeguards? Why or why not?

2. Should so-called offline data brokers be allowed to buy and sell personal information without the permission of the individual whose personal information is being bought and sold? Why or why not?

3. Should digital privacy be legislated or should the data collection industry be encouraged to adopt voluntary guideline for digital privacy? Take a position and defend your position.

Create Central

www.mhhe.com/createcentral

Internet References

CMO.com
  http://www.cmo.com/articles/2014/4/3/big_data_ethics_tran.html
Seattle Times
  http://seattletimes.com/html/businesstechnology/2024604324_pfconsumershakedownsxml.html
The Nation
  http://www.thenation.com/article/177849/we-need-privacy-laws-digital-era

Article   Prepared by: Eric Teoro, *Lincoln Christian University*

Sharing, With a Safety Net

Somini Sengupta

Learning Outcomes

After reading this article, you will be able to:

- Describe issues related to the activity of minors posting on the web.

- Recognize the pros and cons of requiring companies to delete the postings of minors.

- Understand the complexity of businesses adhering to diverse state laws.

Kids. The reckless rants and pictures they post online can often get them in trouble, by compromising their chances of getting into a good college or even landing them in jail. What to do about such lapses vexes parents, school officials, the Internet companies that host their words and images—and the law.

Now California legislators are trying to solve the problem with the first measure in the country to give minors the legal right to scrub away their online indiscretions. The legislation puts the state in the middle of a turbulent debate over how best to protect children and their privacy on the Internet, and whether states should even be trying to tame the Web.

The governor, Jerry Brown, has taken no position on the bill. He has until mid-October to sign it, after which, without his signature, the legislation becomes law.

California is often in the vanguard when it comes to digital privacy. It was the first state to require companies to report data breaches, and it requires Websites and mobile apps to post privacy policies that explain how personal information is used. A recently passed law requires Websites to tell users whether they honor browsers' do-not-track signals.

The right-to-delete, or eraser, provision is part of a broader bill that prohibits Websites, which have "actual knowledge" that a minor is using the site based on a profile and activity on the site, from running ads for a range of products—including alcohol, spray paint, tattoos, tanning beds, and e-cigarettes. The eraser section compels online sites to let users under 18 delete rants, tweets, pictures, status updates, and other material.

Although many companies, including Facebook and Twitter, already offer this option to their users, the California bill would make it a right across the Internet for children who live in that state.

"Kids and teenagers often self-reveal before they self-reflect," said James Steyer, chief executive of Common Sense Media, a San Francisco-based advocacy group that pushed for the law. "It's a very important milestone."

The rash revelations by a Texas teenager, Justin Carter, on Facebook last February—a threatened school shooting his family insists was sarcastic, made in the heat of playing a video game—landed him in a Texas jail on a felony terrorism charge for nearly 6 months. His father, Jack, favors the California legislation, but wonders if it would go far enough.

"They should be allowed to delete it, but then again is it really deleted?" Mr. Carter, 39, of San Antonio, said in an interview this week.

Also, Mr. Carter said, if his son had deleted the conversation that someone reported to the authorities, would the deletion be seen as destroying evidence?

His son, now 19, is out on a bond, pending trial. Any law trying to tame the Internet, he said, is likely to run into turbulence.

"It's a whole new territory, it grew faster than the laws did," Mr. Carter said. "We're trying to come up with things to make it all neat. There's collateral damage—my son being one of them."

Critics of an eraser law see pitfalls. They warn that in trying to protect children, the law could unwittingly put them at risk by digging deeper into their personal lives. To comply with the law, for example, companies would have to collect more information about their customers, including whether they are under 18 and whether they are in California.

There are also practical concerns. If other states pass similar laws, companies would be forced to devise multiple policies for the underage residents of different states—confusing consumers and creating unwieldy requirements for Web businesses that are essentially stateless, except for issues like collecting sales tax. The Internet, opponents of the law say, should be regulated by a uniform set of rules, not piecemeal by the states.

"This is well-meaning legislation but there are concerns about it," said Stephen Balkam, president of the Family Online Safety Institute, which advises companies like Facebook and Microsoft on online safety issues.

Mr. Balkam said he favored Congressional oversight in issues like children's online privacy and, if necessary, regulation by the Federal Trade Commission. "Where California leads, others follow," he said. "I think it will be a mess."

Some supporters of the bill say Internet companies got off easy. The eraser bill does not, for example, require companies to remove the deleted data from its servers altogether, nor does it offer any way to delete material that has been shared by others; a sensational picture that has gone viral, in other words, can't be purged from the Internet.

And it is nothing like the right-to-be-forgotten measure that legislators in Europe have been pressing for. That proposal would, at its core, allow all Europeans, not just children, to delete their online personal information; several amendments to the plan address freedom of expression concerns.

"It's an important first step, but there's more to be done," Mr. Steyer said.

Mr. Steyer's organization, which participated in a safety advisory group with Facebook but soon left after disagreements with the company's approach, has been pushing for more aggressive legislation. Those efforts in 2011 led members of Congress to propose a measure that would have allowed parents to scrub material posted by their children. Criticized by free speech advocates, the bill went nowhere, though Senator Edward J. Markey, Democrat of Massachusetts, who was a co-sponsor, plans to introduce it again later this year.

Short of federal privacy laws in general, states have been passing laws on a host of privacy matters, in many cases following California's lead.

"Often you need to comply with the most restrictive state as a practical matter because the Internet doesn't really have state boundaries," said Mali Friedman, a lawyer in the San Francisco office of Covington & Burling, a national law firm.

Critical Thinking

1. How should businesses engage minors in online formats?
2. To what degree should minors be held accountable or responsible for what they post?
3. What are the ethical implications of eraser laws?

Create Central

www.mhhe.com/createcentral

Internet References

CNN
   http://www.cnn.com/2013/07/12/tech/social-media/facebook-jailed-teen/
Family Online Safety Institute
   http://www.fosi.org
The New Yorker
   http://www.newyorker.com/magazine/2014/09/29/solace-oblivion

Article   Prepared by: Eric Teoro, *Lincoln Christian University*

A Risky Way to Get Deadbeat Clients to Pay: Shame Them Online

Karen E. Klein

Learning Outcomes

After reading this article, you will be able to:

- Understand the controversial nature of publically shaming another.

- Describe methods for holding customers responsible to pay for goods and services.

Self-employed writer and designer Mikey Rox doesn't like to use it, but every once in a while he turns to a sure-fire method to collect money from clients who don't pay him what they owe. "I send e-mail after e-mail, month after month, and I get the same, sad sob story or 'the check is in the mail,'" he says. "Or they don't communicate at all."

When every other avenue has been exhausted, Rox has twice posted polite yet pointed questions about his overdue bills on clients' Facebook (FB) pages. It worked both times: "I've gotten immediate responses and payments right away. Shaming these deadbeats on Facebook is my last resort," Rox says.

Whether you call it shaming or, more gently, "accountability," freelancers are using social media to solve a perennial problem of not getting paid on time.

After years of being advised to fork out the funds to sue, send bills to collection services for partial returns, or write off losses as "lessons learned," small business owners have some newfound leverage with bad clients. After all, companies may be intent on privately wearing out small vendors they see as powerless, but their marketing departments can't as easily ignore situations that go public on Twitter (TWTR) feeds or LinkedIn (LNKD) profiles.

Shelley Seale, a freelance travel and lifestyle writer, tried the tactic in August 2013. A travel publication owed her $800 for several articles she'd contributed, she says, but months went by without payment despite her "bugging and bugging them" about her unpaid invoices. Finally, in desperation, she posted on the publication's Facebook page and tweeted a message asking "why haven't you paid your writer as agreed?" She tagged both the publication and the editor's personal Twitter handle.

"Within a couple of hours he contacted me by direct message on Twitter, very defensive, and 24 hours later I had the money via PayPal (PYPL)," Seale recalls. "He followed up with an e-mail chastising me and saying, 'You didn't have to do that.' I responded, 'Well, obviously I did have to, since you ignored me for months.'"

Efficient as it may be, the tactic is definitely controversial. First off, it could get you into hot water legally, says Stephen P. Dem, a longtime Encino (Calif.) collection attorney who represents many self-employed people. "Of course we have free speech, and there are safeguards there. But there are legal ramifications of bad-mouthing a business publicly, not least of which is facing the wrath of a millionaire who could sue you and force you to spend thousands on a legal defense," he says.

Kenneth C. Wisnefski, founder and chief executive of digital marketing agency WebiMax, recognizes that "calling out delinquent payers via social media is something that has begun to gain steam, but I feel it is a very slippery slope. Damaging people on social media can reflect poorly, because it crosses an etiquette barrier—it can make your business, in some cases, look very small and extremely confrontational."

It's better to adopt business practices that minimize the chances of nonpayment, many experts say. That involves financial vetting of clients, using legal contracts to avoid payment disputes, and requiring upfront deposits and incremental payments during the job. Freelancers Union, which advocates for the self-employed, has a contract creator on its website that freelancers can use before taking on new clients.

Susan Liautaud, a Stanford University ethics lecturer and consultant who founded London-based consulting business Susan Liautaud & Associates, recommends such tactics over taking to social media. "A culture of smearing people on the Web is a very dangerous place to go," she says. "However unethical the creditor's behavior may be, that behavior doesn't justify bad behavior on the part of another. Shaming campaigns are not respectful, and they're not a dignified way to treat a client."

When a website design client stiffed Andy Valde, owner of Chicago creative services business Rockvibe Productions, for $500 a few years ago, he couldn't bring himself to take the pay dispute public. "It seemed very unprofessional, so I decided never to do that," he says, though he admits it was tough to see the client drumming up new business with the site he'd designed.

Other freelancers are not apologizing. "I absolutely would do it again," Rox says. Even if he doesn't get paid, he figures other small business owners will be warned off working for a bad client. "It's not like I'm burning a bridge. I'm certainly not going to work with those people again."

And Seale, for her part, doesn't worry about damaging her own reputation. "I had so many writers and editors contacting me and saying, 'Good for you.' This is one of those negative aspects of being a freelancer, and we're finally finding a recourse for the small guy," she says. "I don't feel bad at all."

Critical Thinking

1. Is it ethically acceptable to shame a nonpaying client online or in other public forums? Why or why not?

2. What methods could individuals use to ensure suppliers, business partners, or customers fulfill their obligations?

3. What role should shame play in our culture? In business?

Create Central

www.mhhe.com/createcentral

Internet References

Forbes
  http://www.forbes.com/sites/davidnicholson/2014/05/30/get-paid-quicker-use-smart-tech-and-shame-the-delayers/
Wired
  http://www.wired.com/2013/07/ap_argshaming/

KLEIN is a Los Angeles-based writer who covers entrepreneurship and small-business issues.

Article   Prepared by: Eric Teoro, *Lincoln Christian University*

Challenges of Governing Globally

A strong understanding of the three distinct corporate governance systems around the world will help managers conduct business more effectively in other countries.

MARC J. EPSTEIN

Learning Outcomes

After reading this article, you will be able to:

- Describe different governance systems.

- Understand factors that affect Board performance.

S hortly after New Year's Day in 2009, just 6 months after Satyam and its politically influential chairman, Rama-linga Raju, were honored by the World Council for Corporate Governance, the company and its senior leadership became the subject of the largest corporate fraud investigation in India's history. Raju admitted to fabricating 70 billion rupees ($1.5 billion) of Satyam's assets and 95 percent of the previous year's revenue. Despite its record for good governance, this large, respected outsourcing firm saw its market value fall more than 80 percent in 24 hours. Long before the confession, shareholders had expressed dissatisfaction with Raju's leadership. Many charged that the board of directors and its members failed to meet their basic responsibilities.

Senior executives aren't the only perpetrators of corporate fraud. A scandal at Volkswagen (VW), Germany's largest carmaker, erupted in 2005 when it was discovered that managers and labor representatives had received improper benefits from the company and its suppliers. A quid-pro-quo agreement had developed between managers and labor that centered around the important role that union representatives play on German boards (workers' representatives have 50 percent of the seats on the supervisory boards of companies with 2,000 or more employees). In return, the local government, which was the controlling shareholder of the corporation with only 18 percent

ownership (the voting rights of any single share-holder are limited to 20 percent), was satisfied with the ability to guarantee regional job security. Yet it seemed that the other shareholders may not have been receiving equal benefits, and the VW board found itself unable or unwilling to protect its minority owners from actions that didn't maximize the returns to everyone.

Not all corporate governance failures involve financial fraud. In 2010, BP, one of the world's largest oil and gas companies, saw its market value fall by more than 50 percent in less than 60 days after the infamous explosion at a deepwater drilling rig off the US Gulf Coast. The incident killed 11 employees and resulted in the largest marine oil spill in history, costing BP billions of dollars in compensation for victims and cleanup costs. The government investigation of the explosion revealed numerous causes and guilty parties. Many people have suggested that BP's board failed to put the right processes in place to ensure that reasonable safety measures were taken to prevent such a disaster.

These stories occur far too often in corporations all over the world. Enron, WorldCom, and Tyco in the US and Parmalat in Italy immediately come to mind. Sometimes these failures are fraud, and sometimes they're the result of poor oversight. Nevertheless, they have caused us to reexamine the structures, systems, and processes of corporate governance.

As you know, corporate governance is the system by which corporations are directed, controlled, and made accountable to shareholders and other stakeholders. Failures such as those outlined above occur in a wide variety of companies and industries and in different countries around the world. Understanding corporate governance practices globally should be a priority for managers who work in multinational corporations or with international clients.

Table 1   General Characteristics of Global Corporate Governance Systems

	Anglo-American	Communitarian	Emerging Markets
Examples of Countries/Regions	United States, United Kingdom, Australia, Canada, South Africa	Japan, Germany, Belgium, Scandinavia	China, Eastern Europe, India, Brazil, Mexico, Russia
General Characteristics	• Shareholder-centric • Market centered • Unitary board structure • Boards primarily composed of nonexecutive directors (and independent directors) • Common law legal system • High levels of disclosure and more rules on disclosure • Large pay incentives for managers, including pay for performance	• Stakeholder-centric • Bank centered • Two-tier board structure (supervisory & management) • Labor, founding family, and bank are common members—interlocking common • Civil law legal system • Moderate levels of disclosure • Pay incentives moderate	• Stakeholder-centric • Government/Family centered • Board structure varies • Few independent board members • Legal systems relatively weak • Low levels of disclosure • Pay incentives smaller

Understanding corporate governance practices globally should be a priority for managers who work in multinational corporations or with international clients.

Here I'll describe three corporate governance systems—Anglo-American, Communitarian, and Emerging Markets—and provide a comparison that you can use to recognize and evaluate differences in practice. This is a summary of extensive work that I recently completed in response to many inquiries from senior managers who want to better understand how to evaluate corporate and board performance in other countries.

Table 1 summarizes some of the major differences in the general characteristics of each system.

Global Corporate Governance Systems

Corporate governance practices vary globally as a result of significant country differences, such as culture, history, regulatory systems, and economic and financial development. All of you who interact with corporate managers in other countries or have affiliates or subsidiaries throughout the world must understand these differences because it's critical to the evaluation of

corporate board performance and to corporate success. It also has important implications for corporate governance, corporate financial and operational transactions, and global relationships.

Let's look at some of the basic differences.

Anglo-American Corporate Governance System

The Anglo-American system of governance evolved in countries to which the United Kingdom exported its common law legal system during its colonial period, such as the United States, Australia, New Zealand, Canada, and South Africa. Originally developed to protect private landholders from nobility, the common law legal system sets a broad legal precedent that protects shareholders and tries to prevent a company's leaders from acting against shareholder interests.

In the Anglo-American system, corporations focus primarily on the shareholder and aim to maximize shareholder wealth. Directors usually are elected by shareholders and can be replaced if shareholders aren't satisfied with the company's financial results. The system emphasizes transparency and disclosure about a company's audited financial status, board composition, and corporate strategy.

Since well-developed financial markets heavily influence corporate governance practices, the Anglo-American system is considered market based with a large share of corporate ownership traded frequently on large, public exchanges. Under this system, corporate boards are structured as unitary boards and are composed primarily of nonexecutive directors (directors who aren't company employees) who represent the interests of large shareholders. These boards also have independent directors with little financial interest in the future performance of the firm. Critics of this system have argued that boards are frequently too large (with as many as 20 members) and that directors have often failed to dedicate enough time to their roles.

Communitarian Corporate Governance System

A Communitarian corporate governance system has evolved in much of continental Europe and in Japan. This system has its origins in the Romano-Germanic civil law codes developed more than a millennium ago. Instead of relying on strong legal protections for investors, performance is regulated through statutes, codes, and relationships with stakeholders.

The Communitarian system is relationship based, which provides for a stakeholder-centric approach to governance and focuses on a broader set of stakeholders that often includes lenders, members of supply chains, customers, employees, and the community. These relationships allow stakeholders to wield strong control over corporations and hold them accountable. In Germany and Japan, for example, it's common for companies and banks to cross-invest in their suppliers and customers, creating associations of corporations that play an active role in deciding corporate governance standards. Boards often include representatives from various stakeholders who are representing their own interests. A banking representative may be interested in a decision's impact on the corporation but also on the bank he or she works for. Similarly, a union representative on the board is interested in the impact of a decision on the corporation and its shareholders but particularly on the workers that the union represents. This stakeholder orientation provides for a broader set of interests and representation on the board.

Corporate governance under the Communitarian system relies heavily on banks instead of capital markets for financing, and representatives from these banks often sit on the board of directors of a company that they finance. This system generally uses a two-tier board structure, dividing board functions between a supervisory board and a management board.

Critics of the system have argued that it fails to protect minority shareholders and lacks representation for outside investors.

Emerging Markets Corporate Governance System

Emerging Markets countries—such as China, Brazil, India, Mexico, Russia, and much of Eastern Europe—still have relatively young legal systems that haven't fully developed the legal framework necessary to classify their corporate governance systems into the other categories. In China, for example, the first corporations were founded centuries after countries with more defined corporate governance systems began their corporate history. These countries also differ in legal traditions, language, and culture, so it's still uncertain how corporate governance will likely evolve there.

Yet there are some recognizable patterns. The lack of defined legal systems means that shareholders often have few credible legal protections, so boards are expected to vigorously monitor and protect shareholder interests. Also, low levels of disclosure and a lack of transparency often make it difficult for shareholders to exercise informed control over the company.

Corporate governance in Emerging Markets countries tends to be stakeholder-centric and centered around family or government relationships. In addition, large corporate shareholders dominate boards and are well-known worldwide. For example, about 30 Korean family groups that are organized as chaebols (business conglomerates) control almost 40 percent of that country's economy. There's also a large amount of state participation. Even in countries where the government has privatized its corporate holdings, it often retains significant control over corporations by regulating equity markets or influencing board members. For example, often the government retains a regulatory interest in supervising large transactions that have an impact on the state. (All governments do this to some extent, but it's far more common in the Emerging Markets countries.)

Roles of the Board Globally

Though significant differences in corporate governance practices exist, some general principles are present globally that are critical for effective corporate governance. Boards of directors are usually expected to fulfill three separate but related roles: accountability, senior-level staffing and evaluation, and strategic oversight. (For more details on roles and responsibilities of corporate boards, see Marc J. Epstein and Marie-Josée Roy, "Corporate Governance Is Changing: Are You a Leader or a Laggard?" *Strategic Finance,* October 2010, pp. 31–37.)

Accountability

In Anglo-American countries, boards of directors traditionally have been responsible for holding managers accountable to shareholders. In the Communitarian system, it's common for the corporation, management, and board to also be accountable to other stakeholders, such as employees, suppliers, and customers. In the Emerging Markets system, boards are typically accountable to the controlling shareholders in the corporation, which can be the state, a family group, or a corporate conglomerate. Thus, it's common to have representatives of these other stakeholders on boards in non-Anglo-American countries.

Senior-Level Staffing and Evaluation

Evaluating senior management, determining their compensation, and having important input to senior staffing decisions are important roles for the board in all three governance systems. But there are important application differences. In the Anglo-American system, many corporations pay managers a huge amount of compensation for their performance in exchange for relentless attention to financial returns. In the Communitarian and the Emerging Markets systems, pay levels, performance-based pay, and the role of the board in determining pay are considerably smaller.

Strategic Oversight

In all three governance systems, strategic oversight is an important board role. In the Anglo-American system, managers focus on strategy formulation, and the board, though providing some oversight, often plays a more passive role in approving important strategic moves. In the Communitarian system, the management board is more assertive in its strategic oversight role and is often more involved in the formulation of strategy than in oversight only. And in the Emerging Markets system, many board members view the formulation and oversight of strategy as the primary role of the board.

Though these specific roles manifest themselves differently in different settings, they greatly impact the mechanisms that ensure managers fulfill shareholder expectations regarding corporate performance.

Strategic oversight is an important board role in all three governance systems.

Internal Determinants of Corporate Boards

How successfully a board performs its duties depends on several internal factors that differ substantially among the three global governance systems (see Table 2). These factors may affect managers' roles and interactions with the board, as well as their compensation. They include:

1. Board composition,
2. Board systems and structure, and
3. Performance evaluation and compensation systems.

Board Composition

Board composition choices determine board competencies, skills, and power structures. Many corporate governance experts and international guidelines advocate increased board member independence and increased numbers of nonexecutive directors on boards, yet the role of nonexecutive and independent directors is markedly different in each corporate governance system.

In the Anglo-American system, boards are composed primarily of nonexecutive directors who represent the interests of large shareholders, as well as independent directors with no significant financial interest in the future performance of the firm. Usually, there are stringent requirements for board independence since these board members often have a significant amount of power. In Canada, for example, 70 percent of companies have independent directors serving as their board chair.

In the Communitarian system, independent directors are less common but still hold a considerable amount of power. Since national codes and companies typically don't stress the independence of board directors, most corporation board members in Japan, Italy, and much of continental Europe are internal.

Table 2   Internal Determinants of Corporate Governance Systems

Corporate Governance Mechanism	Anglo-American	Communitarian	Emerging Markets
Board Composition, Systems, & Structure			
Board composition	• Balance between internal and independent directors	• Few independent directors	• Independent directors rare
Board structure	• Unitary	• Two-tier	• Varies
Board accountability	• Shareholders	• Stakeholders (including entire value chain and employees)	• Stakeholders and government or founding family
Executive compensation	• Large performance pay	• Moderate performance pay	• Little performance pay

This is partly because of codetermination laws that mandate high levels of employee participation on the supervisory board.

The Emerging Markets system features many of the regulatory requirements of the Anglo-American system with regard to independent directors, but truly independent directors are uncommon and wield little power relative to controlling interests on the board. In China, for example, listed companies are required to have two independent directors. Despite these requirements, many believe that Chinese directors show few signs of true independence and are still strongly influenced by the government.

Board Systems and Structure

Board systems and structure are the mechanisms typically used to translate board roles, responsibilities, and composition into decisions. They also vary significantly across governance systems.

Again, in the Anglo-American system, a unitary board typically combines executive directors (company executives who are on the corporate board) and nonexecutive directors. Boards usually are organized into committees—such as audit, nomination, and compensation—that perform much of the board's functions.

In the Communitarian system, the executive directors and nonexecutive directors are divided into two separate entities. The management board, composed mainly of senior-level management, is primarily responsible for managerial decisions, such as strategy, marketing, and product development. The supervisory board, composed of company insiders, such as employees, as well as company outsiders, such as independent accountants, is primarily responsible for overseeing executive management, accounting, senior-level staffing, and evaluation. Employees also can play a significant role in determining the composition of the supervisory board. Shareholders elect the supervisory board, and the supervisory board appoints members of the management board. In Germany, employees elect a third to a half of the members of the supervisory board. In addition, representatives from founding families or national banks may also serve on this board.

In the Emerging Markets system, the board structure varies between countries and even among corporations in the same country. Some corporations have adopted the two-tier board structure of Communitarian countries, and others utilize the unitary board structure of the Anglo-American system. The largest shareholders, usually the state or family groups, often are permitted to control the boards.

Performance Evaluation and Compensation Systems

Performance evaluation and compensation systems also differ among governance systems. In the Anglo-American system, boards are expected to perform rigorous evaluations of senior manager and corporate performance. It's common to structure executive compensation so that a large percentage of that pay is tied to the financial performance of the corporation. Evaluation procedures only recently have become part of corporate governance in the Communitarian system, and most companies in the Emerging Markets system lack explicit evaluation mechanisms. In the two latter systems, large performance-based pay is significantly less common and accounts for a much smaller percentage of overall executive compensation than in Anglo-American countries.

External Determinants of Corporate Board Systems

External factors also affect how boards of directors perform their roles and responsibilities. Three that determine key components of corporate governance are:

1. Markets,
2. Legal systems, and
3. Ownership and control structures.

These mechanisms (see Table 3) ensure that corporations act according to national expectations regarding corporate governance. An understanding of these external factors will provide managers with insight into board regulation, objectives, operations, and decisions.

Markets

The existence of markets for ownership and control of corporations is an important aspect of corporate governance since the threat of takeovers increases when mechanisms for governance fail. Takeovers are most common in the Anglo-American system, particularly in the United States while the existence of a controlling shareholder in the Communitarian and Emerging Markets systems lessens the likelihood of a takeover.

Beyond corporate control, stock markets determine the returns available to stockholders in a corporation and diversify ownership. In the Anglo-American system, these markets are quite active. More than 6,000 domestic companies are listed publicly in the United States, and more than 1,000 are listed in the United Kingdom. But only a relatively small number of firms are listed in Communitarian countries. In Germany, for example, there are fewer than 500 listed companies. In Emerging Markets, stock exchanges are developing rapidly, although there is a great deal of variation across countries. China, for example, has become a "dominant force" in the initial public offering (IPO) market in the last 2 years with its large exchange in Hong Kong. Yet in Mexico, only a small percentage of transfers occurs through the public markets.

Market listing requirements play another important role in corporate governance. In the Anglo-American system, these

Table 3   External Determinants of Corporate Governance Systems

Corporate Governance Mechanism	Anglo-American	Communitarian	Emerging Markets
Markets			
Financial markets	• Strong and active	• Weak and not commonly used	• Volatile
Investment purpose	• Short-term return	• Long-term return	• Policy and political goals
Methods of finance	• Financial markets	• Bank credit and retained earnings	• Private and state-owned banks
Legal Systems			
Legal history	• Common law system	• Civil law system	• Combined systems that are still rapidly evolving
Transactional methods	• Contracts	• Relationship-based transactions	• Relationship-based transactions
Ownership & Control Structures			
Ownership structure	• Diverse individual and institutional ownership	• Concentrated family and corporate ownership	• Concentrated family, corporate, and government ownership
Minority shareholder protections	• Strong	• Moderate	• Weak
Dominant control	• Voting and board representation	• Cross-holding, pyramidal groups, lending relationships	• Internal mechanisms and external mechanisms

regulations have become a dominant mechanism for implementing corporate governance reforms. Several large stock exchanges in Anglo-American countries have adopted mandatory listing requirements that include more stringent corporate governance measures, such as the qualification and roles of board members, having a majority of independent directors, and having a requirement for certain committees such as audit and compensation for publicly traded companies. Many Communitarian and Emerging Markets stock exchanges have followed suit more recently.

Legal Systems

Legal systems affect other aspects of corporate governance, including investor protection for minority shareholders, ownership structure, and financial markets. They also are an important aspect of how investors are protected. The Anglo-American corporate governance system, developed from the common law tradition, often exhibits the best legal protection for investors and tends to provide better enforcement of these laws. The Communitarian corporate governance system, derived from the civil law system, has developed other mechanisms to ensure that capital is allocated efficiently. These include concentrated ownership and control, mandatory dividends, and limited equity markets. Countries in the Emerging Markets system have even fewer shareholder protections than in civil law countries and

have evolved a severely concentrated ownership structure to compensate for these weak protections. In addition, the state often plays a much more active role as a corporate owner.

Ownership and Control Structures

Concentrated ownership and minority control mechanisms can be viewed as corporate governance mechanisms that evolve in the absence of basic shareholder protections. As a result, the most concentrated ownership structures are usually in Emerging Markets economies. One of the most glaring examples of this concentration is in China, where the state still owns majority holdings in most of the large firms, and Hong Kong, where a small group of business tycoons controls most large companies through concentrated shareholdings.

There's considerable ownership concentration in Communitarian countries as well. In Germany and Japan, for example, large banks, corporate groups, or families can control large portfolios of companies. Although these groups don't always hold majority stakes, they use a variety of tactics to steer the company in the direction that they prefer. These tactics include cross-shareholding, where two or more companies controlled by the same family group or government invest in each other, and pyramidal shareholding, where a company owns a sizable minority stake in a holding company that owns smaller stakes in more companies.

In Anglo-American countries, financial institutions, including pension funds, own more than 60 percent of all equity capital, yet ownership is quite dispersed. In this system, countries typically lack a controlling shareholder, so officers and directors have more control over decisions. This means that boards are responsible for ensuring that these decisions are in the best interests of the shareholders.

Closely related to ownership and control of corporations are the existence and enforcement of minority shareholder rights. These rights deal with voting privileges, corporate meetings, and dividends. For example, can major shareholders control corporate decisions, and must these decisions be for the benefit of the entire corporation, for all of its shareholders, for all of its stakeholders, or for only the small limited set of controlling shareholders? For an individual small owner of stock, the Anglo-American system provides far more protection both by regulation and through the legal system. In other systems, small shareholders must often just go along with what a major shareholder wants whether it is in their best interests or not.

In Emerging Markets economies, the state is frequently the controlling owner and can use its political power to derive wide control over corporations. In China, for example, rules surrounding the boards of directors of major corporations and financial markets are structured to give the state control over corporations. Even in countries where the state has started to turn control of corporations over to the private sector—such as in India, Brazil, and Russia—governments continue to wield significant power because of their ability to control the legal framework and market environment.

Understanding the Systems Is Critical

As corporations become more global, senior financial executives constantly deal with international contractors, licensees, affiliates, suppliers, and subsidiaries. Since these global associations and entities are often subject to different regulatory regimes and corporate governance systems, their decision-making processes can provide surprises. They may choose to ignore that your bid is the lowest and choose a higher-cost bid from a controlling shareholder, but it may be that the decision is to choose a contract from a controlling shareholder that benefits their relationship and benefits the other corporation—who is a common shareholder on multiple entities. Also, it may seem strange to a US manager that a corporation might decide to make decisions that benefit the environment or the labor union over shareholders since the US model is shareholder focused. Remember: The other systems aren't better or worse, but they *are* different—and it's important for managers to understand this as they are doing

business in other countries. To better understand decisions and constraints and to conduct business around the world more effectively, executives must understand the context, regulations, and processes of corporate governance in other countries. Without this understanding, evaluating and/or improving performance globally is difficult.

Note

1. This article draws heavily from Marc J. Epstein, "Governing Globally: Convergence, Differentiation, or Bridging," in Eds. Antiono Davila, Marc J. Epstein, and Jean-François Manzoni, *Performance Measurement and Management Control: Global Issues,* Emerald: UK, 2012.

Critical Thinking

1. What are the salient characteristics of the three different global corporate governance systems presented in the article? List the characteristics and be prepared to discuss them during class.

2. What are the implications for placing a firm's code of ethics in a host country plant given different governance systems in the host country than in the home country?

3. What are the internal determinants of corporate boards?

4. What are the external determinants of corporate boards?

5. How do differing legal systems in various countries affect corporate governance?

6. How do differing legal systems in various countries affect implementation of a firm's ethics programs?

Create Central

www.mhhe.com/createcentral

Internet References

Emerging Markets ESG
http://www.emergingmarketsesg.net/esg/wp-content/uploads/2011/01/Three-Models-of-Corporate-Governance-January-2009.pdf

Finnbay
http://www.finnbay.com/media/news/insider-versus-outsider-convergence-governance-systems/

Social Science Research Network
http://papers.ssrn.com/sol3/papers.cfm?abstract_id=2049764

MARC J. EPSTEIN is Distinguished Research Professor of Management at the Jesse H. Jones Graduate School of Business at Rice University in Houston, Texas. He also is a member of IMA®. You can reach Marc at (713) 348-6140 or epstein@rice.edu.

Article   Prepared by: Eric Teoro, *Lincoln Christian University*

Conceptualizing a Framework for Global Business Ethics

WILLIAM J. KEHOE

Learning Outcomes

After reading this article, you will be able to:

- Trace the history of business ethics literature.

- Describe unethical business practices being conducted in a global market.

- Develop a system that promotes global business ethics.

The imperative of globalization arguably is one of the more significant changes experienced by business in the past several decades (Levitt, 1983; Kehoe and Whitten, 1999; Hill, 2001; Cateora and Graham, 2002; Czinkota, Ronkainen, and Moffett, 2002; Keegan, 2002; Griffin and Pustay, 2003; Hill, 2003; Lascu, 2003; Yip, 2003). In pursuing globalization, firms analyze, and debate various entry strategies to host-country markets; carefully consider the appropriateness of sourcing equipment, financing, materials, personnel, and other factors of production across the global arena; argue the merits of operating in a home-country currency versus host-country currencies; and study the cultures of host countries. However, the challenges of implementing an ethical system globally sometimes are addressed only as an afterthought, particularly when an ethical problem occurs.

This manuscript addresses the importance of developing and implementing an ethical framework to facilitate the application of ethics across the expanse of a global firm's operating arena. Prior to presenting the framework, the field of global business ethics is summarized, and the more interesting, well-conceptualized, and significant literature in the field is reviewed. Then, unethical business practices in global business are identified and discussed, so as to present a platform for the development of a framework for global business ethics. The framework is conceptualized and discussed and implementation suggestions for management are presented.

Global Business Ethics as a Field of Study

Almost a decade ago, DeGeorge (1994) opined, "business ethics is still a young field, and its international dimensions have scarcely been raised, much less adequately addressed." While still relatively a young field, the literature base of global business ethics is developing rapidly and has a richness of content.

Literature of 1960s and 1970s

Among the more interesting and well-conceptualized literature in the field during the 1960s and 1970s is the work of such scholars as Baumhart (1961) introducing the concept of ethics in business and exploring the ethics of business practitioners. Raths, Harmin, and Simon (1966) provided important underpinnings on values and teaching for the new field of business ethics; Smith (1966) advanced a theory of moral sentiments; Boulding (1967) provided important underpinnings to business ethics in his scholarly examination of value judgments in economics; and Perlmutter (1969) reflected on the difficult evolution of a multinational corporation. Other notable literature of the period includes work by Kohlberg (1971) conceptualizing stages of moral development, by Bowie (1978) developing an early taxonomy of ethics for multinational corporations, and by Carroll (1979) presenting a model of corporate social performance.

Literature of the 1980s

Moving to the 1980s, significant scholarship included such literature as Engelbourg (1980) in a significant examination of the early history of business ethics and Drucker (1981) examining the concept of business ethics. Nash (1981), enlivening Bowie's (1978) taxonomy, posited 12 questions for managers to ask when considering the ethical aspects of a business decision and offered a taxonomy of shared conditions for successful ethical inquiries. Berleant (1982) explored problems of ethical consistency in multinational firms, raising questions relevant to this day.

Laczniak (1983) developed one of the first primers in ethics for managers. McCoy (1983), in a classic article, presented a parable that is used to differentiate corporate and individual ethics. Donaldson (1985) reconciled international norms with ethical business decision-making, Kehoe (1985) examined ethics, price fixing, and the management of price strategy, and Lacaznik and Murphy (1985) published a book of ethical guidelines for marketing managers. Ferrell and Gresham (1985) conceptualized a contingency framework for understanding ethical decision-making, Hoffman, Lange, and Fedo (1986) examined ethics in multinational corporations, and Murphy (1988) focused on processes for implementing business ethics. The literature period of the 1960s/1970s/1980s closed with a comprehensive work by Donaldson (1989) examining the ethics of international business.

Overall, the literature of the 1960s/1970s/1980s tended to be descriptive in methodology, nature, and tone. Of course, a descriptive nature is to be expected, as business ethics was an embryonic field at that time then. The literature introduced ethical concepts and theories to academics and practitioners in business. It anchored the field of business ethics, conceptualized its early content, developed taxonomies, and established the importance and the validity of the concept of ethics in business with both academics and practitioners.

Literature of the Early 1990s

The period of the early 1990s saw the field of business ethics begin to flourish conceptually, empirically, and operationally. Bowie's (1990) article on business ethics and cultural relativism signaled a movement from the field's descriptive tone toward higher levels of abstraction and inquiry. DeGeorge (1990) authored a book chapter examining international business systems and morality, while Donaldson (1992) presented a classic article on the language of international corporate ethics. Koehn (1992) examined the ethic of exchange, an important article in that the concept of exchange is a central underpinning of business. Velasquez (1992) explored questions of morality and the common good in international business. DeGeorge (1993) addressed the concept of competing with integrity. Green (1993) placed business ethics in a wider global context, while Kehoe (1993) examined theory and application in business ethics.

The Business Ethics Quarterly heralded a defining moment in the scholarship of business ethics by publishing an entire issue (January 1994) devoted to international business ethics. Nicholson (1994) presented a framework for inquiry in organizational ethics, the first such framework in the literature. Fraedrich, Thorne, and Ferrell (1994) assessed the application of cognitive moral development theory to business ethics. Rossouw (1994) addressed the ethics of business in developing countries, an important article given that many ethical abuses occur in developing countries.

Delener (1995) advanced earlier scholarship on ethical issues in international marketing, Smith (1995) described marketing strategies for an ethics era, while Rogers, Ogbuehi, and Kochunny (1995) raised troubling questions of the ethics of transnational corporations in developing countries. Perhaps fittingly, given the emerging questions about ethics of transnational corporations, the Caux Roundtable's Principles for Business (1995) were published at this time, believed to be the first international code of ethics created through collaboration of business leaders in Europe, Japan, and the United States (Skelly, 1995; Davids, 1999).

Literature of the Later 1990s

Donaldson (1996), perhaps building from the troubling questions about ethics in the early 1990s, examined values in tension when home-country ethics are employed in host-country markets away from a home country. Bowie (1997) posited the moral obligations of multinational corporations, while Johnson (1997) foreshadowed ethics during turbulent times as he examined ethics in brutal markets. Kung (1997) reminded scholars that globalization calls for a global ethic. Becker (1998) applied the philosophy of objectivism to integrity in organizations. Costa (1998) argued that moral business leadership is an ethical imperative, and Dunfee (1998), in an article based on a 1996 speech, explored the marketplace of morality from the focus of a theory of moral choice. Hasnas (1998), in an article subtitled "a guide for the perplexed," attempted to clarify the field of business ethics in an interesting article examining three leading normative theories of business ethics—the stockholder theory, the stakeholder theory, and the social contract theory.

A more scholarly tone in business ethics is found particularly in works by Brock (1998), questioning whether corporations are morally defensible and by Collier (1998), theorizing the ethical organization. Other significant literature includes Ferrell (1998) examining business ethics in a global economy, Bowie (1999) reaffirming the place of a Kantian perspective in business ethics, and Buller and McEvoy (1999) examining how to create and to sustain an ethical capability in a multinational corporation. Lantos (1999) considered how to motivate moral corporate behavior, Mackenzie and Lewis (1999) focused on the case of ethical investing, and Weaver, Trevino, and Cochran (1999) posited corporate ethics programs as control systems.

In each of these articles of the later 1990s, a more scholarly, more theoretical, and less descriptive approach is manifest than in many earlier articles in the field, particularly in the literature of the 1960s, 1970s, and early 1980s.

A New Century's Literature

Continuing the scholarly tone of the later 1990s, Chonko and Hunt (2000) presented an important retrospective analysis and prospective commentary on ethics and marketing management, while Freeman (2000) examined business ethics at the millennium. Robin (2000) developed a hierarchical framework of ethical missions and a model of corporate moral development. Velasquez (2000) considered globalization and the failure of ethics. Werhane (2000) authored a seminal work on global capitalism in the 21st century—a work that foreshadows the level of analysis and depth of scholarship to which business ethics aspires and which it must attain.

A question for consideration is whether business ethics is moving toward a postmodern phase (Carroll, 2000; Gustafson, 2000), in which it is not the rules of ethics but rather the "questions that raise issues of responsibility" that will guide business ethics to its tomorrows beyond. Is the field moving toward an interesting future for scholarship in ethics in which content and issues about ethical issues not envisioned in the early 1980s will emerge for serious reflection and scholarship? Contents and issues such as a cross-cultural comparison of ethical sensitivity (Blodgett, Lu, Rose, and Vitell, 2001); myth and ethics (Geva, 2001); an examination of questions at the intersection of ethics and economics (Hosmer and Chen, 2001); ethics and perceived risk (Cherry, 2002); ethics and privacy (Connolly, 2000; McMaster, 2001); ethics and stakeholder theory (Cragg, 2002; Jensen 2002; Kaufman, 2002; Orts and Strudler, 2002); religiosity and ethical behavior (Weaver and Agle, 2002), and multinationality and corporate ethics (van Tulder and Kolk, 2001; Singer, 2002). All of these emergent areas of reflection and scholarship are areas of inquiry important in a home country, but exponentially more critical for examination as organizations move increasingly to host-country markets throughout the world.

From Literature Emerges Imperatives for Research

As the tomorrows emerge for the field of business ethics, several imperatives flow from an examination of the extant literature. One, the field of business ethics, over the past several decades, has been descriptive in nature and tone. It is imperative that business ethics rises above its descriptive beginning. Second, is the necessity to develop a replication tradition. It is troubling that the field of business ethics is somewhat lacking of a replication tradition, possibly due to being an emergent field of inquiry. There is little replication in the field, even into the 1990s or so it seems. A third imperative, possibly related to the lack of a replication tradition or perhaps causative of a lack of replication, concerns a low heuristic power of much of extant research. It is imperative that scholars in the field replicate research and build from and upon the research of others.

Diversity in Understanding of Ethics

Just as there is diversity in research in business ethics, so, too, is there diversity in the understanding of systems of ethics in the conduct of global business, a diversity of understanding that is a function of a host of economic, political, religious, and social variables that define the differences between peoples, nations, and cultures. As an example, Donaldson and Dunfee (1994), postulated that "Muslim managers may wish to participate in systems of economic ethics compatible with the teachings of the Prophet Muhammad, European and American managers may wish to participate in systems of economic ethics giving due respect to individual liberty, and Japanese managers may prefer systems showing respect for the value of the collective." In each of these situations and in similar situations within the many countries of the world, a given system of ethics, particularly a system of ethics that is home-country specific, may not be accepted, respected, understood, or practiced by host-country nationals.

While the ethics of individuals differ around the world and while a system of ethics from a home country may not be embraced by host-country nationals, managers of global firms nevertheless must raise ethics in the consciousness of their employees regardless of where employees are assigned in the world or whatever their national origins. In raising ethical consciousness, it is insufficient to do so simply by establishing a code of ethics in an organization. Rather, management must develop an ethical culture across an organization (O'Mally, 1995) and put in place an organizational structure or framework for ethics, perhaps a framework such as is advocated in this manuscript.

By advocating an ethical culture as well as having an ethical framework, Paine (1994) argued that the reputation of a firm is enhanced and its relationships with its constituencies are strengthened. Sonnenberg and Goldberg (1992) found that employees feel better about a firm and perform at higher levels when they sense ethics as part of its culture. As a result, it is posited in this research that a firm will realize higher-level results when a concern for ethics pervades the organization and is a part of its culture.

A concern for ethics and ethical values must be developed for a global firm to be holistic, to be greater than the sum of its many parts, whether a firm and its operating units are located in the home country and/or in host countries. Global holism is a necessity for success in global business and requires that "the organization has shared beliefs, attitudes, and values," including a system of ethics, which, when taken together, "creates a consistency in the way the firm treats customers, vendors, other business partners, and each other, wherever business is being done" (Daniels and Daniels, 1994). A concern for ethics in global business is a major responsibility of management, is an integral aspect (Roddick, 1994) of international trade, contributes to global holism, and is an imperative for success in global business (Trevino, Butterfield, and McCabe, 1998).

Unethical Practices in Global Business

There are many ways in which a firm might engage in unethical business practices in the global business arena, hopefully inadvertently rather than deliberately. Unethical corporate behavior may have genesis in a lack of understanding of, or an appreciation for, the culture of a host country in which a firm is operating. Many examples of unethical practices are reported in the literature. Presented below are examples developed by Kehoe (1998) and selected by a panel of executives as being among the most egregious. Since being developed as 12 examples in 1998, the research has been updated to include 15 examples reported in the following paragraphs in no particular order of significance.

- The first egregious example is an unethical practice of making of payments, often unrecorded, to officials in a host country in the form of bribes, kickbacks, gifts, and/or other forms of inducement (Landauer, 1979; Kimelman, 1994; Rossouw, 2000; Sidorov, Alexeyeva, and Shklyarik, 2000; Economist Reporter, 2002c; Hanafin, 2002). These payments often are made in spite of prohibitions of the US Foreign Corrupt Practices Act (1977) against such practices.

- A second egregious example is management representing a firm as financially healthier than its actual condition. This allegedly occurred by managers requiring employees to alter forecasts, plans, and budgets in order to mirror market expectations (Fuller and Jensen, 2002), to report sales or business activity at inflated levels (Leopold, 2002), or to inflate pro forma earnings (Roman, 2002). Additionally, some managers allegedly established complex and off-balance-sheet financial structures (Colvin, 2002; Economist Editorial, 2002; Elins, 2002; McLean, 2002; Zellner and Arndt, 2002; Zellner, France, and Weber, 2002) with assets of dubious quality designed to cause an organization to appear financially healthier than was actually its true condition.

- A third egregious example is for an individual to use a position within a firm to advance one's personal wealth at the expense of others, as is alleged to have occurred in Enron (Colvin, 2002; Elins, 2002; McLean, 2002; Nussbaum, 2002; Schmidt, 2002; Schwartz, 2002; Zellner, Anderson, and Cohn, 2002) and Nortel Networks Corporation (Crenshaw, 2002).

- A fourth egregious example, related to the first, second, and third examples and as equally egregious, and is a situation of management punishing those employees who come forward to report or blow a whistle about an unethical practice or practices (Alford, 2001; Economist Reporter, 2002a, 2002b; Mayer and Joyce, 2002). Posited as perhaps even more egregious is to ignore or to marginalize a whistleblower, alleged to have occurred in the Enron bankruptcy situation (Arndt and Scherreik, 2002; Krugman, 2002; Mayer and Joyce, 2002; Morgenson, 2002; Sloan and Isikoff, 2002; WSJ Editorial, 2002; Zellner, Anderson, and Cohn, 2002).

- A fifth example is the marketing of products abroad that have been removed from a home-country market due to health or environmental concerns. Examples given by Hinds (1982) include chemical, pharmaceutical, and pesticide products, as well as contraceptive devices, which were removed from the US market allegedly for being unsafe to the environment and/or to health, but for which marketing in other countries was continued, and, in some cases, was accelerated.

- Marketing products in host countries that are in questionable need or which are detrimental to the health, welfare, and/or economic well-being of consumers is a sixth egregious unethical practice. An often-cited example (Willatt, 1970; Post, 1985; French and Granrose, 1995; Ferrell, Fraedrich, and Ferrell, 2002) is the marketing of infant formula in developing countries by Nestle S.A. (www.nestle.com). Parents in developing countries are alleged to have been unable to afford the formula, unable to read directions to use the formula appropriately, unable to find sanitary sources of water for preparing the formula, and not to have needed the formula until Nestle convinced them that its use was necessary. Another example (White, 1997; Ferrell, Fraedrich, and Ferrell, 2002) is marketing of cigarettes in developing countries by advertising that implies that most people in the United States smoke and that smoking is "an American thing to do."

- A seventh example is a firm operating in countries that are known to violate human rights and/or failing to be an advocate for human rights in such countries. During the apartheid era in South Africa, US firms were criticized for doing business in the country and for failing to advocate human rights by publicly opposing the discrimination, oppression, and segregation of apartheid (Deresky, 1994; Sethi and Williams, 2001).

- An eight example is a firm moving jobs from a home country to low-wage host countries. When this occurs, workers in the home country are hurt because of loss of jobs (Kehoe, 1995), while workers in a host country are exploited by low wages. For example, Ballinger (1992) argued that Nike's (www.nike.com) profits increased due, in part, to the lower wages paid to workers in Nike-contracted plants outside the United States. Employees in these plants allegedly worked in excess of 10 hours per day, six days a week, for a weekly salary of less than US $50 for their efforts. The Associated Press (1997) reported that employees in Nike-contracted plants in Vietnam were paid US 20 ¢ per hour for working a 12-hour day. Encouragingly, reports in *The New York Times* (Staff Report, 1997), *Time* (Saporito, 1998), and *Fortune* (Boyle, 2002) imply that Nike is correcting the alleged abuses of employees in contracted plants in Vietnam.

- Utilizing child labor (Nichols et.al., 1993) in host countries when the law in a firm's home country prohibits such use is the ninth example of an unethical practice. While the use of child labor in a host country may be a necessity to support a child and her/his family, be preferable to unemployment, and not be of a concern to the host government, is it ethical to use children as laborers? In the past several years, a group of firms, including Nike, Reebok, L.L. Bean, Liz Claiborne, and Toys R Us, committed to a policy of prohibiting the employment of children younger than 15 years of age in factories in host countries (Headden, 1997; Bernstein, 1999; Singer, 2000). Additionally, Toys R Us has requested suppliers to seek SA 8000 certification, an international standard certifying working conditions (Singer, 2000).

- Tenth is a practice of operating in countries whose environmental standards are lax, or, the converse, being lax in respect for a host country's environment. In the Amazon, global corporations are reported (Thomson and Dudley, 1989) to have ignored their own and the host country's environmental guidelines in extracting oil. In Ireland, global firms are suspected (Keohane, 1989) of ignoring environmental regulations and to be illegally dumping hazardous waste throughout the country. In several countries, large agriculture conglomerates are bioengineering and genetically modifying crops, perhaps to the determent of the environment, animals, and people (Comstock, 2000). Finally, an emerging issue under the tenth example is the dumping of waste materials in less-developed host countries, sometimes waste of a hazardous nature that would require special handling in a home country but which is dumped carelessly in host countries (Ferrell, Fraedrich, and Ferrell, 2002).

- Eleventh is operating in a host country with a lower regard for workers' health and well-being than in the home country. Japanese companies are alleged (Itoh, 1991) to have over worked their employees both in Japan and in host countries and to have been indifferent to their health. Union Carbide is alleged (Daniels and Radebaugh, 1993) to have operated a plant in Bhopal, India with lower safety standards than its plants in more developed countries.

- Conducting business in a developing nation in such a manner as to dominate the nation's economy is a 12th example of an unethical practice. Several rubber companies have been accused of dominating the economies of the developing nations in which they operated rubber plantations. Such domination has been called *dependencia* (Turner, 1984), and has been shown to be damaging to a host country's economy, demoralizing to its people, and of questionable ethics.

- A 13th example is intervening in the affairs of a host country through such activities as influence peddling or other efforts to affect local political activity. In Italy, for example (Anonymous, 1993a), an investigation was undertaken into the alleged illegal financing of political parties by Italian business firms, as well as by foreign business entities operating in the country.

- Taking actions abroad that would be unpopular, controversial, unethical, or illegal in the home country is a 14th example. For instance, MacKenzie (1992) raised the controversial issue of whether, given advances in DNA research, a business firm has a right to patent a life form? Officials at the European Parliament in Brussels debated the legal and moral issues of this question. While a conclusion has not been reached, assuming an affirmative conclusion, may a non-European firm, operating in a European market, patent life forms in Europe if such patenting activity is unethical or illegal in the firm's home country?

- A 15th and final example is an egregious practice of a firm reinvesting little of the profit realized in a host country back in that country due to a restrictive covenant in corporate policy requiring that a majority of profit earned in a host country be repatriated back to the home country. This means that a global firm may reinvest very little back in a host country, and the citizens of the country may be exploited as a result.

Conceptualizing a Framework for Global Business Ethics

It is posited in this research that a framework for ethics is needed for firms engaged in global business across the many cultures that are encountered. A framework that points a firm safely along the global road—a code for the road, as in the lyrics of Crosby, Stills and Nash (1970), "you, who are on the road, must have a code that you can live by. . . ." Is it possible to design such a framework and to develop a code by which global businesses might live? Where do managers begin the process?

The framework for global business ethics presented here has eight stages. A firm ideally should progress through all eight stages in designing and implementing a global ethical system. The framework begins with the stage of understanding the orientation of a firm, and concludes with recommendations for promulgating and using a framework of global business ethics.

Step One—Orientation of a Firm

The first step in a framework for global business ethics is to define a firm's orientation in the global business arena. A firm may participate in global business as an exporter, a multinational firm, a multilocal multinational firm, a global firm, or some combination of these methods. Each of these methods of participation moves a firm further from being a domestic firm and gives it an increasing array of experiences in world markets. The orientation of a firm may be ethnocentric—home-country oriented; polycentric—adaptive to host countries; or geocentric—open to using the best resources wherever they are available in the world. Each of these orientation positions has implications for ethics.

As an exporter, the orientation of a firm may be generalized as primarily ethnocentric. The logic-in-use of an exporter may be generalized as being that home-country approaches should be applied wherever in the world the firm may operate. This ethnocentric logic means that home-country approaches to ethics are considered to be superior to those elsewhere in the world and may be applied whenever possible.

When a firm moves toward multinational operations, management's orientation will evolve, as the result of the experiences in host countries, from an ethnocentric viewpoint of an exporter toward a polycentric orientation as its managerial logic-in-use. This orientation recognizes that a firm must adapt to the unique aspects of each national market in which it operates. The logic-in-use is broadened by a willingness to adapt the home-country's ethical system in the various host countries in which the firm operates. This willingness to adapt its home-country ethical system is strengthened as a firm focus astutely on each host country, develops a multilocal approach to its multinational operations, brings host-country national into management positions, and grants greater autonomy from the home-country parent. All of these things heighten a firm's willingness to adapt and/or to customize its ethical system to fit the culture of a host country.

When a firm evolves to being a global firm, management's orientation becomes geocentric, with an acceptance of and openness to concepts, ideas, processes, and people from throughout the world, including approaches to ethics. The implication of a geocentric orientation is that a firm will be more amenable to addressing values that are inherent in the culture of a host country as a system of ethics is developed.

In developing a framework for global business ethics, a global firm, with a geocentric orientation of its management, is posited to be more open to using a system of global ethics than is an exporter, whose orientation tends to be ethnocentric. In terms of orientation, a global firm generally exhibits a greater readiness to develop ethical systems that appreciate and include the diversity of culture differences found in the world. An exporter, by contrast, is a domestic firm and is posited generally to prefer home-country ethical systems.

Step Two—Differences and Similarities Between Countries

The second step toward a framework for global business ethics is to appreciate and understand the differences and similarities between countries. In global business, there obviously are significant differences between peoples, countries, and cultures. This diversity adds richness to the experience of living on the earth, but may be problematic in establishing an ethical culture in a firm.

Comparing any two countries in regard to ethics in business would find striking differences as well as similarities. For example, consider a comparison of Japan and the United States.

Japan's business culture is characterized (Shimada, 1991) as having excessive corporate competition and a focus on rationality in decision making, based on economic factors at the expense of human factors. Itoh (1991) reported that Japanese managers are criticized for being indifferent to the health of their employees. Hammer, Bradley, and Lewis (1989) found cases of influence-peddling scandals involving leading business executives and Japanese politicians. In fact, breaches in business ethics was suggested by Whenmouth (1992) to be part of the system of doing business in Japan, with unethical behavior having origins deep in the country's cultural tradition.

In comparison, business in the United States has experienced some of the same ethical lapses as in Japan. For example, Labich (1992) presented evidence showing that for some US managers, ethics had an economic basis. These managers became lax in regard for ethics during difficult economic times, but returned to a stronger appreciation of ethics when business conditions improved. The increasing number of whistleblowing cases in the United States argues that something may be remiss in corporate ethics programs (Driscoll, 1992; Dworkin and Near, 1997; Mayer and Joyce, 2002). Research by Sandroff

(1990) and others found such ethical abuses as lying to employees and clients, expense account padding, favoritism, nepotism, sexual harassment, discrimination, and taking credit for the work of others are part of US business culture. All of which has led to an increasing number of business firms offering in-house training in ethics (Hager, 1991), developing games and simulations in ethics (Ireland, 1991), establishing permanent ethics committees (Labrecque, 1990), publishing codes of ethics (Court, 1988), and contracting with ethics' consulting firms for advice and programs, in what Cordtz (1994) has called an *ethicsplosion.* One consulting firm, Transparency International, is reported (Anonymous, 1993b) to have programs to improve ethics and standards of conduct, and to have worked with companies to prevent bribe paying in the conduct of global business.

Step Three—Identify Things of Broad Agreement

While there are differences and similarities in the appreciation for ethics among countries of the world, and while there are differences and similarities in lapses of ethics among businesses from various countries, there are things about ethics to which peoples across the world may agree. This is the third step in the framework. To identify those things, or values, in which there may be common agreement around the world.

Valasquez (1992, p. 30) identified the *global common good* as an area of worldwide agreement. He argued that individuals in international business have a responsibility to contribute to the global common good, including "maintaining a congenial global climate, . . . maintaining safe transportation routes for the international flow of goods, . . . maintaining clean oceans, . . . and the avoidance of global nuclear war. The global common good is that set of conditions that are necessary for the citizens of all or of most nations to achieve their individual fulfillment. . . . "

Beyond the aspects of a global common good to which people in international business might agree, there are certain attributes of life in any society to which a majority might agree (Kehoe, 1994). These include such values and principles (Goodpaster, Note 383-007) as, obeying the law; not harming others; respecting the rights and property of others; never lying, cheating, or stealing; keeping promises and contracts; being fair to others; helping those in need; and encouraging and reinforcing these values in others, all of which Goodpaster called *moral common sense.* These moral values are reaffirmed and enlarged by Scott (2002) in identifying honest communications, respect for property, respect for life, respect for religion, and justice as important organizational moral values.

Another example of attributes to which people throughout the world agree is found in a code of ethics of Rotary International. The attributes to which some 1.2 million Rotarians in 162 countries (Rotary, 2002) agree are: truth telling, fairness to others, goodwill toward others, and acting in ways beneficial to others. These concepts are embodied in a code called the 4-Way Test of Rotary International. The code, consisting of 24 words, is as follows: 1. Is it the truth? 2. Is it fair to all concerned? 3. Will it build goodwill and better friendships? 4. Will it be beneficial to all concerned?

Step Four—Find Voice to Express Agreement

Having identified the things of broad agreement, the fourth step of the framework is to identify a voice or way of expressing those things. Understanding voice is important because it is arguably likely that there are different voices used by people in different countries to express the same value or ethical concept. In fact, within the same country, an ethical concept may be voiced differently (Gilligan, 1982) by men than by women. The challenge is to find a voice or moral language appropriate for each culture wherein a global firm may operate. The challenge further is to recognize when a change in voice is required in order to express an ethical concept in a different culture.

In order to find a voice appropriate for situations in global business ethics, an underpinning of ethical theory is an initial step. In brief, ethical theory might be presented from a teleological or a deontological frame.

Teleological theory is concerned with the *consequences* of an action or business decision. The teleological principle of utilitarianism requires that an individual act in a way to produce the greatest good for the greatest number. In acting in this manner, an individual considers not only self in a decision or action, but the impact of the act on others. An individual applying utilitarianism in decision-making "would determine the effects of each alternative and would select the alternative that optimizes the satisfactions of the greatest number of people." (Kehoe, 1993, p. 16).

Deontological theory is concerned with the *rules* used to arrive at an action or a decision rather than the consequences of the action; that is, deontological theory is rule based, whereas teleological theory is consequences based. The deontological principle of the categorical imperative (Kant, 1785) is: "Act only according to that maxim by which you can at the same time will that it should be a universal law." In other words, the categorical imperative proscribes that individuals only do those things that they can recommend to others. That is, there are certain things that must be done in order to maintain basic humanity in a society, just as there certain things that must be practiced by individuals to maintain order in an organization. These things make up the shared moral values of an organization and are a part of its ethical culture. For example, a manager who does not participate in bribery because he or she could not admit or recommend it to others may be said to be adhering to the categorical imperative. Likewise, as other individuals in a firm adhere to the categorical imperative, it becomes a shared moral value and a part of the ethical culture of a firm.

Kidder (1994) conceptualized an example of shared moral values. He surveyed "ethical thinkers" from around the world and identified eight shared moral values that have broad application across cultures. These included love, truthfulness, fairness, freedom, unity, tolerance, responsibility, and respect for life.

A second example of shared moral values is by DeGeorge (1994). He suggested that there are moral norms that cross cultures that may be used to develop ethical standards for global business. Examples of such shared moral norms are truthfulness, respect for property, fairness, and trust.

Research by Scott (2002) elevated a third example of shared moral values. Arguing that the most important organizational value for analysis is an organization's moral values, she identified five moral values for organizations—justice, honest communication, respect for property, respect for life, and respect for religion.

Perhaps the most useful example of shared moral values is by Donaldson (1992). He analyzed six moral languages for their appropriateness in global business ethics. The languages were: virtue and vice; self-perfection through self control; maximization of human welfare; avoidance of human harm; rights and duties; and social contract. He argues (Donaldson, 1992, p. 280) that "the former three (virtue and vice; self perfection through self control; maximization of human welfare) are inappropriate for establishing a system of ethics in global business," while the "latter three (avoidance of human harm; rights and duties; social contract) are deontological ethical languages with the capacity to establish minimum rather than perfectionist standards of behavior" and are, therefore, better suited for addressing ethical issues in global business. These moral languages give voice to ethics in global business.

Step Five—Use Voice to Develop Ethical Statements

Generalizing from the conclusions concerning the appropriateness of moral languages for global business ethics, the fifth step of the framework emerges. That step is to use voice to develop ethical statements or codes of ethics.

It is posited that the voice used in a framework for global business ethics should be deontological rather than teleological, and minimum rather than perfectionist. This means that the statements developed in a framework for global business ethics should be rule based and be minimum in standard. Said another way, simpler and shorter statements are more appropriate in developing a framework for global business ethics. Parsimony must be the guiding principle in using voice to develop ethical statements.

Step Six—Separate Core and Peripheral Values

Being guided by voice to use rule based, minimum in standard, simple, and short statements, a global business organization, as a sixth step, should determine the core values to be included in its ethical framework and in its global code of ethics. Then identify the peripheral values that may be altered or even deleted from its global code of ethics according to the culture of a host country. This means, for example, if a global firm's home country is the United States, and if it operates also in China, India, Mexico, and Russia, its global code of ethics should contain core-value statements of the home country as well as statements common across all the countries, but may contain different peripheral-value statements in each of the host countries.

It is an imperative that individuals in a global firm understand its core values and its peripheral values. Collins (1995) defined a core value as something a firm would hold even if it became a competitive disadvantage. Donaldson (1996) identified three core values that have basis in Western and non-Western culture and religious traditions—respect for human dignity, respect for basic rights, and good citizenship through support of community institutions. He postulated (Donaldson, 1996, p. 53) that core values "establish a moral compass for business practice. They can help identify practices that are acceptable and those that are intolerable—even if the practices are compatible with a host country's norms and laws. Dumping pollutants near people's homes and accepting inadequate standards for handling hazardous materials are two examples of actions that violate core values. Similarly, if employing children prevents them from receiving a basic education, the practice is intolerable" and violates core values.

To separate core and peripheral values, consider this situation. If the core values of a firm include acknowledging human equality, promoting human welfare, providing high-quality products, having fair prices, contributing to the community, and compliance with national laws, these values should be reflected in a firm's global code of ethics and promulgated to all host-country subsidiaries. If, however, a firm believes that relationships among employees, with customers, and with suppliers are best addressed at the country level, these are peripheral values to be addressed in ethical statements developed by employees in each operating location. In brief, a firm, as noted by Laczniak and Murphy (1993), should strive to have a single worldwide policy on ethics to address its core values, those values never to be compromised, but may allow addenda to its worldwide core-value policy on ethics to address peripheral values that are inherent in the culture of a host country.

Step Seven—Writing a Global Code of Ethics

The seventh step of the framework concerns writing a global code of business ethics that will be a central part of a firm's framework for global business ethics. A global code cannot and should not be written at the home-country headquarters. Rather, contributions to the code must be sought from around the world. Individuals from throughout a firm's global expanse must be involved in developing the code. This means that a committee or task force that is charged with developing the code should have representation from each geographic region in which a firm operates, or even, if possible, from each host country. Likewise, individuals from across functions and levels of hierarchy should be included, so that the result is a multi-functional, multilevel, and multinational task force. The goal must be to be as inclusive as possible in developing a global code of ethics.

Global inclusiveness is important so that a code does not contain only the concepts, ideas, prejudices theories, values, and words of a firm's home country. This is part of using voice to develop a global code. A firm's values that are reflected in a code must be stated in a globally inclusive manner. This is not easily accomplished. It can only be accomplished by being as globally inclusive in voice as possible in writing the code. This implies that those charged with developing a global code of ethics must be empowered to be in close and regular contact wherever located in the world. This may mean that a firm regularly uses teleconferencing while developing the code. It also may mean that meetings of the task force are held regularly in various host countries while the code is being developed. Put simply, a global code of ethics cannot and should not be developed solely in a home-country venue.

Step Eight—Promulgating and Using a Global Code of Ethics

The final step of a framework for global business ethics is to promulgate and use the code of ethics. This means that the code must be translated effectively to the language of each host country. In each host country, some process for ethics representation should be arranged. It may be that a manager is assigned responsibility for ethics in addition to other duties, or preferably an ethics officer is designated formally in each country. That individual should be charged with promulgating the code of ethics, encouraging its use, and managing and refining the firm's framework for global business ethics. The posited result of having a framework of global business ethics is that there should be higher levels of ethical behavior across a global firm when a framework is in place, as was reported by Ferrell and Skinner (1988) with codes of ethics in domestic firms. Simply put, ethics must be made "salient and be part of an ongoing

conversation" within an organization (Freeman, 2001). The goal of developing a framework for global business ethics is to have ethics often considered, rather than seldom or never considered in the conduct of global business (Kehoe, 1998).

Conclusion

A mosaic of diversity continues to shine brilliantly across the landscape of global business. It is a landscape of business firms, large and small, operating in various ways in an increasing number of the countries of the world. It is a landscape of diverse cultures, with differing appreciations for and understandings of ethics. It is a landscape of individual managers encountering choices that reflect all the ambiguities, differences, and subtleties of a global mosaic of diversity. It is a landscape of people unified by shared moral values and of global firms in which ethics must be an imperative.

More than 40 years ago, Berle (1954) made a statement that is relevant for today's global corporations. The statement addressed ethics and the responsibilities of management. "The really great corporation management must consider the kind of community in which they have faith and which they will serve and which they intend to help construct and maintain. In a word, they must consider the ancient problems of the good life and how their operations in the community can be adapted to affording or fostering it."

The framework conceptualized in this research is anchored in a concept of shared moral values and developed by using moral languages to give meaning to ethics across cultures. The framework allows for a firm to remain loyal to its core values in situations involving questions of ethics, but allows different peripheral-value statements in host countries. When developing a framework for global business ethics, contributions must be sought from throughout the world. This means that individuals from throughout a firm's global expanse must be involved in developing the framework. Such a global corporate community developed framework will contribute to a concept of ethics being embraced throughout a firm, and to ethics being a word often spoken by employees throughout a firm, rather than a word seldom spoken or never spoken.

A report of the Center for Business Ethics (Hoffman, 2000) noted "business ethics is no longer a set of national initiatives, if it ever was. It is now a global affair." Anywhere a firm operates in the world, its activities must be ethical and adapted to affording or fostering the good life. This is an ethical imperative. Simply yet profoundly stated (Freeman, 2002), "ethics is about the most important parts of our lives and must be center stage" in any activity whether of a business or a personal nature. The practice of ethics in global business is posited to enhance a global corporation, uplift it and its stakeholders, and ensure that its actions foster the good life.

References

Alford, C. Fred (2001). *Whistleblowers: Broken Lives and Organizational Power.* Ithaca, NY: Cornell University Press.

Anonymous (1993a). "The Purging of Italy, Inc.," *Economist,* March 20, pp. 69–70.

Anonymous (1993b). "Clean, Not Laundered," *Economist,* May 8, p. 78.

Arndt, Michael and Susan Scherreik (2002). "Five Ways to Avoid More Enrons," *Business Week,* February 18, pp. 36–37.

Associate Press Report (1997). "Conditions Deplorable at Nike's Vietnamese Plants," *The Daily Progress,* March 28, p. A2.

Ballinger, Jeffrey (1992). "The New Free-Trade Hall," *Harper's,* August, pp. 45–47.

Baumhart, Raymond C. (1961). "How Ethical Are Businessmen?" *Harvard Business Review,* July/August, pp. 6–12.

Becker, Thomas E. (1998). "Integrity in Organizations," *Academy of Management Review,* Volume 23 (1), pp. 154–161.

Berle, A. A. (1954). *The 20th Century Capitalist Revolution.* New York, NY: Harcourt, Brace and World, pp. 166–176.

Berleant, Arnold (1982). "Multinationals and the Problem of Ethical Consistency," *Journal of Business Ethics,* 3, August, pp. 185–195.

Bernstein, Aaron (1999). "Sweatshops: No More Excuses," *Business Week,* November 8, pp. 104–106.

Blodgett, Jeffrey G., Long-Chaun Lu, G. M. Rose and S. J. Vitell (2001). "Ethical Sensitivity to Stakeholder Interests: A Cross-Cultural Comparison," *Journal of the Academy of Marketing Science,* Volume 29 (2), pp. 190–202.

Boulding, Kenneth (1967). "The Basis of Value Judgments in Economics," in Sidney Hook, ed., *Human Values and Economic Policy.* New York, NY: New York University Press.

Bowie, Norman E. (1978). "A Taxonomy for Discussing the Conflicting Responsibilities of a Multinational Corporation," in Norman E. Bowie, *Responsibilities of Multinational Corporations to Society.* Arlington, VA: Council of Better Business Bureaus, pp. 21–43.

Bowie, Norman E. (1990). "Business Ethics and Cultural Relativism," in Peter Madsen and Jay M. Shafritz, eds., *Essentials of Business Ethics.* New York, NY: Penguin Books, pp. 366–382.

Bowie, Norman E. (1997). "The Moral Obligations of Multinational Corporations," in Norman E. Bowie, ed., *Ethical Theory and Business.* Upper Saddle River, NJ: Prentice-Hall, pp. 522–534.

Bowie, Norman E. (1999). *Business Ethics: A Kantian Perspective.* New York, NY: Blackwell Publishers.

Boyle, Matthew (2002). "How Nike Got Its Swoosh Back," *Fortune,* Volume 145, June 11, p. 31.

Brock, Gillian (1998). "Are Corporations Morally Defensible?" *Business Ethics Quarterly,* Volume 8, October, pp. 703–721.

Buller, Paul F. and Glen M. McEvoy (1999). "Creating and Sustaining Ethical Capability in the Multinational Corporation," *Journal of World Business,* 34 (4), pp. 326–343.

Business Ethics Quarterly (1994, Volume 4, January). Issue devoted entirely to international business ethics, pp. 1–110.

Carroll, Archie B. (1979). "A Three-Dimensional Conceptual Model of Corporate Social Performance," *Academy of Management Review,* Volume 4, pp. 497–505.

Carroll, Archie B. (2000). "Ethical Challenges for Business in the New Millennium," *Business Ethics Quarterly,* Volume 10, Number 1, pp. 33–42.

Cateora, Philip R. and John L. Graham (2002). *International Marketing.* New York, NY: McGraw-Hill Companies, Inc.

Caux Roundtable, Principles for Business. (1995). *Society for Business Ethics Newsletter,* May, pp. 14–15.

Cherry, John (2002). "Perceived Risk and Moral Philosophy." *Marketing Management Journal,* Volume 12, Issue 1, pp. 49–58.

Chonko, Lawrence B. and Shelby D. Hunt (2000). "Ethics and Marketing Management: A retrospective and Prospective Commentary," *Journal of Business Research,* 50, pp. 235–244.

Collier, Jane (1998). "Theorising the Ethical Organization," *Business Ethics Quarterly,* Volume 8, October, pp. 621–654.

Collins, James M. (1995). "Change Is Good—But First, Know What Should Never Change," *Fortune,* May 29, p. 141.

Colvin, Geoffrey (2002). "Wonder Women of Whistleblowing," *Fortune,* August 12, p. 56.

Comstock, Gary L. (2000). *Vexing Nature? On the Ethical Case Against Agricultural Biotechnology.* Boston, MA: Kluwer Academic Publishers.

Connolly, P. J. (2000). "Privacy as Global Policy," *InfoWorld,* September 11, pp. 49–50.

Cordtz, Dan (1994). "Ethicsplosion," *Financial World,* August 16, pp. 58–60.

Costa, John Dalla (1998). The Ethical Imperative: *Why Moral Leadership Is Good Business.* Reading, MA: Addison-Wesley.

Court, James (1988). "A Question of Corporate Ethics," *Personnel Journal,* September, pp. 37–39.

Cragg, Wesley (2002). "Business Ethics and Stakeholder Theory," *Business Ethics Quarterly,* Volume 12, Number 2, April, pp. 113–142.

Crenshaw, Albert B. (2002). "Nortel Executive Quits Amid Accusations," *The Washington Post,* February 12, pp. E1 and E4.

Crosby, Stills and Nash. (1970).

Czinkota, Michael R., Ilkka A. Ronkainen and Michael H. Moffett (2002). *International Business.* Fort Worth, TX: Harcourt College Publishers.

Daniels John D. and L. H. Radebaugh (1993). *International Dimensions of Contemporary Business.* Boston, MA: PWS-Kent Publishing Company, pp. 79–80.

Daniels John L. and N. Caroline Daniels (1994). *Global Vision: Building New Models for the Corporation of the Future.* New York, NY: McGraw-Hill, Inc., p. 12.

Davids, Meryl (1999). "Global Standards, Local Problems," *Journal of Business Strategy,* January/February, pp. 38–43.

DeGeorge, Richard T. (1990). "The International Business System, Multinationals, and Morality," in Richard T. DeGeorge, *Business Ethics.* New York, NY: Macmillan Publishing Company.

DeGeorge, Richard T. (1993). *Competing With Integrity in International Business.* New York, NY: Oxford University Press.

DeGeorge, Richard T. (1994). "International Business Ethics," *Business Ethics Quarterly,* Volume 4, January, pp. 1–9.

Delener, Nejdet, ed. (1995). *Ethical Issues in International Marketing.* New York, NY: International Business Press.

Deresky, Helen (1994). *International Management.* New York, NY: Harper Collins College Publishers, pp. 516–519.

Donaldson, Thomas (1985). "Multinational Decision Making: Reconciling International Norms," *Journal of Business Ethics,* December, pp. 357–366.

Donaldson, Thomas (1989). *The Ethics of International Business.* New York, NY: Oxford University Press.

Donaldson, Thomas (1992). "The Language of International Corporate Ethics," *Business Ethics Quarterly,* Volume 2, July, pp. 271–281.

Donaldson, Thomas (1996). "Values in Tension: Ethics Away From Home," *Harvard Business Review,* September–October, p. 53.

Donaldson, Thomas and T. W. Dunfee (1994). "Toward a Unified Conception of Business Ethics: Integrative Social Contracts Theory," *Academy of Management Review,* April, p. 261.

Driscoll, Lisa (1992). "A Better Way to Handle Whistle Blowers: Let Them Speak," *Business Week,* July 27, p. 36.

Drucker, Peter (1981). "What is Business Ethics?" *The Public Interest,* Spring, pp. 18–37.

Dunfee, Thomas W. (1998). "The Marketplace of Morality: Small Steps Toward a Theory of Moral Choice," *Business Ethics Quarterly,* Volume 8, January, pp. 127–145.

Dworkin, Terry M. and J.P. Near (1997). "A Better Statutory Approach To Whistle Blowing," *Business Ethics Quarterly,* Volume 7, January, pp. 1–16.

Economist Reporter (2002a). "In Praise of Whistleblowers," *The Economist,* January 12, pp. 13–14.

Economist Reporter (2002b). "As Companies Cut Costs They Cut Corners Too. Time to Blow the Whistle?" *The Economist,* January 12, pp. 55–56.

Economist Reporter (2002c). Special Report: Bribery and Business," *The Economist,* March 2, pp. 63–65.

Elins, Michael (2002). "Year of the Whistleblower," *Business Week,* December 16, pp. 106–110.

Engelbourg, Saul (1980). *Power and Morality: American Business Ethics, 1840–1914.* Westport, CT: Greenwood Press.

Ferrell, O. C. (1998). "Business Ethics in a Global Economy," *Journal of Marketing Management,* Volume 9 (1), pp. 65–71.

Ferrell, O. C. and L. G. Gresham (1985). "A Contingency Framework for Understanding Ethical Decision Making," *Journal of Marketing,* 49 (Summer), pp. 87–96.

Ferrell, O. C. and S. J. Skinner (1988). "Ethical Behavior and Bureaucratic Structure in Marketing Research Organizations," *Journal of Marketing Research,* 25 (February), pp. 103–109.

Ferrell, O. C., John Fraedrich and Linda Ferrell (2002). *Business Ethics.* Boston, MA: Houghton Mifflin.

File: Framework for Global Business Ethics, RR&R, 2003.

Fraedrich, John, Debbie M. Thorne and O. C. Ferrell (1994). "Assessing the Application of Cognitive Moral Development Theory to Business Ethics," *Journal of Business Ethics,* 13, pp. 829–838.

Freeman, R. Edward (2000). "Business Ethics at the Millennium," *Business Ethics Quarterly,* Volume 10, January, pp. 169–180.

Freeman, R. Edward (2001). Presentation to the FBI/UVA Annual Meeting, University of Virginia, December 12, 2001.

Freeman, R. Edward (2002). Presentation to Beta Gamma Sigma Ethics Symposium, University of Virginia, February 1, 2002.

French, Warren A. and John Granrose (1995). *Practical Business Ethics.* Englewood Cliffs, NJ: Prentice-Hall, Inc.

Fuller, Joseph and Michael C. Jensen (2002). "Just Say No to Wall Street," *Working Paper 02-01,* Tuck School of Business, Dartmouth College and Harvard Business School.

Geva, Aviva (2001). "Myth and Ethics in Business," *Business Ethics Quarterly,* Volume 11, October, pp. 575–597.

Gilligan, Carol (1982). *In a Different Voice: Psychological Theory and Women's Development.* Cambridge, MA: Harvard University Press.

Goodpaster, Kenneth E. (Note 383-007). "Some Avenues for Ethical Analysis in General Management," *Harvard Business School Note 383-007,* p. 6.

Green, Ronald M. (1993). "Business Ethics in a Global Context," in Ronald M. Green, *The Ethical Manager.* New York, NY: Macmillan Publishing Company.

Griffin, Ricky W. and Michael W. Pustay (2003). *International Business.* Upper Saddle River, NJ: Prentice Hall.

Gustafson, Andrew (2000). "Making Sense of Postmodern Business Ethics," *Business Ethics Quarterly,* Volume 10, July, pp. 645–658.

Hager, Bruce (1991). "What's Behind Business' Sudden Fervor for Ethics?," *Business Week,* September 23, p. 65.

Hammer, Joshua, Bradley Martin and David Lewis (1989). "The Dark Side of Japan, Inc.," *Newsweek,* January 9, p. 41.

Hanafin, John J. (2002). "Morality and Markets in China," *Business Ethics Quarterly,* Volume 12 (January), 1–18.

Hasnas, John (1998). "The Normative Theories of Business Ethics: A Guide for the Perplexed," *Business Ethics Quarterly,* Volume 8, January, pp. 19–42.

Headden, Susan (1997). "A Modest Attack on Sweatshops," *U. S. News and World Report,* April 28, p. 39.

Hinds, M. (1982). "Products Unsafe at Home Are Still Unloaded Abroad," *The New York Times,* August 22, p. 56.

Hill, Charles W. L. (2001). *International Business.* New York, NY: McGraw-Hill.

Hill, Charles W. L. (2003). *Global Business Today.* New York, NY: McGraw-Hill.

Hoffman, W. Michael (2000). *Business Ethics: Reflections for the Center.* Waltham, MA: Center for Business Ethics, p. 6.

Hoffman, W. Michael, A.E. Lange, and D. A. Fedo, eds. (1986). *Ethics and the Multinational Enterprise.* Lanham, MD: University Press of America.

Hosmer, LaRue T. and Feng Chen (2001). "Ethics and Economics: Growing Opportunities for Research," *Business Ethics Quarterly,* Volume 11, October, pp. 599–622.

Ireland, Karin (1991). "The Ethics Game," *Personnel Journal,* March, pp. 72–75.

Itoh, Yoshiaki (1991). "Worked to Death in Japan," *World Press Review,* March, p. 50.

Jensen, Michael C. (2002). "Value Maximization, Stakeholder Theory and the Corporate Objective Function," *Business Ethics Quarterly,* Volume 12, Number 2, April, pp. 235–256.

Johnson, Elmer W. (1997). "Corporate Soulcraft in the Age of Brutal Markets," *Business Ethics Quarterly,* Volume 7, October, pp. 109–124.

Kant, Immanuel (1785). *Foundations of the Metaphysic of Morals,* L. W. Beck, translator. New York, NY: Bobbs-Merrill, 1959, p. 39.

Kaufman, Allen (2002). "Managers' Double Fiduciary Duty: To Stakeholders and To Freedom," *Business Ethics Quarterly,* Volume 12, Number 2, April, pp. 189–214.

Keegan, Warren J. (2002). *Global Marketing Management.* Upper Saddle River, NJ: Prentice Hall.

Kehoe, William J. (1985). "Ethics, Price Fixing, and the Management of Price Strategy," in Gene R. Laczniak and Patrick E. Murphy, eds., *Marketing Ethics: Guidelines for Managers.* Lexington, MA: D. C. Heath and Company, pp. 71–83.

Kehoe, William J. (1993). "Ethics in Business: Theory and Application," *Journal of Professional Services Marketing,* Volume 9, Number 1, pp. 13–25.

Kehoe, William J. (1994). "Ethics and Employee Theft," in John E. Richardson, ed., *Annual Editions: Business Ethics.* Guilford, CT: The Dushkin Publishing Group.

Kehoe, William J. (1995). "NAFTA: Concept, Problems, Promise," in B. T. Engelland and D. T. Smart, eds., *Marketing: Foundations For A Changing World.* Evansville, IN: Society for Marketing Advances, pp. 363–367.

Kehoe, William J. (1998). "The Environment of Ethics in Global Business," *Journal of Business and Behavioral Sciences,* Volume 4, Fall, pp. 47–56.

Kehoe, William J. and Linda K. Whitten (1999). "Structuring Host-Country Operations: Framing a Research Study," *Proceedings of the American Society of Business and Behavioral Sciences,* Volume 5, pp. 1–9.

Keohane, K. (1989). "Toxic Trade Off: The Price Ireland Pays for Industrial Development," *The Ecologist,* 19, pp. 144–146.

Kidder, R.M. (1994). *Shared Values for a Troubled World: Conversations with Men and Women of Conscience.* San Francisco, CA: Jossey-Bass, pp. 18–19.

Kimelman, John (1994). "The Lonely Boy Scout," *Financial World,* August 16, pp. 50–51.

Koehn, Daryl (1992). "Toward an Ethic of Exchange," *Business Ethics Quarterly,* Volume 2, July, pp. 341–355.

Kohlberg, Lawrence (1971). "Stages of Moral Development as a Basis for Moral Education," in C. M. Beck, B. S. Crittenden and E. V. Sullivan, eds., *Moral Education.* Toronto, Canada: University of Toronto Press.

Krugman, Paul (2002). "A System Corrupted," *The Wall Street Journal,* January 18, p. C1.

Kung, Hans (1997). "A Global Ethic in An Age of Globalization," *Business Ethics Quarterly,* Volume 7, July, pp. 17–32.

Labich, Kenneth (1992). "The New Crisis in Business Ethics," *Fortune,* April 20, pp. 167–176.

Labrecque, Thomas G. (1990). "Good Ethics Is Good Business," *USA Today: The Magazine of The American Scene,* May, pp. 20–21.

Laczniak, Gene R. (1983). "Business Ethics: A Manager's Primer," *Business,* January–March, pp. 23–29.

Laczniak, Gene R. and Patrick E. Murphy (1985). *Marketing Ethics: Guidelines for Managers.* Lexington, MA: D. C. Heath and Company.

Laczniak, Gene R. and Patrick E. Murphy (1993). *Ethical Marketing Decisions: The Higher Road.* Boston, MA: Allyn and Bacon.

Landauer, J. (1979). "Agency Will Define Corrupt Acts Abroad by U. S. Businesses," *The Wall Street Journal,* September 21, p. 23.

Lantos, Geoffrey P. (1999). "Motivating Moral Corporate Behavior," *Journal of Consumer Marketing,* Volume 16 (3), pp. 222–233.

Lascu, Dana-Nicoleta (2003). *International Marketing.* Cincinnati, OH: Atomic Dog Publishing.

Leopold, Jason (2002). "En-Ruse? Workers at Enron Sat They Posed as Busy Traders to Impress Visiting Analysts," *The Wall Street Journal,* February 7, pp. C1 and C13.

Levitt, Theodore. (1983). "The Globalization of Markets," *Harvard Business Review,* May–June, pp. 92–93.

Mackenzie, Craig and Alan Lewis (1999). "Morals and Markets: The Case for Ethical Investing," *Business Ethics Quarterly,* Volume 9, July, pp. 439–452.

MacKenzie, Debora (1992). "Europe Debates the Ownership of Life," *New Scientist,* January 4, pp. 9–10.

Mayer, Caroline E. and Amy Joyce (2002). "Blowing the Whistle," *The Washington Post,* February 10, pp. H1 and H4–H5.

McCoy, Bowen H. (1983). "The Parable of the Sadhu," *Harvard Business Review,* September/October, pp. 103–108.

McLean, Bethany (2002). "Monster Mess: The Enron Fallout has Just Begun," *Fortune,* February 4, pp. 93–96.

McMaster, Mark (2001). "Too Close for Comfort," *Sales & Marketing Management,* July, pp. 42–48.

Morgenson, Gretchen (2002). "Enron Letter Suggests $1.3 Billion More Down the Drain," *The New York Times,* January 17, pp. C1 & C10.

Murphy, Patrick E. (1988). "Implementing Business Ethics," *Journal of Business Ethics,* Volume 7, pp. 907–915.

Nash, Laura L. (1981). "Ethics Without the Sermon," *Harvard Business Review,* November/December, pp. 79–90.

Nichols, Martha, P. A. Jacobi, J. T. Dunlop and D. L. Lindauer (1993). "Third World Families at Work: Child Labor or Child Care?," *Harvard Business Review,* January–February, pp. 12–23.

Nicholson, Nigel (1994). "Ethics in Organizations: A Framework for Theory and Research," *Journal of Business Ethics,* 13, pp. 581–596.

Nussbaum, Bruce (2002). "Can You Trust Anybody Anymore?" *Business Week,* January 28, pp. 31–32.

O'Mally, Shaun F. (1995). "Ethical Cultures—Corporate and Personal," *Ethics Journal,* Winter, p. 9.

Orts, Eric W. and Alan Strudler (2002). "The Ethical and Environmental Limits of Stakeholder Theory," *Business Ethics Quarterly,* Volume 12, Number 2, April, pp. 215–233.

Paine, Lynn S. (1994). "Managing for Organizational Integrity," *Harvard Business Review,* March–April, pp. 106–117.

Perlmutter, Howard W. (1969). "The Tortuous Evolution of the Multinational Corporation," *Columbia Journal of World Business,* January–February, pp. 11–14.

Post, James M. (1985). "Assessing the Nestle Boycott," *California Management Review,* Winter, pp. 113–131.

Raths, Louis E., Merrill Harmin and Sidney Simon (1966*). Values and Teaching.* Columbus, OH: Merrill Publishing.

Robin, Donald P. (2000). *Questions and Answers About Business Ethics: Running an Ethical and Successful Business.* Cincinnati, OH: Dame, Thompson Learning.

Roddick, Anita (1994). "Corporate Responsibility," *Vital Speeches of the Day,* January 15, pp. 196–199.

Rogers, Hudson P., Alponso O. Ogbuehi, and C. M. Kochunny (1995). "Ethics and Transnational Corporations in Developing Countries: A Social Contract Perspective" in Nejdet Delener, ed., *Ethical Issues in International Marketing.* New York, NY: International Business Press, pp. 11–38.

Roman, Monica (2002). "Deflating those Pro Forma Figures," *Business Week,* January 28, p. 50.

Rossouw, G. J. (1994). "Business Ethics in Developing Countries," *Business Ethics Quarterly,* Volume 4, January, pp. 43–51.

Rotary (2002). "Rotary at a Glance," *The Rotarian,* January, p. 44. See also the Rotary International website at www.rotary.org/aboutrotary/4way.html.

Sandroff, Ronni (1990). "How Ethical Is American Business? The Working Woman Report," *Working Woman,* September, pp. 113–129.

Saporito, Bill (1998). "Taking a Look Inside Nike's Factories," *Time,* Volume 151, Issue 12, pp. 52–53.

Schmidt, Susan (2002). "Lawmaker Challenges Skilling's Denials," *The Washington Post,* February 12, pp. E1 and E5.

Schwartz, John (2002). "An Enron Unit Chief Warned and Was Rebuffed," *The New York Times,* February 20, pp. C1 and C4.

Scott, Elizabeth D. (2002). "Organizational Moral Values," *Business Ethics Quarterly,* Volume 12, Number 1, January, pp. 33–55.

Sethi, S. Prskash and Oliver F. Williams (2001). *Economic Imperatives and Ethical Values in Global Business: The South African Experience and International Codes Today.* South Bend, IN: University of Notre Dame Press.

Shimada, Hauro (1991). "The Desperate Need for New Values in Japanese Corporate Behavior," *Journal of Japanese Studies,* Winter, pp. 107–125.

Sidorov, Alexey, Irina Alexeyeva and Elena Shklyarik (2000). "The Ethical Environment of Russian Business," *Business Ethics Quarterly,* Volume 10, October, pp. 911–924.

Singer, Andrew W. (2000). "When it Comes to Child Labor, Toys R Us Isn't Playing Around," *Ethikos,* May/June, pp. 4–14.

Singer, Peter (2002). "Navigating the Ethics of Globalization," *The Chronicle of Higher Education,* October 11, pp. B7–B10.

Skelly, Joe (1995). "The Rise of International Ethics," *Business Ethics,* March/April, pp. 2–5.

Sloan, Allen and Michael Isikoff (2002). "The Enron Effect," *Newsweek,* January 28, pp. 34–35.

Smith, Adam (1966). *The Theory of Moral Sentiments.* New York, NY: Kelley Publishers.

Smith, N. Craig (1995). "Marketing Strategies for the Ethics Era," *Sloan Management Review,* Summer, pp. 85–97.

Sonnenberg, Frank K. and Beverly Goldberg (1992). "Business Integrity: An Oxymoron?," *Industry Week,* April 6, pp. 53–56.

Staff Report (1997). "Nike Suspends a Vietnam Boss," *The New York Times,* p. C3.

Thomson, Roy and Nigel Dudley (1989). "Transnationals and Oil in Amazonia," *The Ecologist,* November, pp. 219–224.

Trevino, Linda K., K. D. Butterfield and D. L. McCabe (1998). "The Ethical Context of Organizations: Influences on Employee Attitudes and Behaviors," *Business Ethics Quarterly,* Volume 8, July, pp. 447–476.

Turner, Louis (1984). "There's No love Lost Between Multinational Companies and the Third World," in W. M. Hoffman and J. M. Moore, eds., *Business Ethics.* New York, NY: McGraw-Hill Book Company, pp. 394–400.

U. S. Foreign Corrupt Practices Act (1977). www.usdoj.gov/criminal/fraud/fcpa/dojdocb.htm

van Tulder, Rob and Ans Kolk (2001). "Multinationality and Corporate Ethics," *Journal of International Business Studies,* Volume 32 (2), pp. 267–283.

Velasquez, Manual (1992). "International Business, Morality, and the Common Good," *Business Ethics Quarterly,* Volume 2, January, p. 30.

Velasquez, Manual (2000). "Globalization and the Failure of Ethics," *Business Ethics Quarterly,* Volume 10, January, pp. 343–352.

WSJ Editorial (2002). "Enron's Sins," *The Wall Street Journal,* January 18, p. A10.

Weaver, Gary R., Linda K. Trevino and Philip L. Cochran (1999). "Corporate Ethics Programs as Control Systems," *Academy of Management Journal,* Volume 42 (1), pp. 41–57.

Weaver Gary R. and Bradley R. Agle (2002). "Religiosity and Ethical Behavior In Organizations," *Academy of Management Review,* Volume 27, Number 1, pp. 77–97.

Werhane, Patricia H. (2000). "Exporting Mental Models: Global Capitalism in the 21st Century," *Business Ethics Quarterly,* Volume 10, January, pp. 353–362.

Whenmouth, Edwin (1992). "A Matter of Ethics," *Industry Week,* March 16, pp. 57–62.

White, Anna (1997). "Joe Camel's World Tour," *The New York Times,* April 23, p. A31.

Willatt, Norris (1970). "How Nestle Adapts Products to Its Markets," *Business Abroad,* June, pp. 31–33.

Yip, George S. (2003). *Total Global Strategy II.* Upper Saddle River, NJ: Prentice Hall/Pearson Education, Inc.

Zellner, Wendy and Michael Arndt (2002). "The Perfect Sales Pitch: No Debt, No Worries," *Business Week,* January 28, p. 35.

Zellner, Wendy, Stephanie F. Anderson and Laura Cohn (2002). "The Whistle Blower: A Hero and a Smoking-Gun Letter," *Business Week,* January 28, pp. 34–35.

Zellner, Wendy, Michael France and Joseph Weber (2002). "The Man Behind the Deal Machine," *Business Week,* February 4, pp. 40–41.

Critical Thinking

1. What are important considerations in developing a global code of ethics?

2. Should a firm change its home-country code of ethics when operating in another country? Why or why not?

3. Of the eight-stage framework for developing a global code of ethics presented in the article, what stage do you believe is most critical for a firm operating in the global business arena? Why is it a critical stage?

4. How should a firm promulgate its code of ethics in countries in which it operates?

Create Central

www.mhhe.com/createcentral

Internet References

Association of Corporate Council
    http://www.acc.com/legalresources/quickcounsel/daiagcoc.cfm

Ethics Resource Center
    http://www.ethics.org/files/u5/LRNGlobalIntegrity.pdf

Article   Prepared by: Eric Teoro, *Lincoln Christian University*

Taking Your Code to China

KIRK O. HANSON AND STEPHAN ROTHLIN

Learning Outcomes

After reading this article, you will be able to:

- Recognize the difficulty of developing a global standard for ethical behavior in business.

- Describe the unique challenges in conducting business in China.

- Develop a schema for promoting ethical business practices in China.

Introduction

The proliferation of codes of conduct and ethical standards among American and European companies has been dramatic over the past 20 years. It is rare today to find a large publicly held company in the West that does not have some type of ethics code and is not involved in the growing dialog over global standards of conduct. But one of the most difficult challenges facing these companies is how to apply these codes and these ethical standards to the companies' operations in developing countries, particularly in Africa, the Middle East, and Asia. Among these cases, perhaps the most urgent challenge is for each company to decide how to adapt and apply its code to operations in China. Companies such as Rio Tinto, Google, and Foxconn are recent case studies in ethical conflicts arising from doing business in China.

With pressures for human rights, environmental sensitivity, and fighting corruption rising in their domestic homelands and in global commerce, nothing is more critical to these companies' reputation and success than learning how to "take their code to China."

This article presents the learning of the two authors and companies they have consulted and worked with over the last 10 years in China. Our experience is that Western companies have generally progressed very slowly in applying their codes to their operations in China. This article summarizes why it is so difficult to do so, and what the most successful companies are doing to make it work.

Pressures for a Global Standard of Company Behavior

The fundamental problem any company faces in creating a global commitment to ethical behavior in its own organization is that cultural, competitive, economic, and political conditions vary significantly from country to country. It is often said that ethical values themselves differ significantly between countries. From our experience, however, we believe values do not differ as much as common practice—or how companies typically behave. Actual behavior, of course, depends on historical patterns, government regulation and enforcement, social pressures and acceptance, and the moral resolve of the actors. While corruption is common in many countries of the world, one cannot really say that corruption is welcomed or valued anywhere. There are anticorruption coalitions among domestic companies in almost every national setting. Even in those countries with the most corruption, there is an awareness of the corrosive effects it brings to the country, and the drag corruption creates for economic development.

Nonetheless, there are some value and cultural differences of significance, and different countries that are at different stages of development often have different priorities for social and economic progress. Further, the national and local governments in host countries present different challenges depending on their history and leadership.

Western companies really have little choice whether to "take their code to China" and to the other countries they operate in. They are facing four key developments which make "taking their codes" to wherever they operate more important and often more difficult. The first is that global companies are under increasingly insistent demands, both legal and from key constituencies in their home countries to adopt and implement standards of behavior abroad that match those at home. The United States' Foreign Corrupt Practices Act (FCPA), which was passed in 1977, makes some forms of corruption abroad crimes in the United States; in 1999 almost all OECD countries signed similar laws.

Because home country constituencies will not tolerate different (i.e. lower) ethical standards abroad, most large Western companies adopt and implement "global codes of conduct" which are expected to guide company behavior to be the same across all countries in which the firm operates. Many companies have commented that, from a purely practical point of view, adherence to a single global standard of behavior reduces the incidence of rogue local behavior, and rationalizations that the firm's conduct must be "adapted" to local conditions.

The second development is a growing global movement, reflected in an increasing number of developing countries, to deal seriously with bribery and corruption. Thirty-eight countries have now signed up to the OECD's 1997 anticorruption convention, leading to a spatter of cross-border prosecutions. Local constituencies in host countries then pressure companies from developed Western countries to join the reform coalitions to counter corruption. Local affiliates of Transparency International are most significant in this development.

The third development is a growing global dialog on "global standards" for business behavior. The United Nations Global Compact is an initiative launched in 1999 at the World Economic Forum in Davos by former Secretary General Kofi Anan but enthusiastically continued under his successor Ban Kee Moon. Companies and NGOs in over 80 countries have pledged to follow the 10 principles of the Global Compact in the crucial area of human rights, labor conditions, environmental protection and anticorruption. Similar efforts are being pursued in specific industries and in specific dimensions of corporate behavior such as employment policies and environmental behavior. Efforts such as these to promote a global standard of behavior are making it more difficult to operate under different practices in different countries. Such pressure requires companies to commit publicly to various global standards, which are then reinforced in their own company codes.

Finally, the explosive growth of the global media in all its forms has led to an increasing scrutiny of corporate behavior, even in the most distant and remote areas of the developing world. It has become difficult for a company to behave differently abroad without it coming to the attention of its home and host country constituencies. Corporate sweatshops, or environmental practices, can be documented by amateur reporters with cellphone cameras, even in the most restricted societies. Such disclosure dramatically increases pressures on Western companies to behave by a single global standard.

The Realities of Operating in Developing Countries

In each country where a company operates, it must confront a set of unique realities in applying its code of corporate behavior. Among the most important are the following:

Cultural expectations and standards—Each country has a set of cultural standards, or more informal expectations, that may conflict with the ethical standards the company operates by elsewhere. While some cultural expectations are benign—modes of greeting and signs of respect—others can be more problematic. In some societies, vendors are often selected primarily because they are a "related company" or are operated by a local employee's family or by a relative of a government official. In other societies, it is expected that potential business partners will develop a deep and reciprocal relationship before a contract is signed. In discussing China, the cultural tradition of gift giving to support such relationships can be a particularly problematic issue to manage.

Social and business community pressure to conform—Foreign companies operating in any society can be very disruptive, whether it is their pay scales or their insistence on arms-length contracting practices. When the foreign company operates by standards that challenge or constitute implied criticisms of local practices, there will be significant pressure on the foreign firm to conform to local practices, lest their presence create greater costs for indigenous firms, or create dissatisfaction in the local firm's workforce. The Western firm may find itself frozen out of business opportunities or subjected to selective regulatory enforcement if it is considered to be "disruptive."

Local management's comfort and loyalty to local standards—Foreign companies seek to hire local managers as quickly as possible and for as many positions as possible. Often local managers, particularly more senior managers already experienced in local companies, have adopted the local values and ways of doing things. Changing these managers' ways of operating can be particularly difficult.

Priorities of economic and political development—The national and local governments of host countries have many priorities and needs, and often choose to focus on issues unimportant to foreign firms while ignoring issues central to these newcomers. Chinese government decisions about how to deal with copyright violations, liberty issues such as access to the internet, and expressions of dissent may create significant difficulties for Western firms.

Western companies as targets of opportunity—Finally, any firm entering a developing country is a target for opportunistic individuals who seek to take advantage of the firm, particularly the substantial investment capital it plans to commit. They may negotiate deals overly favorable to the local partner, and may enmesh the firm in ethically questionable activities before it knows the local situation well enough to avoid such entanglements. Any firm must exercise particular caution until it develops an understanding of the local culture and acquires trusted business partners.

Special Reasons Why Operating in China Is Harder

China, as the "Middle Kingdom," is acutely proud of its long and complex history and culture. There is a widespread conviction that everything which comes from outside China needs a profound process of adaptation and inculturation in order to become accepted and relevant in the Chinese context. Companies seeking to implement "global standards" are sometimes met with distrust and disdain.

A second consideration is that there is a respect for local hierarchies that appears to be all-pervasive in Chinese society. There is a perceived need to give face to influential officials and individuals, which reflects the history of Chinese dynasties and has become distinctly different than the democratic traditions of other countries. A number of behavior patterns reflect this Imperial style. There are rituals and cultural patterns designed primarily to maintain social stability through these hierarchical relationships. On the level of companies and institutions this means that company leaders tend to be given the status of benevolent dictators who are accountable to no one. The way up to the top positions in many organizations may be paved more by one's ability to flatter a senior person at the right moment than by one's competency.

A third consideration, drawn from the long and revered Confucian tradition is the focus of the morally refined person, a "qunzi," who is expected to inspire much more moral behavior than the mere observance of the law. It is felt that the law cannot quite be trusted to ensure that the rights of every individual to be safeguarded. In its place, family bonds remain the strongest social reference, as also reflected strongly in the Confucian tradition. Thus, doing business with family members is often preferred to conducting arms-length transactions.

Finally, it is also true that the recent history of foreign aggression toward China, such as during the Opium wars or the Japanese invasion and massacres in the 1930s and 1940s, are featured frequently in the media and emerge frequently in the memory of the Chinese. These concerns erupt periodically, and affect attitudes toward all Western companies, not just those from the United Kingdom or Japan. There is a particular sensitivity to the perceived aggression of US support for Taiwan, for example. Eruptions of such feelings can delay or derail deal making and normal operations at unexpected moments.

The Chinese Context in 2010

After the end of the so-called "Cultural Revolution" from 1966 until 1976 and the turmoil of the "Gang of Four," China has witnessed the strongest economic growth in history due to the policies the paramount leader Deng Xiaoping introduced in 1978. Special economic zones have been opened in Shenzhen and other cities in China and foreign companies from the United States and Europe now have substantial investments, as well as substantial manufacturing and outsourcing operations to China.

Not surprisingly, the prospect of getting their teeth into a new huge market created the illusion for many foreign firms that enormous and immediate profits would be theirs for the taking. This has been almost always proven to be an illusion from the very beginning. It has been an extremely difficult challenge to be able to compete in China where the web of relationships—"guanxi" in Chinese—especially with government officials—seems to be crucial for one's success. It took the Swiss Multinational firm Nestle, which settled into Mainland China in 1983, 20 years in order to reach profitability. Many joint ventures—such as Pepsi Cola with its partner in Sichuan, Danone with Wahaha—were arranged in haste and have experienced a long and dreadful divorce and seemingly endless litigation. The Chinese companies involved, mostly state owned enterprises, seemed able to appeal to some government body or appeal publicly to nationalistic pride and xenophobic resentment in order to justify an opportunistic escape from their foreign partnership obligations. Despite a still wide spread "Gold Rush Mentality" to make the big deal quickly, a large majority of foreign business ventures have ended in failure or only limited success.

A major element of discomfort of Western companies in 2010 stems from the ambiguous role of the Chinese government dealing with the phenomenon of wide spread corruption which seems to be deeply engrained in the society. On one side, there have been serious attempts from the Central Government since the 1990s to curb corruption with various anticorruption campaigns. This has been more than lip service. Several actions have shown how steps have been taken. After the appointment of Zhu Rongji as Prime Minister in 1998 a whole empire of corruption, smuggling, and prostitution collapsed in the Eastern province of Fujian as bold actions were taken. The year 2006 sticks out as a year when a number of prominent multinationals such as Whirlpool, McKinsey, and ABB were punished by the Chinese government due to their kickback payments to the local government in Shanghai. In the same year the mayor, Mr. Cheng Liangyu, was sacked. During the last National Parliament Congress, blunt statements denouncing wide spread corruption stunned the public.

However, the same government—especially on lower levels—seems to represent a culture of deeply engrained patterns of soliciting favors and the rampant abuse of power. According to a survey among prominent business schools in China, including Hong Kong and Macau, a record number of 49 percent of the respondents thought that interacting with lower level government officials would most likely bring them into conflict with their personal value system.

There is a noticeable rise of public concern in China regarding business and government misbehavior. A number of recent incidents have had a significant impact on the Chinese public. When news broke out in 2007 that more than a thousand people, including children and disabled people, were being abused in kiln mines in the Shanxi province, it became surprising news coverage and a national tragedy. The link between the most brutal abuse of human beings and corrupt officials (and also local media) who have been paid to keep their mouth shut became obvious to everyone. An indigenous consumer movement, already strong in Hong Kong and Macau, has grown stronger in the wake of the lead paint scandals in the toy industry, the tainted milk scandals in Anhui Province (2001) and Hebei Province (2008), and the gas explosion in Northern China on the Songhua River in November 2005. This explosion stands out as the most devastating ecological disaster in recent history. The clean up will take at least 10 more years under the best circumstances.

It is said the Chinese citizen is also awakening to personal responsibility. The earthquake, which occurred in Wenchuan in the Sichuan province on May 12, 2009, provoked such a surprising outpouring of help and mutual assistance that even critical newspapers were hailing the birth of a civil society in China. Public philanthropy and public scrutiny of powerful companies and government officials are both evidence of a growing civil society.

While stories in the West emphasize limitations on the media in China, and there is the tight control from government censorship, it also seems that the so called "New Media"—a term for aggressive investigative journalism—with newspapers like Southern Weekly, Caijing, and China Newsweek—has had a significant impact in featuring stories of the abuse of power by some local officials. This new media has presented stories about both exemplary and shoddy behavior by Western companies operating in China.

There is even an emerging study of ethics and responsibility for the next generation of Chinese leaders. The Central Party School has not only been engaged in integrating Business Ethics and Corporate Social Responsibilities program within their curriculum, but also invited law professors and other experts from other countries to their school in order to engage in a serious debate about the rule of law and how civil society may be implemented in China. And according to a survey conducted by Jiaotong University, Shanghai, 39 percent of the business schools in China do actually include CSR and business ethics in their program.

Background Issues in Implementing a Code in China

There is much debate in China on several major issues which influence how a code is implemented. The first is the question whether the values of a company's Chinese employees are similar to those of their Western counterparts. Some Party ideologues are strongly arguing that Chinese values are divergent from the rest of the world. If there were no common ground, it would indeed be hard to implement in China the same code used in the West. By contrast, when China joined the World Trade Organization (WTO), in July 2001 it was presumed that the internationally accepted standards of the WTO could be implemented in China, that there were enough common values.

Another debate has been developed regarding the term of "Dignity," a term commonly used in recent Chinese government statements. What in Western terminology might be termed as "human rights" appears quite similar to the Chinese term of "Dignity" (zuiyan). Some suggest this represents a commitment to common values and may provide a language to address concerns important to Western companies.

Many Western executives operating in China have come to believe the goal to achieve in implementing a code must be far more than the formal agreement and legal compliance sought in the West. We believe implementing global standards in China will only work if they are formally agreed to AND take into account several aspects of the exceeding complex Chinese organizational culture.

For example, it is a good rule in China to assume that at the beginning of a project or implementation that "Nothing Is Clear." A common source of irritation is that partnerships and projects are formally agreed to, but too hastily arranged. Western companies assume all important details have been taken care of, when they have not. Often, a kind of very brief honeymoon is celebrated, followed by a long and painful divorce due to neglect of informal relationships and agreements, which must also be developed. Countless case studies document this pattern. In the most notorious cases, such as the breakdown of the joint venture between the French company, Danone, with its Chinese partner Wahaha, the relationship deteriorated so badly that the respective governments felt compelled to step in and impose a truce. It is, therefore, wise to understand that any successful cooperation with Chinese partners, or even one's own employees, takes much more time. It is frequently a necessary strategy to adopt stronger methods of control if common agreements are to be properly understood and honored. It is unfortunately common that a Western company's first partnership ends up in failure.

When a misunderstanding arises, one should adopt the Confucian self-critical attitude in figuring out the reasons for such a failure rather than putting the blame on the Chinese side. Most often, it will be the neglect of informal agreements and relationships. Only in a deeper relationship and through much more informal and formal communication can the true meaning of agreements in China be clarified.

Another area of general concern in implementing codes is that Western companies often do not appreciate the strong divide between the city and the countryside in China. Implementing agreements and employee and partner standards can be harder in some rural conditions. Roughly two-thirds of the Chinese still live in the countryside where carefully orchestrated rituals are even more important to the successful implementation of agreements. For example, in some circumstances a host may insist on offering hospitality with excessive drinking. While in the cities the foreign guest may be able to politely refuse at some point to continue with the drinking games, in the countryside it may be considered rude to stop the dynamics of getting drunk together.[1] Clearly, a company must find ways of limiting participation in the most objectionable practices. Besides excessive drinking games, there are some banquets and karaoke sessions where women are hired to act as prostitutes. Such objectionable practices can create significant legal exposure for a company as well.

Codes must be written and implemented with an understanding of extensive new legislation in China addressing labor conditions, corruption, whistleblowing, sexual harassment, consumer, and environmental issues. Despite the difficulties of introducing a global ethics code in China, there are opportunities for Western companies to contribute significantly to the implementation and success of these new laws, all of which will make the companies' task easier in the future. There is an interest in growing segments of the government and the Chinese business community to see these laws made effective.

Finally, Western companies must keep abreast of developments in a growing commitment to the rule of law. In many ways, Hong Kong represents a model of the implementation of the Rule of Law in the Chinese context. Hong Kong, which reverted to China in 1997, continues its role as a beacon of clean government. Forty years ago rampant cases of corruption were common in Hong Kong. However, due to the establishment of the Independent Commission against Corruption (ICAC), significant headway has been made in diminishing corruption so that now Hong Kong ranks besides Singapore as the cleanest country in Asia. This has encouraged greater transparency concerning corruption in other parts of China.

The conclusion of the recent publication of the Anticorruption report of Mr. Xiao Yang (2009) who served as Supreme Judge in the PRC has been very clear. He argued that corruption on Mainland China has strongly increased in the last 15 years and has involved more and more Ministries. He argued for the implementation of an institution modeled on ICAC designed to investigate and prosecute cases of abuse cases of public.

Shaping Your Code to Fit China

The first choice every company faces is whether to operate by global standards or to adjust and adapt to local norms. Our experience suggests there is always some adherence to local norms, though not always by changing the actual words in the code, and hopefully, this adherence is within the framework of global standards a company claims to follow wherever it operates. However, in some settings, more adjustments and more recognition of the ethical traditions of the host country may be necessary. We think this is true of China.

We have observed the most successful Western firms in China following these steps to "take their codes to China":

Inculturate Your Code

The term "inculturation" represents a compromise between unchanging global standards and complete local accommodation. "Inculturation" in China has a long history. The Roman Catholic Church has sought, since the time of Matteo Ricci, a Jesuit priest who came to China in 1583, of "inculturating" the Christian message to Chinese conditions. For Ricci and even for Catholics today, religious "inculturation" indicates the dynamic process when key values enshrined in the Gospel such as truth, honesty, and charity are not just imposed from outside, but get truly integrated within a given culture. This process makes possible global consistency with local sensitivity. This is most important in countries like China that have a history of foreign domination and a sensitivity to imperialistic behavior.

For the company choosing to operate in China, inculturation means adhering to global principles that have specific local meanings and therefore, local rules. The most obvious example is gift giving. In a gift giving culture like China, a company would find it hard to adhere to an absolute "no gift" policy as some companies adopt elsewhere in the world. An inculturated gift policy would permit gift giving, albeit tightly limited, but also scaled so that larger gifts, again within a firmly established upper limit, would be permitted to higher executives or officials. An inculturated Chinese policy would also even permit small but scaled gifts to government officials, as this is in China a show of respect. A top value of $75 or $100 for the highest corporate or government official visited is viable and allows the Western company to respect and adhere to local cultural gift-giving practice, but not to engage in bribery. The company also must make it absolutely clear that gifts of any greater value are forbidden.

Inculturation would also recognize the cultural tradition of relationship building and the necessary entertainment to that purpose. However, a Western company should very explicitly and clearly communicate the limits on the value and frequency of such entertainment. Inculturation in China should also recognize the particular context of ethics hotlines and of whistle blowing. With particular adjustments, even this Western concept can be made to work in China, as noted below.

Make the Company Code Consistent with Chinese Laws

China is proud of the progress made in recent years in promulgating and adopting regulatory standards and laws that protect the interests of employees, consumers, and shareholders. It is a necessary step in taking ones's code to China to assess the alignment of these local laws (many very recently adopted) and the company's code of conduct. This process must, of course, be an ongoing one, making future adjustments to the company's code as new laws are adopted in China.

Align Your Code with Chinese Concepts and Slogans of Key Government Officials

In addition to the laws adopted by the National Congress and Communist Party rules adopted by the every 5-year Central Party Congress, Chinese party and government leaders introduce key phrases or slogans which are meant to organize and direct the path of Chinese economic and social development.

Under Jiang Zemin the former President of the PRC, there was considerable attention to the "Three Represents," a doctrine by which the all-powerful Communist Party of China represented the masses of people, the productive forces of society, and the culture. The key message was the preeminence of the Party, but the detailed message gave room to cast corporate codes and decisions as advocating the masses, the development of productive capacity, and even the proper cultural development of China. Under the first 5-year term of Hu Jintao, the current President of China, the concept of "Harmonious Society" was adopted as a preeminent national goal. Later, Hu promoted the concept of "a Scientific Society" wherein, among other things, empirical data and facts should drive decisions more than bias or entrenched interests.

Tying corporate norms and standards of conduct to that objective can strengthen corporate efforts, both because employees understand the alignment of corporate objectives, but also because the company could occasionally secure government help in enforcing its code that it would not otherwise receive.

Incorporate References to Global Standards Embraced by the Chinese

Over the past 10 years, the Chinese government has participated in the formulation of, and conferences on, many international codes and standards. The United Nations Global Compact has 195 signatories in China. The WTO code was widely publicized to Chinese industries in 2001 when China officially joined the WTO. References to these documents and standards strengthen acceptance of a company's global code.

Publish the Code in Bilingual Format

A company code should be published in both English and in Chinese language versions, perhaps side by side. Any Chinese company and every Western company operating in China will have English speakers, and they or other employees will be eager to *compare* the actual English words with the Chinese characters chosen as direct translations. And of course, any company will have Chinese speakers who do not read English. Translation into Chinese demonstrates a seriousness of purpose and a commitment to enforce the code, which must be addressed in the published document.

Introduce the Code in the Chinese Way

Too often, ethics codes are introduced in the United States and in Western Europe by email or by distribution of a printed booklet, perhaps with a card to return acknowledging receipt of the code. This approach will simply not work in China.

Chinese employees will expect that any code or standard they are actually expected to follow will be introduced with considerable time available for discussion, objection, and clarification, and in a workshop conducted in their own dialect. At minimum, they will expect to be able to argue about adaptations to the Chinese context, and the particular Chinese characters used to translate the English or European language concepts. Rather than interpret this as dissent and obfuscation, those introducing the code should consider it a productive opportunity to explain the code and get good feedback on the application of the code to the Chinese context.

Other aspects of the introduction should proceed much as they do in the West. The code must be introduced by line officers of the company with a seriousness that convinces employees that these are actually to be the desired standards. Training must address the most common dilemmas employees will face to give clear and understandable signals about the type of behavior expected. Specific examples are more important in the Chinese context because employees will have generally experienced the rollout of multiple initiatives that have had little impact and less staying power.

Education regarding the code must be given to all new hires. Education in the code must be tailored to the several hierarchical levels within the firm, including senior executives, middle managers, and hourly employees.

Do Whistleblowing the Chinese Way

Without giving up the principle of reporting violations, a Chinese hotline can be positioned and promoted as a "Help line" designed to advise employees on how a particular action should be taken. This approach has been used by many companies in the

West. Further, because of the sensitivity to reporting on a senior, there must be greater opportunity for an employee to have his or her complaint treated as genuinely confidential and anonymous. There is a greater sensitivity to cases where the complaint, by its very nature, might be traced back to an individual employee. A Chinese help line will require more promotion and explanation, and may be more effective if it is structured to have complaints dealt with by the highest authority in a company—for example, by the board of directors. Because of deference to hierarchy, only the board can effectively address wrongdoing by senior level officials.

Extending the Code to Business Partners

There is a growing understanding among Chinese businesses that American and European companies must extend their standards and codes to their business partners, and have a right to expect their partners to adhere to the same standards. In the past, too many Western companies have thrown up their hands and despaired of actually influencing the behavior of business partners, accepting signed assurances of compliance but not really expecting adherence. Today, more Western companies are vetting their partners for their capacity and willingness to conform to codes, and then are monitoring and assessing compliance over time.

The first step in the process must be the selection of partners who have the basic capacity to be in alignment with the values and code of the Western firm. This requires due diligence, either by the company's own managers, or by a firm hired explicitly to evaluate potential partners. Such due diligence is usually hard to accomplish, and virtually every firm reports one or more disasters trying to integrate business partners into the business's activities. Nonetheless, Chinese firms, particularly those with experience operating in an international business environment, and firms with experience in previous partnerships with Western companies, can be effective and ethical local partners. In China, there has developed a language often used to describe projects and companies capable of operating by such standards. This is known as operating by "international standards" as opposed to Chinese or local standards. Projects are said to be built to or operating by international standards. Chinese businesses are said to be "international standards companies." Such firms are more likely to be effective partners.

Preparing Local Leadership to Enforce Your Code in China

As in virtually all settings where a company seeks to infuse a code and its standards into actual behavior, local leadership will exercise the strongest influence in China. Chinese executives

and managers will be anxious to adopt the latest developments in leadership. It is important to position the code as a key part of cutting edge and modern management.

An extended dialog with the chief local official regarding the code before it is introduced is essential. Only a local executive can identify the unavoidable points of stress in the implementation of a code. A local executive will expect to be consulted on the "inculturation" process, and may be the best source of ideas for doing this successfully without abandoning the firm's global standards. And only a local executive can highlight where enforcement must be emphasized.

Much has been made regarding the wisdom of having a Chinese national or a foreign passport holder as a Western company's top officer in China. Both have risks for the implementation of a corporate code of conduct. The foreign executive enforcing the code may make the code seem more foreign and less practical in the local context. On the other hand, some Chinese executives may not believe in the code as fully, or may go through the motions without truly requiring adherence within the organization. A Chinese executive who genuinely believes in the code may be more effective in getting compliance from the organization, or recognizing lip service when it is being given.

Company leaders, both at the Western headquarters and in China, need to create a system of accountability—of monitoring and auditing compliance with the code. This is even more important in China than it is in the West. There are so many initiatives and slogans thrown at Chinese managers, that they are looking for signals that this one is not merely lip service. Too often they conclude that ethics codes are not serious because they are introduced in ineffective ways and without the accountability and follow-up.

It is absolutely essential to the success of any code that the offending employee or manager must be subject to firing, and that occasionally an employee does get fired for violating the code. Even more so than in the West, it is critical all understand that the behavior of senior managers and executives be subject to the code, and risk dismissal if they violate the code. There is a predisposition to believe the code is both lip service and/or applied selectively on lower level employees, and not to those higher in the hierarchy.

In summary, we believe Western companies following the preceding principles can and are making genuine progress "taking their codes to China" and establishing a truly global standard of behavior in their firms.

Note

1. Obviously, such games may seriously harm the health of those who are unable to put a timely end to this ritual. Recently, there have again been reports of death of government officials due to excessive drinking.

References

Organization for Economic Co-operation and Development. (2009). *Ratification Status as of March 2009.*

Retrieved from www.oecd.org/dataoecd/59/13/40272933.pdf The Foreign Corrupt Practices Act of 1977 § 15 U.S.C. § 78dd-1(1977).

United Nations Global Compact Office. (2005). *The ten principles.* Retrieved from www.unglobalcompact.org/AboutTheGC/TheTenPrinciples/index.html

United Nations Global Compact Office. (2010). *Participant search* [Data File]. Retrieved from www.unglobalcompact.org/participants/search?business_type=all&commit=Search&cop_status=all&country[]=38&joined_after=&joined_before=&keyword=&organization_type_id=& page=1&per_page=100&sector_id=all

Yang, X. (2009). Fantan baogao (Anti-Corruption Report). Beijing: Law Press.

Critical Thinking

1. What are the realities facing a firm when applying its code of ethics in other countries?

2. What are the reasons why operating in China with a code of ethics is harder than elsewhere in the world?

3. How should a code of ethics be shaped to fit China's marketplace?

4. How should a firm prepare its local managers to enforce a code of ethics in China?

Create Central

www.mhhe.com/createcentral

Internet References

Forbes
http://www.forbes.com/sites/russellflannery/2010/08/17/on-the-front-line-in-china-challenging-business-ethics/

Institute of Business Ethics
http://www.ibe.org.uk/userfiles/chinaop.pdf

Markula Center for Applied Ethics
http://www.scu.edu/ethics/publications/ethicalperspectives/business-china.html

Article   Prepared by: Eric Teoro, *Lincoln Christian University*

Wal-Mart Hushed Up a Vast Mexican Bribery Case

DAVID BARSTOW, ALEJANDRA XANIC, AND JAMES C. MCKINLEY JR.

Learning Outcomes

After reading this article, you will be able to:

- Describe the facts related to Wal-Mart's Mexican bribery case.

- Recognize the need for strong internal controls to promote ethical behavior.

- Recognize that ethical breaches of omission can be as serious as ethical breaches of commission.

In September 2005, a senior Wal-Mart lawyer received an alarming e-mail from a former executive at the company's largest foreign subsidiary, Wal-Mart de Mexico. In the e-mail and follow-up conversations, the former executive described how Wal-Mart de Mexico had orchestrated a campaign of bribery to win market dominance. In its rush to build stores, he said, the company had paid bribes to obtain permits in virtually every corner of the country.

The former executive gave names, dates and bribe amounts. He knew so much, he explained, because for years he had been the lawyer in charge of obtaining construction permits for Wal-Mart de Mexico.

Wal-Mart dispatched investigators to Mexico City, and within days they unearthed evidence of widespread bribery. They found a paper trail of hundreds of suspect payments totaling more than $24 million. They also found documents showing that Wal-Mart de Mexico's top executives not only knew about the payments, but had taken steps to conceal them from Wal-Mart's headquarters in Bentonville, Ark. In a confidential report to his superiors, Wal-Mart's lead investigator, a former F.B.I. special agent, summed up their initial findings this way: "There is reasonable suspicion to believe that Mexican and USA laws have been violated."

The lead investigator recommended that Wal-Mart expand the investigation.

Instead, an examination by The *New York Times* found, Wal-Mart's leaders shut it down.

Neither American nor Mexican law enforcement officials were notified. None of Wal-Mart de Mexico's leaders were disciplined. Indeed, its chief executive, Eduardo Castro-Wright, identified by the former executive as the driving force behind years of bribery, was promoted to vice chairman of Wal-Mart in 2008. Until this article, the allegations and Wal-Mart's investigation had never been publicly disclosed.

But *The Times*'s examination uncovered a prolonged struggle at the highest levels of Wal-Mart, a struggle that pitted the company's much publicized commitment to the highest moral and ethical standards against its relentless pursuit of growth.

Under fire from labor critics, worried about press leaks and facing a sagging stock price, Wal-Mart's leaders recognized that the allegations could have devastating consequences, documents and interviews show. Wal-Mart de Mexico was the company's brightest success story, pitched to investors as a model for future growth. (Today, one in five Wal-Mart stores is in Mexico.) Confronted with evidence of corruption in Mexico, top Wal-Mart executives focused more on damage control than on rooting out wrongdoing.

In one meeting where the bribery case was discussed, H. Lee Scott Jr., then Wal-Mart's chief executive, rebuked internal investigators for being overly aggressive. Days later, records show, Wal-Mart's top lawyer arranged to ship the internal investigators' files on the case to Mexico City. Primary responsibility for the investigation was then given to the general counsel of Wal-Mart de Mexico—a remarkable choice since the same general counsel was alleged to have authorized bribes.

The general counsel promptly exonerated his fellow Wal-Mart de Mexico executives.

When Wal-Mart's director of corporate investigations—a former top F.B.I. official—read the general counsel's report, his appraisal was scathing. "Truly lacking," he wrote in an e-mail to his boss.

The report was nonetheless accepted by Wal-Mart's leaders as the last word on the matter.

In December, after learning of *The Times*'s reporting in Mexico, Wal-Mart informed the Justice Department that it had begun an internal investigation into possible violations of the Foreign Corrupt Practices Act, a federal law that makes it a crime for American corporations and their subsidiaries to bribe foreign officials. Wal-Mart said the company had learned of possible problems with how it obtained permits, but stressed that the issues were limited to "discrete" cases.

"We do not believe that these matters will have a material adverse effect on our business," the company said in a filing with the Securities and Exchange Commission.

But *The Times*'s examination found credible evidence that bribery played a persistent and significant role in Wal-Mart's rapid growth in Mexico, where Wal-Mart now employs 209,000 people, making it the country's largest private employer.

A Wal-Mart spokesman confirmed that the company's Mexico operations—and its handling of the 2005 case—were now a major focus of its inquiry.

"If these allegations are true, it is not a reflection of who we are or what we stand for," the spokesman, David W. Tovar, said. "We are deeply concerned by these allegations and are working aggressively to determine what happened."

In the meantime, Mr. Tovar said, Wal-Mart is taking steps in Mexico to strengthen compliance with the Foreign Corrupt Practices Act. "We do not and will not tolerate noncompliance with F.C.P.A. anywhere or at any level of the company," he said.

The Times laid out this article's findings to Wal-Mart weeks ago. The company said it shared the findings with many of the executives named here, including Mr. Scott, now on Wal-Mart's board, and Mr. Castro-Wright, who is retiring in July. Both men declined to comment, Mr. Tovar said.

The Times obtained hundreds of internal company documents tracing the evolution of Wal-Mart's 2005 Mexico investigation. The documents show Wal-Mart's leadership immediately recognized the seriousness of the allegations. Working in secrecy, a small group of executives, including several current members of Wal-Mart's senior management, kept close tabs on the inquiry.

Michael T. Duke, Wal-Mart's current chief executive, was also kept informed. At the time, Mr. Duke had just been put in charge of Wal-Mart International, making him responsible for all foreign subsidiaries. "You'll want to read this," a top Wal-Mart lawyer wrote in an Oct. 15, 2005, e-mail to Mr. Duke that gave a detailed description of the former executive's allegations.

The Times examination included more than 15 hours of interviews with the former executive, Sergio Cicero Zapata, who resigned from Wal-Mart de Mexico in 2004 after nearly a decade in the company's real estate department.

In the interviews, Mr. Cicero recounted how he had helped organize years of payoffs. He described personally dispatching two trusted outside lawyers to deliver envelopes of cash to government officials. They targeted mayors and city council members, obscure urban planners, low-level bureaucrats who issued permits—anyone with the power to thwart Wal-Mart's growth. The bribes, he said, bought zoning approvals, reductions in environmental impact fees and the allegiance of neighborhood leaders.

He called it working "the dark side of the moon."

The Times also reviewed thousands of government documents related to permit requests for stores across Mexico. The examination found many instances where permits were given within weeks or even days of Wal-Mart de Mexico's payments to the two lawyers. Again and again, *The Times* found, legal and bureaucratic obstacles melted away after payments were made.

The Times conducted extensive interviews with participants in Wal-Mart's investigation. They spoke on the condition that they not be identified discussing matters Wal-Mart has long shielded. These people said the investigation left little doubt Mr. Cicero's allegations were credible. ("Not even a close call," one person said.)

But, they said, the more investigators corroborated his assertions, the more resistance they encountered inside Wal-Mart. Some of it came from powerful executives implicated in the corruption, records, and interviews show. Other top executives voiced concern about the possible legal and reputational harm.

In the end, people involved in the investigation said, Wal-Mart's leaders found a bloodlessly bureaucratic way to bury the matter. But in handing the investigation off to one of its main targets, they disregarded the advice of one of Wal-Mart's top lawyers, the same lawyer first contacted by Mr. Cicero.

"The wisdom of assigning any investigative role to management of the business unit being investigated escapes me," Maritza I. Munich, then general counsel of Wal-Mart International, wrote in an e-mail to top Wal-Mart executives.

The investigation, she urged, should be completed using "professional, independent investigative resources."

The Allegations Emerge

On Sept. 21, 2005, Mr. Cicero sent an e-mail to Ms. Munich telling her he had information about "irregularities" authorized "by the highest levels" at Wal-Mart de Mexico. "I hope to meet you soon," he wrote.

Ms. Munich was familiar with the challenges of avoiding corruption in Latin America. Before joining Wal-Mart in 2003, she had spent 12 years in Mexico and elsewhere in Latin America as a lawyer for Procter & Gamble.

At Wal-Mart in 2004, she pushed the board to adopt a strict anticorruption policy that prohibited all employees from "offering anything of value to a government official on behalf of Wal-Mart." It required every employee to report the first sign of corruption, and it bound Wal-Mart's agents to the same exacting standards.

Ms. Munich reacted quickly to Mr. Cicero's e-mail. Within days, she hired Juan Francisco Torres-Landa, a prominent Harvard-trained lawyer in Mexico City, to debrief Mr. Cicero. The two men met three times in October 2005, with Ms. Munich flying in from Bentonville for the third debriefing.

During hours of questioning, Mr. Torres-Landa's notes show, Mr. Cicero described how Wal-Mart de Mexico had perfected the art of bribery, then hidden it all with fraudulent accounting. Mr. Cicero implicated many of Wal-Mart de Mexico's leaders, including its board chairman, its general counsel, its chief auditor and its top real estate executive.

But the person most responsible, he told Mr. Torres-Landa, was the company's ambitious chief executive, Eduardo Castro-Wright, a native of Ecuador who was recruited from Honeywell in 2001 to become Wal-Mart's chief operating officer in Mexico.

Mr. Cicero said that while bribes were occasionally paid before Mr. Castro-Wright's arrival, their use soared after Mr. Castro-Wright ascended to the top job in 2002. Mr. Cicero described how Wal-Mart de Mexico's leaders had set "very aggressive growth goals," which required opening new stores "in record times." Wal-Mart de Mexico executives, he said, were under pressure to do "whatever was necessary" to obtain permits.

In an interview with *The Times*, Mr. Cicero said Mr. Castro-Wright had encouraged the payments for a specific strategic purpose. The idea, he said, was to build hundreds of new stores so fast that competitors would not have time to react. Bribes, he explained, accelerated growth. They got zoning maps changed. They made environmental objections vanish. Permits that typically took months to process magically materialized in days. "What we were buying was time," he said.

Wal-Mart de Mexico's stunning growth made Mr. Castro-Wright a rising star in Bentonville. In early 2005, when he was promoted to a senior position in the United States, Mr. Duke would cite his "outstanding results" in Mexico.

Mr. Cicero's allegations were all the more startling because he implicated himself. He spent hours explaining to Mr. Torres-Landa the mechanics of how he had helped funnel bribes through trusted fixers, known as "gestores."

Gestores (pronounced hes-TORE-ehs) are a fixture in Mexico's byzantine bureaucracies, and some are entirely legitimate. Ordinary citizens routinely pay gestores to stand in line for them at the driver's license office. Companies hire them as quasi-lobbyists to get things done as painlessly as possible.

But often gestores play starring roles in Mexico's endless loop of public corruption scandals. They operate in the shadows, dangling payoffs to officials of every rank. It was this type of gestor that Wal-Mart de Mexico deployed, Mr. Cicero said.

Mr. Cicero told Mr. Torres-Landa it was his job to recruit the gestores. He worked closely with them, sharing strategies on whom to bribe. He also approved Wal-Mart de Mexico's payments to the gestores. Each payment covered the bribe and the gestor's fee, typically 6 percent of the bribe.

It was all carefully monitored through a system of secret codes known only to a handful of Wal-Mart de Mexico executives.

The gestores submitted invoices with brief, vaguely worded descriptions of their services. But the real story, Mr. Cicero said, was told in codes written on the invoices. The codes identified the specific "irregular act" performed, Mr. Cicero explained to Mr. Torres-Landa. One code, for example, indicated a bribe to speed up a permit. Others described bribes to obtain confidential information or eliminate fines.

Each month, Mr. Castro-Wright and other top Wal-Mart de Mexico executives "received a detailed schedule of all of the payments performed," he said, according to the lawyer's notes. Wal-Mart de Mexico then "purified" the bribes in accounting records as simple legal fees.

They also took care to keep Bentonville in the dark. "Dirty clothes are washed at home," Mr. Cicero said.

Mr. Torres-Landa explored Mr. Cicero's motives for coming forward.

Mr. Cicero said he resigned in September 2004 because he felt underappreciated. He described the "pressure and stress" of participating in years of corruption, of contending with "greedy" officials who jacked up bribe demands.

As he told *The Times*, "I thought I deserved a medal at least."

The breaking point came in early 2004, when he was passed over for the job of general counsel of Wal-Mart de Mexico. This snub, Mr. Torres-Landa wrote, "generated significant anger with respect to the lack of recognition for his work." Mr. Cicero said he began to assemble a record of bribes he had helped orchestrate to "protect him in case of any complaint or investigation," Mr. Torres-Landa wrote.

"We did not detect on his part any express statement about wishing to sell the information," the lawyer added.

According to people involved in Wal-Mart's investigation, Mr. Cicero's account of criminality at the top of Wal-Mart's most important foreign subsidiary was impossible to dismiss. He had clearly been in a position to witness the events he described. Nor was this the first indication of corruption at Wal-Mart de Mexico under Mr. Castro-Wright. A confidential investigation, conducted for Wal-Mart in 2003 by Kroll Inc., a leading investigation firm, discovered that Wal-Mart de Mexico had systematically increased its sales by helping favored high-volume customers evade sales taxes.

A draft of Kroll's report, obtained by *The Times*, concluded that top Wal-Mart de Mexico executives had failed to enforce their own anticorruption policies, ignored internal audits that raised red flags and even disregarded local press accounts asserting that Wal-Mart de Mexico was "carrying out a tax fraud." (The company ultimately paid $34.3 million in back taxes.)

Wal-Mart then asked Kroll to evaluate Wal-Mart de Mexico's internal audit and antifraud units. Kroll wrote another report that branded the units "ineffective." Many employees accused of wrongdoing were not even questioned; some "received a promotion shortly after the suspicions of fraudulent activities had surfaced."

None of these findings, though, had slowed Mr. Castro-Wright's rise.

Just days before Mr. Cicero's first debriefing, Mr. Castro-Wright was promoted again. He was put in charge of all Wal-Mart stores in the United States, one of the most prominent jobs in the company. He also joined Wal-Mart's executive committee, the company's inner sanctum of leadership.

The Initial Response

Ms. Munich sent detailed memos describing Mr. Cicero's debriefings to Wal-Mart's senior management. These executives, records show, included Thomas A. Mars, Wal-Mart's general counsel and a former director of the Arkansas State Police; Thomas D. Hyde, Wal-Mart's executive vice president and corporate secretary; Michael Fung, Wal-Mart's top internal auditor; Craig Herkert, the chief executive for Wal-Mart's operations in Latin America; and Lee Stucky, a confidant of Lee Scott's and chief administrative officer of Wal-Mart International.

Wal-Mart typically hired outside law firms to lead internal investigations into allegations of significant wrongdoing. It did so earlier in 2005, for example, when Thomas M. Coughlin, then vice chairman of Wal-Mart, was accused of padding his expense accounts and misappropriating Wal-Mart gift cards.

At first, Wal-Mart took the same approach with Mr. Cicero's allegations. It turned to Willkie Farr & Gallagher, a law firm with extensive experience in Foreign Corrupt Practices Act cases.

The firm's "investigation work plan" called for tracing all payments to anyone who had helped Wal-Mart de Mexico obtain permits for the previous 5 years. The firm said it would scrutinize "any and all payments" to government officials and interview every person who might know about payoffs, including "implicated members" of Wal-Mart de Mexico's board.

In short, Willkie Farr recommended the kind of independent, spare-no-expense investigation major corporations routinely undertake when confronted with allegations of serious wrongdoing by top executives.

Wal-Mart's leaders rejected this approach. Instead, records show, they decided Wal-Mart's lawyers would supervise a far more limited "preliminary inquiry" by in-house investigators.

The inquiry, a confidential memo explained, would take two weeks, not the 4 months Willkie Farr proposed. Rather than examining years of permits, the team would look at a few specific stores. Interviews would be done "only when absolutely essential to establishing the bona fides" of Mr. Cicero. However, if the inquiry found a "likelihood" that laws had been violated, the company would then consider conducting a "full investigation."

The decision gave Wal-Mart's senior management direct control over the investigation. It also meant new responsibility for the company's tiny and troubled Corporate Investigations unit.

The unit was ill-equipped to take on a major corruption investigation, let alone one in Mexico. It had fewer than 70 employees, and most were assigned to chasing shoplifting rings and corrupt vendors. Just four people were specifically dedicated to investigating corporate fraud, a number Joseph R. Lewis, Wal-Mart's director of corporate investigations, described in a confidential memo as "wholly inadequate for an organization the size of Wal-Mart."

But Mr. Lewis and his boss, Kenneth H. Senser, vice president for global security, aviation and travel, were working to strengthen the unit. Months before Mr. Cicero surfaced, they won approval to hire four "special investigators" who, according to their job descriptions, would be assigned the "most significant and complex fraud matters." Mr. Scott, the chief executive, also agreed that Corporate Investigations would handle all allegations of misconduct by senior executives.

And yet in the fall of 2005, as Wal-Mart began to grapple with Mr. Cicero's allegations, two cases called into question Corporate Investigations' independence and role.

In October, Wal-Mart's vice chairman, John B. Menzer, intervened in an internal investigation into a senior vice president who reported to him. According to internal records, Mr. Menzer told Mr. Senser he did not want Corporate Investigations to handle the case "due to concerns about the impact such an investigation would have." One of the senior vice president's subordinates, he said, "would be better suited to conduct this inquiry." Soon after, records show, the subordinate cleared his boss.

The other case involved the president of Wal-Mart Puerto Rico. A whistle-blower had accused the president and other executives of mistreating employees. Although Corporate Investigations was supposed to investigate all allegations against senior executives, the president had instead assigned an underling to look into the complaints—but to steer clear of those against him.

Ms. Munich objected. In an e-mail to Wal-Mart executives, she complained that the investigation was "at the direction of the same company officer who is the target of several of the allegations."

"We are in need of clear guidelines about how to handle these issues going forward," she warned.

The Inquiry Begins

Ronald Halter, one of Wal-Mart's new "special investigators," was assigned to lead the preliminary inquiry into Mr. Cicero's allegations. Mr. Halter had been with Wal-Mart only a few months, but he was a seasoned criminal investigator. He had spent 21 years in the F.B.I., and he spoke Spanish.

He also had help. Bob Ainley, a senior auditor, was sent to Mexico along with several Spanish-speaking auditors.

On Nov. 12, 2005, Mr. Halter's team got to work at Wal-Mart de Mexico's corporate headquarters in Mexico City. The team gained access to a database of Wal-Mart de Mexico payments and began searching the payment description field for the word "gestoria."

By day's end, they had found 441 gestor payments. Each was a potential bribe, and yet they had searched back only to 2003.

Mr. Cicero had said his main gestores were Pablo Alegria Con Alonso and Jose Manuel Aguirre Juarez, obscure Mexico City lawyers with small practices who were friends of his from law school.

Sure enough, Mr. Halter's team found that nearly half the payments were to Mr. Alegria and Mr. Aguirre. These two lawyers alone, records showed, had received $8.5 million in payments. Records showed Wal-Mart de Mexico routinely paid its gestores tens of thousands of dollars per permit. (In interviews, both lawyers declined to discuss the corruption allegations, citing confidentiality agreements with Wal-Mart.)

"One very interesting postscript," Mr. Halter wrote in an e-mail to his boss, Mr. Lewis. "All payments to these individuals and all large sums of $ paid out of this account stopped abruptly in 2005." Mr. Halter said the "only thing we can find" that changed was that Mr. Castro-Wright left Wal-Mart de Mexico for the United States.

Mr. Halter's team confirmed detail after detail from Mr. Cicero's debriefings. Mr. Cicero had given specifics—names, dates, bribe amounts—for several new stores. In almost every case, investigators found documents confirming major elements of his account. And just as Mr. Cicero had described, investigators found mysterious codes at the bottom of invoices from the gestores.

"The documentation didn't look anything like what you would find in legitimate billing records from a legitimate law firm," a person involved in the investigation said in an interview.

Mr. Lewis sent a terse progress report to his boss, Mr. Senser: "FYI. It is not looking good."

Hours later, Mr. Halter's team found clear confirmation that Mr. Castro-Wright and other top executives at Wal-Mart de Mexico were well aware of the gestor payments.

In March 2004, the team discovered, the executives had been sent an internal Wal-Mart de Mexico audit that raised red flags about the gestor payments. The audit documented how Wal-Mart de Mexico's two primary gestores had been paid millions to make "facilitating payments" for new store permits all over Mexico.

The audit did not delve into how the money had been used to "facilitate" permits. But it showed the payments rising rapidly, roughly in line with Wal-Mart de Mexico's accelerating growth. The audit recommended notifying Bentonville of the payments.

The recommendation, records showed, was removed by Wal-Mart de Mexico's chief auditor, whom Mr. Cicero had identified as one of the executives who knew about the bribes. The author of the gestor audit, meanwhile, "was fired not long after the audit was completed," Mr. Halter wrote.

Mr. Ainley arranged to meet the fired auditor at his hotel. The auditor described other examples of Wal-Mart de Mexico's leaders withholding from Bentonville information about suspect payments to government officials.

The auditor singled out Jose Luis Rodriguezmacedo Rivera, the general counsel of Wal-Mart de Mexico.

Mr. Rodriguezmacedo, he said, took "significant information out" of an audit of Wal-Mart de Mexico's compliance with the Foreign Corrupt Practices Act. The original audit had described how Wal-Mart de Mexico gave gift cards to government officials in towns where it was building stores. "These were only given out until the construction was complete," Mr. Ainley wrote. "At which time the payments ceased."

These details were scrubbed from the final version sent to Bentonville.

Investigators were struck by Mr. Castro-Wright's response to the gestor audit. It had been shown to him immediately, Wal-Mart de Mexico's chief auditor had told them. Yet rather than expressing alarm, he had appeared worried about becoming too dependent on too few gestores. In an e-mail, Mr. Rodriguezmacedo told Mr. Cicero to write up a plan to "diversify" the gestores used to "facilitate" permits.

"Eduardo Castro wants us to implement this plan as soon as possible," he wrote.

Mr. Cicero did as directed. The plan, which authorized paying gestores up to $280,000 to "facilitate" a single permit, was approved with a minor change. Mr. Rodriguezmacedo did not want the plan to mention "gestores." He wanted them called "external service providers."

Mr. Halter's team made one last discovery—a finding that suggested the corruption might be far more extensive than even Mr. Cicero had described.

In going through Wal-Mart de Mexico's database of payments, investigators noticed the company was making hefty "contributions" and "donations" directly to governments all over Mexico—nearly $16 million in all since 2003.

"Some of the payments descriptions indicate that the donation is being made for the issuance of a license," Mr. Ainley wrote in one report back to Bentonville.

They also found a document in which a Wal-Mart de Mexico real estate executive had openly acknowledged that "these payments were performed to facilitate obtaining the licenses or permits" for new stores. Sometimes, Mr. Cicero told *The Times*, donations were used hand-in-hand with gestor payments to get permits.

Deflecting Blame

When Mr. Halter's team was ready to interview executives at Wal-Mart de Mexico, the first target was Mr. Rodriguezmacedo.

Before joining Wal-Mart de Mexico in January 2004, Mr. Rodriguezmacedo had been a lawyer for Citigroup in Mexico. Urbane and smooth, with impeccable English, he quickly won fans in Bentonville. When Wal-Mart invited executives from its foreign subsidiaries for several days of discussion about the fine points of the Foreign Corrupt Practices Act, Mr. Rodriguezmacedo was asked to lead one of the sessions.

It was called "Overcoming Challenges in Government Dealings."

Yet Mr. Cicero had identified him as a participant in the bribery scheme. In his debriefings, Mr. Cicero described how Mr. Rodriguezmacedo had passed along specific payoff instructions from Mr. Castro-Wright. In an interview with *The Times*, Mr. Cicero said he and Mr. Rodriguezmacedo had discussed the use of gestores shortly after Mr. Rodriguezmacedo was hired. "He said, 'Don't worry. Keep it on its way.'"

Mr. Rodriguezmacedo declined to comment; on Friday Wal-Mart disclosed that he had been reassigned and is no longer Wal-Mart de Mexico's general counsel.

Mr. Halter's team hoped Mr. Rodriguezmacedo would shed light on how two outside lawyers came to be paid $8.5 million to "facilitate" permits. Mr. Rodriguezmacedo responded with evasive hostility, records and interviews show. When investigators asked him for the gestores' billing records, he said he did not have time to track them down. They got similar receptions from other executives.

Only after investigators complained to higher authorities were the executives more forthcoming. Led by Mr. Rodriguezmacedo, they responded with an attack on Mr. Cicero's credibility.

The gestor audit, they told investigators, had raised doubts about Mr. Cicero, since he had approved most of the payments. They began to suspect he was somehow benefiting, so they asked Kroll to investigate. It was then, they asserted, that Kroll discovered Mr. Cicero's wife was a law partner of one of the gestores.

Mr. Cicero was fired, they said, because he had failed to disclose that fact. They produced a copy of a "preliminary" report from Kroll and e-mails showing the undisclosed conflict had been reported to Bentonville.

Based on this behavior, Mr. Rodriguezmacedo argued, the gestor payments were in all likelihood a "ruse" by Mr. Cicero to defraud Wal-Mart de Mexico. Mr. Cicero and the gestores, he contended, probably kept every last peso of the "facilitating payments."

Simply put, bribes could not have been paid if the money was stolen first.

It was an argument that gave Wal-Mart ample justification to end the inquiry. But investigators were skeptical, records, and interviews show.

Even if Mr. Rodriguezmacedo's account were true, it did not explain why Wal-Mart de Mexico's executives had authorized gestor payments in the first place, or why they made "donations" to get permits, or why they rewrote audits to keep Bentonville in the dark.

Investigators also wondered why a trained lawyer who had gotten away with stealing a small fortune from Wal-Mart would now deliberately draw the company's full attention by implicating himself in a series of fictional bribes. And if Wal-Mart de Mexico's executives truly believed they had been victimized, why hadn't they taken legal action against Mr. Cicero, much less reported the "theft" to Bentonville?

There was another problem: Documents contradicted most of the executives' assertions about Mr. Cicero.

Records showed Mr. Cicero had not been fired, but had resigned with severance benefits and a $25,000 bonus. In fact, in a 2004 e-mail to Ms. Munich, Mr. Rodriguezmacedo himself described how he had "negotiated" Mr. Cicero's "departure." The same e-mail said Mr. Cicero had not even been confronted about the supposed undisclosed conflict involving his wife. (Mr. Cicero flatly denied that his wife had ever worked with either gestor.) The e-mail also assured Ms. Munich there was no hint of financial wrongdoing. "We see it merely as an undisclosed conflict of interest," Mr. Rodriguezmacedo wrote.

There were other discrepancies.

Mr. Rodriguezmacedo said the company had stopped using gestores after Mr. Cicero's departure. Yet even as Mr. Cicero was being debriefed in October 2005, Wal-Mart de Mexico real estate executives made a request to pay a gestor $14,000 to get a construction permit, records showed.

The persistent questions and document requests from Mr. Halter's team provoked a backlash from Wal-Mart de Mexico's executives. After a week of work, records and interviews show, Mr. Halter and other members of the team were summoned by Eduardo F. Solorzano Morales, then chief executive of Wal-Mart de Mexico.

Mr. Solorzano angrily chastised the investigators for being too secretive and accusatory. He took offense that his executives were being told at the start of interviews that they had the right not to answer questions—as if they were being read their rights.

"It was like, 'You shut up. I'm going to talk,'" a person said of Mr. Solorzano. "It was, 'This is my home, my backyard. You are out of here.'"

Mr. Lewis viewed the complaints as an effort to sidetrack his investigators. "I find this ludicrous and a copout for the larger concerns about what has been going on," he wrote.

Nevertheless, Mr. Herkert, the chief executive for Latin America, was notified about the complaints. Three days later, he and his boss, Mr. Duke, flew to Mexico City. The trip had been long-planned—Mr. Duke toured several stores—but they also reassured Wal-Mart de Mexico's unhappy executives.

They arrived just as the investigators wrapped up their work and left.

A Push to Dig Deeper

Wal-Mart's leaders had agreed to consider a full investigation if the preliminary inquiry found Mr. Cicero's allegations credible.

Back in Bentonville, Mr. Halter and Mr. Ainley wrote confidential reports to Wal-Mart's top executives in December 2005 laying out all the evidence that corroborated Mr. Cicero—the hundreds of gestor payments, the mystery codes, the rewritten audits, the evasive responses from Wal-Mart de Mexico executives, the donations for permits, the evidence gestores were still being used.

"There is reasonable suspicion," Mr. Halter concluded, "to believe that Mexican and USA laws have been violated." There was simply "no defendable explanation" for the millions of dollars in gestor payments, he wrote.

Mr. Halter submitted an "action plan" for a deeper investigation that would plumb the depths of corruption and culpability at Wal-Mart de Mexico.

Among other things, he urged "that all efforts be concentrated on the reconstruction of Cicero's computer history."

Mr. Cicero, meanwhile, was still offering help. In November, when Mr. Halter's team was in Mexico, Mr. Cicero offered his services as a paid consultant. In December, he wrote to Ms. Munich. He volunteered to share specifics on still more stores, and he promised to show her documents. "I hope you visit again," he wrote.

Mr. Halter proposed a thorough investigation of the two main gestores. He had not tried to interview them in Mexico for fear of his safety. ("I do not want to expose myself on what I consider to be an unrealistic attempt to get Mexican lawyers to admit to criminal activity," he had explained to his bosses.) Now Mr. Halter wanted Wal-Mart to hire private investigators to interview and monitor both gestores.

He also envisioned a round of adversarial interviews with Wal-Mart de Mexico's senior executives. He and his investigators argued that it was time to take the politically sensitive step of questioning Mr. Castro-Wright about his role in the gestor payments.

By January 2006, the case had reached a critical juncture. Wal-Mart's leaders were again weighing whether to approve a full investigation that would inevitably focus on a star executive already being publicly discussed as a potential successor to Mr. Scott.

Wal-Mart's ethics policy offered clear direction. "Never cover up or ignore an ethics problem," the policy states. And some who were involved in the investigation argued that it was time to take a stand against signs of rising corruption in Wal-Mart's global operations. Each year the company received hundreds of internal reports of bribery and fraud, records showed. In Asia alone, there had been 90 reports of bribery just in the previous 18 months.

The situation was bad enough that Wal-Mart's top procurement executives were summoned to Bentonville that winter for a dressing down. Mr. Menzer, Wal-Mart's vice chairman, warned them that corruption was creating an unacceptable risk, particularly given the government's stepped-up enforcement of the Foreign Corrupt Practices Act. "Times have changed," he said.

As if to underscore the problem, Wal-Mart's leaders were confronted with new corruption allegations at Wal-Mart de Mexico even as they pondered Mr. Halter's action plan. In January, Mr. Scott, Mr. Duke, and Wal-Mart's chairman, S. Robson Walton, received an anonymous e-mail saying Wal-Mart de Mexico's top real estate executives were receiving kickbacks from construction companies. "Please you must do something," the e-mail implored.

Yet at the same time, records and interviews show, there were misgivings about the budding reach and power of Corporate Investigations.

In less than a year, Mr. Lewis's beefed-up team had doubled its caseload, to roughly 400 cases a year. Some executives grumbled that Mr. Lewis acted as if he still worked for the F.B.I., where he had once supervised major investigations. They accused him and his investigators of being overbearing, disruptive and naive about the moral ambiguities of doing business abroad. They argued that Corporate Investigations should focus more on quietly "neutralizing" problems than on turning corrupt employees over to law enforcement.

Wal-Mart's leaders had just witnessed the downside of that approach: in early 2005, the company went to the F.B.I. with evidence that the disgraced former vice chairman, Mr. Coughlin, had embezzled hundreds of thousands of dollars. The decision produced months of embarrassing publicity, especially when Mr. Coughlin claimed he had used the money to pay off union spies for Wal-Mart.

Meanwhile, Wal-Mart de Mexico executives were continuing to complain to Bentonville about the investigation. The protests "just never let up," a person involved in the case said.

Another person familiar with the thinking of those overseeing the investigation said Wal-Mart would have reacted "like a chicken on a June bug" had the allegations concerned the United States. But some executives saw Mexico as a country where bribery was embedded in the business culture. It simply did not merit the same response.

"It's a Mexican issue; it's better to let it be a Mexican response," the person said, describing the thinking of Wal-Mart executives.

In the midst of this debate, Ms. Munich submitted her resignation, effective Feb. 1, 2006. In one of her final acts, she drafted a memo that argued for expanding the Mexico investigation and giving equal respect to Mexican and United States laws.

"The bribery of government officials," she noted dryly, "is a criminal offense in Mexico."

She also warned against allowing implicated executives to interfere with the investigation. Wal-Mart de Mexico's executives had already tried to insert themselves in the case. Just before Christmas, records show, Mr. Solorzano, the Wal-Mart de Mexico chief executive, held a video conference with Mr. Mars, Mr. Senser, and Mr. Stucky to discuss his team's "hypothesis" that Mr. Cicero had stolen gestor payments.

"Given the serious nature of the allegations, and the need to preserve the integrity of the investigation," Ms. Munich wrote, "it would seem more prudent to develop a follow-up plan of action, independent of Walmex management participation."

The Chief Weighs In

Mr. Scott called a meeting for Feb. 3, 2006, to discuss revamping Wal-Mart's internal investigations and to resolve the question of what to do about Mr. Cicero's allegations.

In the days before the meeting, records show, Mr. Senser ordered his staff to compile data showing the effectiveness of Corporate Investigations. He assembled statistics showing that the unit had referred relatively few cases to law enforcement agencies. He circulated copies of an e-mail in which Mr. Rodriguezmacedo said he had been treated "very respectfully and cordially" by Mr. Senser's investigators.

Along with Mr. Scott, the meeting included Mr. Hyde, Mr. Mars, and Mr. Stucky, records show. The meeting brought the grievances against Corporate Investigations into the open. Mr. Senser described the complaints in Mr. Lewis's performance evaluation, completed shortly after the meeting. Wal-Mart's leaders viewed Mr. Lewis's investigators as "overly aggressive," he wrote. They did not care for Mr. Lewis's "law enforcement approach," and the fact that Mr. Scott convened a

meeting to express these concerns only underscored "the importance placed on these topics by senior executives."

By meeting's end, Mr. Senser had been ordered to work with Mr. Mars and others to develop a "modified protocol" for internal investigations.

Mr. Scott said he wanted it done fast, and within 24 hours Mr. Senser produced a new protocol, a highly bureaucratic process that gave senior Wal-Mart executives—including executives at the business units being investigated—more control over internal investigations. The policy included multiple "case reviews." It also required senior executives to conduct a "cost-benefit analysis" before signing off on a full-blown investigation.

Under the new protocol, Mr. Lewis and his team would only investigate "significant" allegations, like those involving potential crimes or top executives. Lesser allegations would be left to the affected business unit to investigate.

"This captures it, I think," Mr. Hyde wrote when Mr. Senser sent him the new protocol.

Four days after Mr. Scott's meeting, with the new protocol drafted, Wal-Mart's leaders began to transfer control of the bribery investigation to one of its earliest targets, Mr. Rodriguezmacedo.

Mr. Mars first sent Mr. Halter's report to Mr. Rodriguezmacedo. Then he arranged to ship Mr. Halter's investigative files to him as well. In an e-mail, he sought Mr. Senser's advice on how to send the files in "a secure manner."

Mr. Senser recommended FedEx. "There is very good control on those shipments, and while governments do compromise them if they are looking for something in particular, there is no reason for them to think that this shipment is out of the ordinary," he wrote.

"The key," he added, "is being careful about how you communicate the details of the shipment to Jose Luis." He advised Mr. Mars to use encrypted e-mail.

Wal-Mart's spokesman, Mr. Tovar, said the company could not discuss Mr. Scott's meeting or the decision to transfer the case to Mr. Rodriguezmacedo. "At this point," he said, "we don't have a full explanation of what happened. Unfortunately, we realize that until the investigation is concluded, there will be some unanswered questions."

Wal-Mart's leaders, however, had clear guidance about the propriety of letting a target of an investigation run it.

On the same day Mr. Senser was putting the finishing touches on the new investigations protocol, Wal-Mart's ethics office sent him a booklet of "best practices" for internal investigations. It had been put together by lawyers and executives who supervised investigations at Fortune 500 companies.

"Investigations should be conducted by individuals who do not have any vested interest in the potential outcomes of the investigation," it said.

The transfer appeared to violate even the "modified protocol" for investigations. Under the new protocol, Corporate Investigations was still supposed to handle "significant" allegations—including those involving potential crimes and senior executives. When Mr. Senser asked his deputies to list all investigations that met this threshold, they came up with 31 cases.

At the top of the list: Mexico.

After the meeting with Mr. Scott, Mr. Senser had told Mr. Lewis in his performance evaluation that his "highest priority" should be to eliminate "the perceptions that investigators are being too aggressive." He wanted Mr. Lewis to "earn the trust of" his "clients"—Wal-Mart's leaders. He wanted him to head off "adversarial interactions."

Mr. Senser now applied the same advice to himself.

Even as Mr. Halter's files were being shipped to Mr. Rodriguezmacedo, Mr. Stucky made plans to fly to Mexico with other executives involved in the bribery investigation. The trip, he wrote, was "for the purpose of re-establishing activities related to the certain compliance matters we've been discussing." Mr. Stucky invited Mr. Senser along.

"It is better if we do not make this trip to Mexico City," Mr. Senser replied. His investigators, he wrote, would simply be "a resource" if needed.

Ten days after Mr. Stucky flew to Mexico, an article about Wal-Mart appeared in *The Times*. It focused on "the increasingly important role of one man: Eduardo Castro-Wright." The article said Mr. Castro-Wright was a "popular figure" inside Wal-Mart because he made Wal-Mart de Mexico one of the company's "most profitable units."

Wall Street analysts, it said, viewed him as a "very strong candidate" to succeed Mr. Scott.

Case Closed

For those who had investigated Mr. Cicero's allegations, the preliminary inquiry had been just that—preliminary. In memos and meetings, they had argued that their findings clearly justified a full-blown investigation. Mr. Castro-Wright's precise role had yet to be determined. Mr. Halter had never been permitted to question him, nor had Mr. Castro-Wright's computer files been examined, records, and interviews show.

At the very least, a complete investigation would take months.

Mr. Rodriguezmacedo, the man now in charge, saw it differently. He wrapped up the case in a few weeks, with little additional investigation.

"There is no evidence or clear indication," his report concluded, "of bribes paid to Mexican government authorities with the purpose of wrongfully securing any licenses or permits."

That conclusion, his report explained, was largely based on the denials of his fellow executives. Not one "mentioned having ordered or given bribes to government authorities," he wrote.

His report, six pages long, neglected to note that he had been implicated in the same criminal conduct.

That was not the only omission. While his report conceded that Wal-Mart de Mexico executives had authorized years of payments to gestores, it never explained what these executives expected the gestores to do with the millions of dollars they received to "facilitate" permits.

He was also silent on the evidence that Wal-Mart de Mexico had doled out donations to get permits. Nor did he address evidence that he and other executives had suppressed or rewritten audits that would have alerted Bentonville to improper payments.

Instead, the bulk of Mr. Rodriguezmacedo's report attacked the integrity of his accuser.

Mr. Cicero, he wrote, made Wal-Mart de Mexico's executives think they would "run the risk of having permits denied if the gestores were not used." But this was merely a ruse: In all likelihood, he argued, Wal-Mart de Mexico paid millions for "services never rendered." The gestores simply pocketed the money, he suggested, and Mr. Cicero "may have benefited," too.

But he offered no direct proof. Indeed, as his report made clear, it was less an allegation than a hypothesis built on two highly circumstantial pillars.

First, he said he had consulted with Jesus Zamora-Pierce, a "prestigious independent counsel" who had written books on fraud. Mr. Zamora, he wrote, "feels the conduct displayed by Sergio Cicero is typical of someone engaging in fraud. It is not uncommon in Mexico for lawyers to recommend the use of gestores to facilitate permit obtainment, when in reality it is nothing more than a means of engaging in fraud."

Second, he said he had done a statistical analysis that found Wal-Mart de Mexico won permits even faster after Mr. Cicero left. The validity of his analysis was impossible to assess; he did not include his statistics in the report.

In building a case against Mr. Cicero, Mr. Rodriguezmacedo's report included several false statements. He described Mr. Cicero's "dismissal" when records showed he had resigned. He also wrote that Kroll's investigation of Mr. Cicero concluded that he "had a considerable increase in his standard of living during the time in which payments were made to the gestores." Kroll's report made no such assertion, people involved in the investigation said.

His report promised a series of corrective steps aimed at putting the entire matter to rest. Wal-Mart de Mexico would no longer use gestores. There would be a renewed commitment to Wal-Mart's anticorruption policy. He did not recommend any disciplinary action against his colleagues.

There was, however, one person he hoped to punish. Wal-Mart de Mexico, he wrote, would scour Mr. Cicero's records and determine "if any legal action may be taken against him."

Mr. Rodriguezmacedo submitted a draft of his report to Bentonville. In an e-mail, Mr. Lewis told his superiors that he found the report "lacking." It was not clear what evidence supported the report's conclusions, he wrote. "More importantly," he wrote, "if one agrees that Sergio defrauded the company and I am one of them, the question becomes, how was he able to get away with almost $10 million and why was nothing done after it was discovered?"

Mr. Rodriguezmacedo responded by adding a paragraph to the end of his report: They had decided not to pursue "criminal actions" against Mr. Cicero because "we did not have strong case."

"At the risk of being cynical," Mr. Lewis wrote in response, "that report is exactly the same as the previous which I indicated was truly lacking."

But it was enough for Wal-Mart. Mr. Rodriguezmacedo was told by executives in Bentonville on May 10, 2006, to put his report "into final form, thus concluding this investigation."

No one told Mr. Cicero. All he knew was that after months of e-mails, phone calls, and meetings, Wal-Mart's interest seemed to suddenly fade. His phone calls and e-mails went unanswered.

"I thought nobody cares about this," he said. "So I left it behind."

Critical Thinking

1. What is your overall impression about the allegations of bribery being faced by Wal-Mart?

2. Having read the article carefully, preparing talking points for class discussion about the efficacy of Wal-Mart's response to the allegation. Contrast the initial response to a time later when "the Chief (i.e., Mr. Scott) weighs in."

3. If you were an outside consultant advising Mr. Scott on ethical issues involved in the situation of the alleged bribery, what would be your advice?

4. What might Wal-Mart's management have done differently in the aftermath of the bribery allegations?

5. Prepare comments for class discussion on the "case closed" section of the article.

6. What are the lessons to be learned from the allegations of bribery and Wal-Mart's handling of the allegations?

Create Central

www.mhhe.com/createcentral

Internet References

Bloomberg
http://www.bloomberg.com/news/2014-03-26/wal-mart-says-bribery-probe-cost-439-million-in-past-two-years.html

Business Insider
http://www.businessinsider.com/new-details-in-walmart-bribery-scandal-2012-12

New York Times
http://www.nytimes.com/2012/11/16/business/wal-mart-expands-foreign-bribery-investigation.html?pagewanted=all

Article   Prepared by: Eric Teoro, *Lincoln Christian University*

Doing More Good

Here are several ways your company can become a better corporate citizen.

JODI CHAVEZ

Learning Outcomes

After reading this article, you will be able to:

- Recognize the business benefits of good corporate citizenship.

- Create strategy for implementing Corporate Social Responsibility.

Today's challenging economic climate has forced many organizations to reduce spending, release workers, and raise fees to consumers. The result is that businesses of all shapes and sizes are being painted in an unfavorable light, inviting criticism from the public and politicians alike.

But the picture being painted—that of a business culture that abandons the public in pursuit of profits—isn't an accurate one. The most effective counter to this depiction is the rise of corporate responsibility initiatives.

The Committee Encouraging Corporate Philanthropy (CECP), an international forum of business leaders focused on measuring and encouraging corporate philanthropy, recently released its *Giving in Numbers* report for 2011. In the report, the CECP noted that one out of every two businesses had actually increased the amount of funds contributed to charity or community organizations since the onset of the recession in 2007. As a matter of fact, a quarter of companies reported increasing their giving by more than 25 percent. Furthermore, the CECP tracked aggregate total contributions for 110 high-performing companies in 2007–2010 and found that aggregate total giving rose by 23 percent.

Clearly, many successful businesses are actually augmenting their contributions to society and taking the challenge of good corporate citizenship seriously. But why? Of course, the ability to "do more good" for more people carries intrinsic value and tremendous appeal. Yet there are other significant business benefits that arise out of doing more good.

Here we'll explore some of these benefits, and I'll offer practical ways you can begin to make a difference in your company and, ultimately, society.

The Business Case for Being Charitable

The rise of corporate responsibility and citizenship has been two decades in the making. As detailed in "Responsibility: The New Business Imperative," published in the May 2002 issue of *The Academy of Management Executive,* during the 1990s: "Numerous exposés of labor practices in global supply chains pressured multinational brands and retailers to adopt corporate codes of conduct. Later in the decade, pressure—and expectations—increased further, driving firms not only to introduce codes but also to ensure compliance with these codes by their suppliers." Finally, the fall of businesses like Enron and the recent financial collapse and mortgage crisis forced businesses to reexamine their "anything goes" approach to profitability.

All these are crucial steps in the evolution of corporate responsibility. But today the most important driver of corporate responsibility is the belief that good citizenship makes good business sense.

There are several ways it can give you a competitive advantage.

Building a reputation: Companies large and small impact the neighborhoods, cities, and countries they do business in. By aligning your goals with the goals of the community in which you operate, you're more likely to build a mutually beneficial relationship with potential stakeholders, including employees, customers, investors, suppliers, and business partners.

Setting your company apart: Like an innovative product or a new service offering, a strong record of corporate responsibility is a competitive advantage that you can leverage against others in your industry.

Attracting investment: Businesses with strong records of corporate responsibility generate more interest from investors when compared with apathetic competitors. In a study titled "Institutional and Social Investors Find Common Ground," originally published in the *Journal of Investing* and later cited in the comprehensive article "The Business Case for Corporate Social Responsibility" in the *International Journal of Management Review,* author Timothy Smith lays out why this is the case. "Many institutional investors 'avoid' companies or industries that violate their organizational mission, values, or principles . . . [They also] seek companies with good records on employee relations, environmental stewardship, community involvement, and corporate governance."

Reducing costs and risks: Companies that make a concerted effort to contribute to and advance society are more likely to avoid potential penalties or exposure to legal fines and government intervention. This is especially important in a climate of increased regulation and scrutiny. A strong record of corporate citizenship can also help you avoid harm to your reputation and sales that may arise without notice.

Attracting better talent: Great people want to work for great companies. By demonstrating your strong commitment to teamwork, responsibility, community, etc., you can attract employees who share those same values. Furthermore, now may be the opportune time to start reevaluating your corporate responsibility profile so you can connect with future leaders. Research indicates that the Millennial generation, currently entering the workforce in record numbers, is particularly civic minded. Members of this generation want more from their job than just a paycheck—they want an opportunity to make a difference. Why not give it to them and give yourself an edge in the process?

Increasing motivation and retention: In addition to attracting new talent, a demonstrated commitment to corporate responsibility can enhance engagement across your current workforce. It can also help you identify leaders who want to spearhead these important initiatives. This can help you reduce the expenses inherent in high turnover, including recruiting, training, and onboarding, and eliminate productivity gaps that occur when an employee leaves your company.

The Millennial generation wants more from their job than just a paycheck—they want an opportunity to make a difference.

Fostering innovation: By looking beyond the walls of your buildings and understanding the wider impact of your business, you can open your eyes to new opportunities and new avenues for growth. A primary example of this is Xerox, which has shown a continued commitment to sustainability and citizenship in designing "waste free" products and investing in "waste free" facilities. This commitment has led to the development of new products that appeal to corporations, fuel profitability, and set Xerox apart in the marketplace. Toyota is another example of a company that recognized the impact of its business—vehicle emissions—and built a profitable solution to the problem in the form of the popular Prius hybrid. Though other auto manufacturers have followed suit, the development of the Prius and its status as the first commercially viable hybrid gave Toyota a competitive advantage and a leg up on the competition. No matter what product or service you offer, a new perspective gleaned from a commitment to corporate responsibility can help you do the same.

Putting Responsibility into Action

Today, corporate responsibility encompasses many forms, including education about social issues and advancement of different cultures (social responsibility), ensuring the health of the environment (sustainability), and donating funds or time to charitable causes (philanthropy). Corporate responsibility is also concerned with the health and safety of the workforce and providing good working conditions for employees.

With corporate responsibility taking on so many facets, it may be difficult to determine how your company can begin making an impact. The International Institute for Sustainable Development (IISD) recently published *Corporate Social Responsibility: An Implementation Guide for Business* to help companies adapt and facilitate corporate social responsibility. Here is their recommended frame-work for implementation.

Conduct a corporate social responsibility (CSR) assessment: Gather and examine relevant information about your products, services, decision-making processes, and activities to determine your current CSR activity. An effective assessment should give you an accurate understanding of your values and ethics, the CSR issues that are affecting your business now or in the future, key stakeholders, and your leadership's ability to deliver a more effective CSR approach.

Develop a CSR strategy: Using your assessment as a starting point, begin to determine your objectives. Develop a realistic strategy that can help you reach your goals. The IISD recommends these five steps to developing an effective strategy:

- Build support with the CEO, senior management, and employees.
- Research what others (including competitors) are doing.
- Prepare a matrix of proposed CSR actions.
- Develop options for proceeding and the business case for them.
- Decide on direction, approach, boundaries, and focus areas.

Develop commitments: Create a task force to review your objectives and finalize your strategy. The task force should solicit input from key stakeholders—the CEO, department heads, top management, etc.—to gauge their interest and ensure future participation. Using this feedback, prepare a preliminary draft of your CSR commitment, and review this again with those employees who will be affected or who can help effect change. At this point, you can revise and publish your commitments for your internal audience, customers, investors, and potential employees.

Implement CSR commitments: This is the phase where your planning begins to give way to reality. Though each company should approach this critical step in accordance with its unique values and culture, the IISD offers these universal best practices:

- Prepare a CSR business plan.
- Set measurable targets, and identify performance measures.
- Engage employees and others to whom CSR commitments apply.
- Design and conduct CSR training.
- Establish mechanisms for addressing resistance.
- Create internal and external communications plans.
- Make commitments public.

Document progress: It's imperative that you're able to communicate the impact of your efforts to internal and external stakeholders. Reporting tools provide insight into the costs of your initiatives as well as the hard and soft benefits derived from your corporate responsibility program.

Reporting on responsibility initiatives has actually given rise to an entirely new financial model called social accounting. Social accounting is the process of measuring, monitoring, and reporting to stakeholders the social and environmental effects of an organization's actions. Social accounting is conducted by accountants who employ the same tools and knowledge used in traditional financial reporting. Though many larger organizations utilize social accounting, all businesses can benefit from being able to demonstrate the true value of their actions.

In fact, robust social accounting and responsibility reporting is fast becoming the standard for businesses, not the exception. KPMG conducted an *International Survey of Corporate Responsibility Reporting 2011* to review trends of 3,400 companies worldwide, including the top 250 global companies (the G250). The survey indicated that corporate responsibility reporting is undertaken by 95 percent of the G250 and 64 percent of the 100 largest companies across the 34 countries surveyed.

"[Corporate responsibility] has moved from being a moral imperative to a critical business imperative. The time has now come to enhance [corporate responsibility] reporting information systems to bring them up to the level that is equal to financial reporting, including a comparable quality of governance controls and management," said Wim Bartels, global head of KPMG's Sustainability Assurance.

Evaluate and improve: Using the reports and metrics generated, continue to refine your corporate responsibility initiatives. This is critical. Evaluate your performance objectively, identify opportunities for improvement, and engage key stakeholders to plot a course for the future.

The reality of today's economic, political, and social climate necessitates that business leaders rise above their bottom lines and look to make an impact outside their organization. Doing so presents an opportunity to elevate others while elevating your organization.

Critical Thinking

1. What is corporate citizenship?
2. What are the differences between good and bad corporate citizenship?
3. The article suggests a five step process for developing a Corporate Social responsibility strategy. What is your opinion of each of the suggested steps? What other, if any, steps might be added to the five step process?

Create Central

www.mhhe.com/createcentral

Internet References

CSRwire
   http://www.csrwire.com/pdf/JustGoodBusinessCSRwireExcerpt.pdf
Forbes
   http://www.forbes.com/sites/richardlevick/2012/01/11/corporate-social-responsibility-for-profit/
Journal of Economics, Business, and Management
   http://www.joebm.com/index.php?m=content&c=index&a=show&catid=43&id=535

Jodi Chavez is senior vice president of Accounting Principals. You can reach her at Jodi.Chavez@accountingprincipals.com

Article

Prepared by: Eric Teoro, *Lincoln Christian University*

Necessary but Not Sufficient

An Exploration of Where CR Begins—and Ends

PETER A. SOYKA

Learning Outcomes

After reading this article, you will be able to:

- Understand the argument that CSR is good for business.
- Describe various facets of CSR and sustainability.
- Recognize the role of governance and values in promoting CSR and sustainability.

R ecent years have witnessed a proliferation of corporate social responsibility (CSR) and corporate responsibility (CR) programs in many industries, along with media, graduate programs and institutes, and other resources to support and promote them. The underlying concept of CSR/CR is deeply rooted in the conviction that corporations have a variety of obligations to their host societies that go well beyond meeting shareholders' expectations of financial returns. A problem, however, complicates reliance on such an approach to guide the behavior of the organization. Setting aside the CR programs that lack substance and appear to be mainly about public relations (we count more than a few), it is not clear within the CR construct how far the responsibility to address environmental, social, and governance (ESG) concerns extends. Nor is it clear how such concerns should be balanced against the need for the corporation to satisfy the demands of its customers and earn the rate of return required by its owners and other capital providers.

The general rule of thumb appears to be to meet certain required minima (e.g., legal compliance, no use of unreasonable labor practices) and as many other "good" things as resources allow, with the proviso that virtually any demand made by a major customer will receive careful consideration. That is, CSR/CR as commonly understood does not provide a clear means for striking the appropriate balance between obligation

and opportunity, nor does it place sufficient emphasis on incenting the desired behaviors from companies and their employees. The concept of sustainability, as defined in this article (and more fully in my recent book), provides these missing elements. My concept of sustainability combines CSR/CR and related concepts with aggressive, financially driven assessment of opportunities. Such a balanced approach is the only viable way to get United States business at large on a more sustainable path.

Sustainability Defined

In my view, sustainability is a value set, philosophy, and approach that is rooted in the belief that organizations (corporate and otherwise) can and must materially contribute to the betterment of society. Sustainable organizations must balance their needs, aspirations, and limitations against the larger interests of the societies in which they operate. Only organizations that provide goods and/or services that are of value to people and/or society more generally, and are dedicated to excellence, interested in the full development of human potential, and committed to fairness, are likely to be durable (sustainable) over the long term. Fundamentally, sustainable organizations are purpose-driven, with the purpose being an overarching objective larger and less tangible than self-gratification or profit maximization. Indeed, they accept that their conduct and all their activities in totality must yield an overall benefit-to-cost ratio greater than unity. Accordingly, in my formulation of the concept, sustainable organizations are:

- Mission-driven;
- Aware of and responsive to societal and stakeholder interests;
- Responsible and ethical;
- Dedicated to excellence;

- Driven to meet or exceed customer/client expectations; and
- Disciplined, focused, and skillful.

This view places the conventional emphasis on the "three legs of the stool" (economic prosperity, environmental protection, and social equity) within a larger, more integrative context. It also recognizes that each is a key dimension of any coherent concept of sustainable organizations, past or present. The importance of each of the three major elements of sustainability depends on the organization's nature and purpose. Public sector and nonprofit organizations have been formed and structured specifically to provide some combination of products and services that benefit society, whether that involves forecasting the weather, teaching children, or defending the country from military threats. With the exception of agencies and nongovernmental organizations (NGOs) specifically focused on some aspect of sustainability—such as the United States Environmental Protection Agency (EPA) or the Sierra Club—most such organizations have a primary mission to fulfill that is not directly related to either environmental protection or social equity. Nonetheless, by adopting sustainability as a guiding principle, such organizations commit themselves at the very least to ensuring that they limit any adverse impacts of their operations on the environment and treat all stakeholders fairly. Many public sector organizations, including the federal government and its many parts, have been moving decisively in recent years to institute more sustainable behavior.

Only organizations that provide goods and/or services that are of value to people and/or society more generally, and are dedicated to excellence, interested in the full development of human potential, and committed to fairness, are likely to be durable (sustainable) over the long term.

Corporations are in quite a different place. They are not explicitly supported by and accountable to the American taxpayer and have not (generally) been formed to pursue a mission eligible for tax-exempt status as a nonprofit. Some observers believe that in contrast to the work done by the government and nonprofit sectors, the legitimate role of business is to make money for its owners (shareholders), and the more the better. In this view of the world, time and money invested in improving environmental performance, providing safer working conditions, supporting local communities through philanthropic activity, and other such CR behaviors are an unwarranted and unproductive use of the firm's assets. This view, which has been held and promoted with great conviction by many in the business community and academia, is increasingly being challenged.

Recognizing important sustainability issues and acting on them in an enlightened and sophisticated way has been shown to increase revenue growth and earnings and to strengthen firm positions in terms of the factors that drive long-term financial success.

Corporate leaders should accept and, ideally, embrace the concept of sustainability, for two fundamental reasons. One is that United States corporations, as distinct entities holding enumerated legal rights and receiving numerous public benefits, have an obligation not only to comply with all applicable laws and regulations but also to ensure that their conduct does not harm the broader societies of which they are a part and on which they depend for survival. (Unfortunately, many people in the business community and press seem not to recognize how many benefits the United States federal and state governments provide, and how different this largesse is from the situation in many other countries.) The other is that, increasingly, recognizing important sustainability issues and acting on them in an enlightened and sophisticated way has been shown to increase revenue growth and earnings and to strengthen firm positions in terms of the factors that drive long-term financial success. In other words, the argument for embracing corporate sustainability (above and beyond CR) has two elements: It is the right thing to do, and it is the smart thing to do.

Beyond Environment and Philanthropy

Each of these other, more limited concepts has considerable merit. However, none is new or sufficient to both address the needs and interests of the broad set of stakeholders to which most organizations are accountable and to position the firm to avail itself of all related opportunities.

Sustainability is often framed in the media as a campaign to "green" the world or "save the planet." When viewed from an appropriately broad perspective, however, sustainability extends beyond the currently fashionable focus on "greening." Greening is, after all, simply the latest manifestation of public interest in the environment, which has come back into vogue during the past 3 or 4 years following a multiyear hiatus. As an interested party who has watched several incarnations of a growing public/business interest in improving the environmental performance of organizations (and individuals), I find it both heartening and, in some ways, disturbing to observe the eagerness with which many are now embracing everything "green." Greening sounds and feels admirable, but public interest in this topic tends to wax and wane over time. My fear is that it will again fall out of fashion, unless the renewed focus on environmental performance improvement is coupled with considerations of social equity and both are underlain by rigorous economic analysis. Sustainability, defined in this way, provides the only theoretical and practical environmental improvement framework that can be fully justified and maintained during both good and challenging economic times. Therefore, it is robust and "sustainable" enough for the long haul.

My concerns with the terms CSR and CR are somewhat different. Although in most formulations they include the three "legs of the stool," they really are about delineating and acting on the obligations of the modern corporation to society at large. In contrast, and as highlighted above, sustainability should be considered an imperative that applies to all organizations and political entities (countries, states, municipalities). Each of these is challenged to understand and address the broad conditions under which it operates and its relationships with other entities and the natural world. Each also must chart a course on which it can thrive without undermining its asset base or unfairly precluding or limiting the sustainable success of others. In that context, CR can be thought of as one element of a corporate strategy to address the sustainability imperative. Such an element can, for example, identify the concerns of external stakeholders and define and execute processes to ensure that these external interests are respected as the firm pursues its broader business goals. In other words, CR and its analogues can be an important part of (but in any case are a subset of) an organization's approach to sustainability. In particular, CR can, and often does, comprise an organization's efforts to respond to the imperative to promote sustainable development. Similarly, CR can be used to appropriately target a company's philanthropic activities. Or the firm might separately deploy a strategic philanthropy campaign. But by its nature any such activity is far narrower in scope and effect than organizational sustainability. The two should not be confused or, in my view, ever be used interchangeably.

These distinctions are not trivial. Indeed, understanding and resolving them has proven difficult for many organizations and practitioners. Regardless of what words you choose to employ, the key point is that pursuing sustainability at the organizational level is more complex, more important, and more difficult than simply greening the organization to some arbitrary but comfortable level, or becoming more attentive to particular stakeholders and their views. However, substantial rewards can accompany taking on this greater level of difficulty.

Sustainability has emerged directly from the environmental movement and is often focused on key environmental issues and challenges. However, important opportunities exist for corporate leaders to examine social equity and economic issues in parallel with the environmental aspects of their organizations. The concept of sustainability provides an integrative framework to facilitate this thought process. Moreover, in practice, synergies and scale economies often make it possible to address issues having both environmental and social aspects more effectively and economically than would be possible by pursuing separate, unrelated approaches.

Of Governance and Values

Many stakeholders want assurance that the people at the top of the organization have thought through its important environmental and social issues and that they have developed and deployed effective programs, systems, and practices to address them. Sustainability provides an integrating structure that can both guide and explain how corporate leaders meet these expectations and do so in a way that is far more streamlined, sophisticated, and ultimately less time-consuming than would be possible otherwise.

Environmental and social improvement initiatives are continually underused when they are not seen as contributing to core business drivers or creating financial value in any tangible way.

Illegal and, increasingly, unethical behavior is not well tolerated by regulators, customers, suppliers, and other business partners. Such behavior can have severe financial consequences, both immediately and in the longer term. Understanding what is legal requires competence and vigilance on the part of one's general or outside counsel, but understanding what is ethical requires a set of organizational values and business norms. It is now widely understood that well-run companies have a core "DNA" or identity that embodies shared values and aspirations and is independent of any individual. This attribute enables the organization to remain strong and vibrant over an extended period even as people enter and depart from it. Moreover, this type of organizational identity provides many advantages under normal circumstances but is especially critical during crisis situations, when people need to know how to act as well as what to do. Sustainability can serve as a common, unifying principle to guide the thinking and behaviors of all members of the organization. This is important when different members are called on to execute their unique functions, some of which may be in conflict. Moreover, sustainability provides the needed flexibility to address the following realities:

- Environmental, social, and economic considerations must be balanced.
- The way in which they are balanced will differ according to the organization, issue, and circumstance in question.
- This balance will likely change over time.

The complexities of, and interrelationships among, ESG issues require a management approach that combines and considers all these disciplines. Such an approach should address all significant needs and requirements (particularly compliance), surface and resolve conflicts among them, provide consistency and predictability, and be both effective and efficient. In other words, some sort of overarching concept and management structure is required, and sustainability provides the "umbrella" under which many organizations are now organizing their previously disparate internal functions. I am unaware of any competing or alternative concept that has been shown to be workable while providing similar benefits.

The best way to pursue sustainability is to consider the three primary determinants of value for any business enterprise:

- The revenue stream and the customer base that generates it;
- Earnings or, in the case of public sector organizations, effective control of costs and management of capital; and
- Adequate understanding and management of risk.

A sensible sustainability strategy embodies careful consideration of how new initiatives or changes to existing programs might affect all three of these determinants of value. History has shown that absent this orientation, environmental and social improvement initiatives are continually underused because they are not seen as contributing to core business drivers or creating financial value in any tangible way. By the same token, a properly specified sustainability approach imposes a new measure of financial discipline on both internal and external proponents of new "greening" ideas and prospective investments in projects or activities having primarily a social orientation.

My fear is that "greening" will again fall out of fashion, unless the renewed focus on environmental performance improvement is coupled with considerations of social equity, with both underlain by rigorous economic analysis.

Entering the Mainstream

EHS issues have in many cases been managed tactically in United States corporations and public sector agencies. Historically, EHS functions were often housed within, and directed by, the organization's legal department because the focus then was on understanding legal requirements and ensuring compliance. More recently, EHS people have reported through various administrative functions (such as human resources), facility maintenance, or manufacturing management. In short, with few exceptions, EHS has been managed primarily as a facility-based tactical function, rather than as a strategic issue or source of potential broad-spectrum financial value creation. Adopting a sustainability framework can help disrupt, and might even compel, dissolution of organizational silos that exist in many companies. This can create the conditions needed for people across the organization to reach out to one another. They can identify and manage environmental and social issues in ways that limit risk, build brand and market value, and generate new cash flows. In an organization actively pursuing sustainability, achieving better environmental performance or more equitable dealings with stakeholders is not a task to be delegated to someone else. It is an integral part of everyone's job (if only in a small way), from the boardroom to the shop floor.

Critical Thinking

1. What is the relationship of sustainability and corporate responsibility?

2. Using the Internet, identify firms with strong sustainability programs and good corporate responsibility results.

3. For the firms you identified in answering question 2, analysis at least two of those firms on the basis of the six attributes of a sustainable organization presented in the article. Explain how the two firms you chose either exhibit or do not exhibit attributes of a sustainable organization.

4. What is the relationship of ethics and sustainability? To be an ethical firm, does the firm need a sustainability program? Why or why not?

Create Central

www.mhhe.com/createcentral

Internet References

Cranfield University School of Management

http://www.som.cranfield.ac.uk/som/p16919/Knowledge-Interchange/Management-Themes/Corporate-Responsibility-and-Sustainability

Forbes

http://www.forbes.com/sites/brucerogers/2014/04/07/corporate-responsibility-and-sustainability-is-a-competitive-advantage-for-capgemini/

PETER SOKA is founder and president of Soyka & Company. This is the first in a series of excerpts from his new book, *Creating a Sustainable Organization: Approaches for Enhancing Corporate Value Through Sustainability*, reprinted with permission from FT Press, a division of Pearson.

Article   Prepared by: Eric Teoro, *Lincoln Christian University*

Cause for Concern

Water conservation has been billed as the most important environmental issue of the 21st century, yet few American consumers are altering their behaviors—and fewer companies are trying to motivate them to do so.

CHRISTINE BIRKNER

Learning Outcomes

After reading this article, you will be able to:

- Describe initiatives companies are taking to promote water conservation.

- Recognize the importance of aligning behavior with espoused values.

According to the US Environmental Protection Agency, at least two-thirds of the United States is either experiencing or bracing for local, regional, or statewide water shortages. Parts of the United States use up to 80 percent of their available freshwater resources, making future water shortages more probable, according to the United Nations Educational, Scientific and Cultural Organization. Globally, 1.2 billion people live in areas with inadequate water supplies and by 2025, two-thirds of the world will contend with water scarcity, according to the International Water Management Institute.

1.2 Billion people live in areas with inadequate water supplies.

International Water Management Institute.

Did you know that the world's water shortages are that dire? You're not alone if you didn't—and you're in good company if you have yet to do anything about it. A 2011 study by the London-based Chartered Institution of Water and Environmental Management says that consumers around the world are generally unaware of their own water consumption, tend not to change their behavior and have a general lack of knowledge about water management issues.

"Water is still a really inexpensive resource across the country and until water rates go up, the vast majority of people aren't going to think twice about conserving water," says Park Howell, president of Park&Co, a Phoenix-based marketing agency that specializes in sustainability and has worked on nationwide water conservation campaigns. "It's a big environmental issue that's creeping up on consumers that they don't even realize is at their doorstep."

While consumer behaviors have yet to change, such change is inevitable, experts say, which makes water conservation a powerful and prescient cause for companies to get behind—incorporating water-saving strategies into both their day-to-day operations and their marketing plans, and taking the lead on water-based public awareness efforts. "It's going to be the No. 1 environmental issue for North America, if not the entire world, in the next few years [because] the population continues to expand and our infrastructure is not keeping up. Consumer product manufacturers are [realizing] this is going to become much more visible over the next decade and if they're there as a pioneer saying, 'Let us show you how to use our product to save water,' then [they're] the hero," Howell says.

Distilling the Message

Howell is no stranger to effective water-based marketing strategies. In 1999, his firm developed a campaign for the city of Mesa, AZ, aimed at encouraging residents to conserve water. The campaign, called "Water: Use it Wisely," offers simple water conservation tips on a website and in TV, print, and radio ads. Initially used by local utilities, the "Water: Use It Wisely" messaging later was adopted by more than 400 public and private entities across the United States, with corporate sponsors including Lowe's and Home Depot, and is still active nationwide. The campaign model is important, Howell says, because it allows utilities that have limited financial and personnel resources to cobrand a national campaign and benefit from its universal theme: "There are a number of ways to save water, and they all start with you."

"We learned early that people across the country said, 'Don't tell me to save water; show me how,' " Howell says. "The campaign demonstrated to corporations that environmental engagement can be fun, thought-provoking and easy for an individual to do."

Corporate Conservation

Many municipalities have no choice but to promote more positive consumer behaviors regarding water usage and on the corporate side, many companies know that it makes good business sense to change their organizational behaviors when it comes to water usage—whether or not they decide to promote it.

"[Water conservation] is a rapidly growing area in the corporate world," says Brian Richter, director of global freshwater strategies at the Nature Conservancy, an Arlington, VA-based global conservation organization that works with government agencies at local, state and federal levels around the world to evaluate water efficiency. "More and more companies are seeing the need to get involved in looking at their water use: how much they use, where they use it and the certainty or risk associated with that use." Northfield, IL-based Kraft Foods Inc., which has worked with the Nature Conservancy in the past, reduced water consumption at its manufacturing plants by 21 percent from 2005 to 2010 and plans to further reduce water consumption by an additional 15 percent by 2015, according to a company spokesman.

In 2010, Chicago-based MillerCoors initiated a study of water-related supply risks in its supply chain and worked with the Beverage Industry Environmental Roundtable, a partnership of global beverage companies devoted to environmental issues, to create an industry approach to "water footprinting." "Sustainability benefits the business and benefits the environment, and for us, we really want to be a recognized leader in the space," says Kim Marotta, vice president of corporate social responsibility at MillerCoors. "We need to understand the watersheds of where our breweries are located so we protect the quality and quantity of water long term." MillerCoors also sponsors the beverage page on the Mother Nature Network website, which includes news, educational videos, and tips on

sustainability issues such as water conservation best practices for businesses.

Other than industry-focused initiatives and some brand sponsorships of clean water efforts, MillerCoors doesn't engage in much water-related cause marketing yet because other environmental issues, such as recycling, attract more consumer attention, Marotta says.

That organizational rather than cause-marketing-related approach to water conservation isn't atypical among American businesses. At Atlanta-based Coca-Cola Co., most water conservation efforts are conducted behind the scenes as well, at least in the United States. As part of its partnership with the Nature Conservancy, Coca-Cola worked with academics at the Global Environment & Technology Foundation on a report detailing methods by which companies can measure and account for the benefits of water conservation work in communities and watersheds. Coca-Cola and the Nature Conservancy also worked with private land owners and cooperatives in north Texas to expand grasslands and reintroduce native species to restore prairies, which helps with water quality.

> ## By 2025, two-thirds of the world will contend with water scarcity.
>
> International Water Management Institute.

"We have evolved in our understanding and response to water issues over the last decade," says Greg Koch, Coca-Colas managing director of global water stewardship. "We've recognized the stresses water is under, from quality, to quantity, to droughts and scarcity. Plant performance is important and we've maintained that, but . . . it's not enough for us to take care of the water we need for our business because water is so fundamental to life. It's in our vested business interest to play a role in watersheds and communities, and in awareness and education."

Richter says that companies must first get a handle on their own water usage before they can engage in any meaningful water-related cause marketing initiatives. "It's difficult for a company to take a position of encouraging its consumers to be responsible for their water use until the company assumes the responsibility for its own water."

From a Drip to a Deluge

Coca-Cola therefore is navigating the "water as a corporate cause" strategy carefully, introducing only a few water conservation programs domestically until consumers are more receptive to water-related messaging. Instead, Cokes environmental messaging in the United States focuses on recycling and species conservation efforts, such as the company's recent holiday campaign in which Coke cans and bottles were white rather than red to support the World Wildlife Fund's polar bear conservation programs. These efforts more closely match the American consumer's mindset, says Lisa Manley, Coca-Cola's director of sustainability communications. "Consumer interests vary country by country. We need to understand areas of interest within our sustainability area that are most relevant to a particular community and work to tailor our communications against those. Here in the United States, we've seen a lot more interest around packaging and recycling. In [global] markets, we see more of a defined interest around water," Manley says.

Overseas, Coca-Cola is doing more overt water conservation initiatives, including running ads such as the one in its Latin American marketing campaign, "Every Bottle Tells a Story," that features a man doing water stewardship work in communities in Mexico. And during the FIFA World Cup in South Africa in 2010, Coca-Cola ran ads promoting the Replenish Africa Initiative, which helps bring water to drought-ridden communities throughout the continent.

Coca-Cola's site-specific and consumer-sensitive strategy is wise, experts say. "[Water conservation] is certainly not on the forefront of American consumers' minds, but it is on the forefront of global consumers' minds," says Karen Barnes, vice president of insight at Shelton Group Inc., a Knoxville, TN-based advertising agency focused on bringing sustainability to the mass market.

When corporations are ready to engage American consumers on water conservation awareness, though, they could take a page from the play-book of Piscataway, NJ-based faucet and toilet maker American Standard Brands. American Standard's water conservation efforts are organic in that the company's products handle consumers' water use, so water conservation as a corporate cause is an obvious fit. Jeannette Long, vice president of digital marketing, doesn't deny that fact but says that by promoting water efficiency, both the company and the environment can benefit.

Water conservation is part of American Standard's DNA, she says. "Every product that we make is a water receptacle or has water that passes through it, so we feel like it's our responsibility to design products that will function exceptionally well and use as little water as possible. The bathroom accounts for 75 percent of water used in the home, so if we're designing the products, it's our responsibility to create the best product and still protect our natural resources."

American Standard recently teamed up with the Environmental Protection Agency on a water conservation program called WaterSense and developed water-efficient faucets, showerheads and toilets. As part of that program, American Standard worked to change consumer perception that water-efficient appliances don't perform as well as regular appliances, Long says. "Our biggest goal is to convince consumers that more water does not equal better performance. We've reduced water in the faucet category by 20 percent and in the showerhead category by 40 percent, and we do testing to ensure that the performance the customer's going to experience is exactly the same as when they used more water."

To tout its products' water- and money-saving capabilities, American Standard conducted the Responsible Bathroom campaign from late 2009 to early 2011. The campaign included print, TV and mobile marketing, with trailers featuring American Standard product exhibits stopping at home shows around the country. "It was critical for us to demonstrate that you don't need as much water. [We] came up with demonstrations that showed, 'This toilet flushes 24 golf balls with 20 percent less water,'" Long says. "Everybody walked away saying, 'Wow, that's impressive.'"

Responsible Bathroom ads promoted water-saving behaviors, emphasizing that a family of four, for instance, can save 16,000 gallons of water a year by using water-saving appliances and water-efficient practices. The campaign included a Responsible Bathroom Sweepstakes, which gave away vacations to families who submitted creative ways to save water. A water calculator on the Responsible Bathroom section of American Standard's website also estimated the cost savings of using water-efficient appliances.

Getting consumers to adopt water-saving habits is a challenge, Long admits. "Some of them won't be interested in water conservation, but there is this message that says: 'You're going to use less water; your performance is going to be just as good, actually better than when you were using more water, and you're going to save money on your water bill. You're going to save energy because you're not heating as much water for your shower and your faucets.' We talk to them on that side, for people who aren't environmentally conscious."

To introduce future generations to the issue of water conservation, American Standard partners with the Green Education Foundation on a curriculum for New Jersey schools that shows children how much water is being used in the bathroom. Students conduct audits of plumbing products, figuring out how much water they could save if they replaced fixtures in their school. "We were effective [in] bringing younger generations into it because they are more socially minded as they start to hear about natural resources being used up," Long says.

The company also donated $1 million to the Nature Conservancy's water conservation awareness programs in 2010, and works with organizations such as the International Association of Plumbing and Mechanical Officials and the EPA on plumbing infrastructure testing. American Standard also meets with congressmen about issues that relate to the plumbing industry and water conservation, all of which are important to the end consumer.

Howell applauds American Standard's conservation efforts. "They've got products that use water and facilitate the flow of water, so they're a good corporate citizen, going out of their way to build water savings into the product and teach the behavior change. Technology alone is not going to save this planet, no matter how energy-efficient the showerhead," he says.

For Cleveland-based Great Lakes Brewing Co., which sells a water-based product with a water-related brand name, water conservation also is a natural fit. "Our product is made of 95 percent water, so it's the main ingredient of our product," says Saul Kliorys, environmental programs manager at Great Lakes. "We've called our company Great Lakes Brewing Co., Lake Erie is one mile away: Those are the reasons we're interested in [water conservation]. It's a resource that's getting scarcer and scarcer."

The brewer's cause marketing efforts include a music festival in Cleveland called Burning River Fest that's dedicated to promoting water conservation. Money raised at the festival goes to water conservation organizations such as the Doan Brook Watershed Partnership in Northeast Ohio, Lake Erie Waterkeeper and a rain harvesting program for urban gardens at Baldwin Wallace College in Berea, Ohio. Great Lakes also works with organizations that conduct educational projects at local schools, including Drink Local, Drink Tap in Cleveland and Tinkers Creek Watershed Partners in Twinsburg, Ohio.

The brewer's water conservation efforts are an obvious tie-in, Kliorys says, and they help to boost the company's brand image. "In Cleveland, folks like our brand a lot, so we asked them why they do, and the primary reason is for the quality of the beer . . . but most people are also supportive of the sustainability initiatives. It's definitely an added benefit."

Be Conservative

As with any cause marketing initiative, authenticity is key to companies' water conservation messages, whether consumer-driven or covert. Water has always been a top priority for MillerCoors as a business, which helps in its bid for authenticity, Marotta says. "Any time you're connecting with a consumer and talking about the importance of any aspect of sustainability, it absolutely needs to be authentic. If you're not walking the walk, then don't talk the talk. If it's about water, you better be operating from the most water-efficient breweries, understanding your footprint and making water

conservation efforts in your supply chain. Otherwise, it's going to be noticeable that its greenwashing and not part of the DNA of the brand," she says. "It's not as though we woke up in 2008 and said: 'Boy, there's some successful sustainability campaigns out there. We should really look at this.' It's [been] a decades-long commitment."

Echoes Coca-Cola's Manley: "Today's consumer is incredibly savvy and incredibly aware of a company matching their behaviors with their messaging, so it would be folly for us to communicate with something that we didn't feel we were engaging in a responsible way around. We've got all of the proof points that one might need to feel comfortable beginning to think about how do you convey the message to consumers— and not just convey it in terms of how do you educate them, but . . . how do you invite them along in the journey? I see it as an area where we'll have increasing engagement with consumers in the future."

"Water is going to be the most important natural resource and environmental issue of the 21st century."

Brian Richter, The Nature Conservancy.

Water will never be just the cause du jour. Rather, it's a matter of survival, the Nature Conservancy's Richter says, so it's a worthwhile investment to get behind water conservation now. "Water is going to be the most important natural resource and environmental issue of the 21st century. Population growth is going to put more and more pressure on limited water supplies, so it's going to be critically important for everyone, especially corporations, to be actively involved in promoting activities that will protect those water supplies and use them more efficiently," he says. "Unlike many other natural resources, water has no substitute."

"Unlike many other natural resources, water has no substitute."

Brian Richter, The Nature Conservancy.

Critical Thinking

1. Do you agree that water conservation is the most important environmental issue of the 21st century? Why or why not?

2. Why do you think so few American consumers are ignoring the need for water conservation?

3. If you live in an area of adequate water, should you be concerned about the reported 1.2 billion people in the world without adequate water supplies? Prepare answers on both sides of this question.

4. How might the need for water conservation be instilled in society?

5. If you were to write a paragraph for inclusion in a firm's code of ethics about the importance of water conservation, what would you write? Be prepared to present and explain your paragraph to your classmates.

Create Central

www.mhhe.com/createcentral

Internet References

Scientific American
    http://www.scientificamerican.com/article/will-water-become-the-chief-commodity-of-the-21st-century/
United States Envronmental Protection Agency
    http://www.epa.gov/greeningepa/water/
Water Culture Institute
    http://www.waterculture.org/Ethics_of_Water_Use.html

Article   Prepared by: Eric Teoro, *Lincoln Christian University*

Commentary: Markets Will Best Guard Environment

JOHN STOSSEL

Learning Outcomes

After reading this article, you will be able to:

• Describe how private property rights and the market system offer an alternative to governmental oversight regarding environmental protection.

• Understand potential problems of commonly held resources.

L ast week I said the Environmental Protection Agency has become a monster that does more harm than good. But logical people say, "What else we got?" It's natural to assume greedy capitalists will run amok and destroy the Earth unless stopped by regulation.

These critics don't understand the real power of private ownership, says Terry Anderson of the Property and Environment Research Center.

"Long before the EPA was a glint in anyone's eye," said Anderson on my TV show, "property rights were dealing with pollution issues."

The worst pollution often happens on land owned by "the people"—by government. Since no one person derives direct benefit from this property, it's often treated carelessly. Some of the worst environmental damage happens on military bases and government research facilities, such as the nuclear research site in Hanford, Washington.

Worse things may happen when government indifference combines with the greed of unrestrained businesspeople, like when the U.S. Forest Service lets logging companies cut trees on public land. Private forest owners are careful to replant and take steps to prevent forest fires. Government-owned forests are not as well managed. They are much more likely to burn.

When it's government land—or any commonly held resource—the incentive is to get in and take what you can, while you can. It's called the "tragedy of the commons."

"No one washes a rental car," says Anderson, but "when people own things, they take care of them. And when they have private property rights that they can enforce, other people can't dump gunk onto the property."

That's why, contrary to what environmentalists often assume, it's really property rights that encourage good stewardship. If you pollute, it's your neighbors who are most likely to complain, not lazy bureaucrats at the EPA.

"Here in Montana, for example, the Anaconda Mining Company, a copper and mining company, ruled the state," says Anderson.

"And yet when it was discovered that their tailings piles (the heaps left over after removing the valuable material by mining) had caused pollution on ranches that neighbored them, local property owners took them to court. (Anaconda Mining) had to cease and desist and pay for damages. . . . They quickly took care of that problem." They also restored some of the land they had mined.

Property rights and a simple, honest court system—institutions that can exist without big government—solve problems that would be fought about for years by politicians, environmental bureaucrats and the corporations who lobby them.

In fact, it's harder to assess the benefits and damages in environmental disputes when these decisions are taken out of the marketplace and made by bureaucracies that have few objective ways to measure costs.

Markets even solve environmental problems in places where environmentalists assume they cannot, such as oceans and other property that can't be carved up into private parcels.

Environmental bureaucrats usually say, to make sure fishermen don't overfish and destroy the stock of fish, we will set a quota for every season. That command-and-control approach has been the standard policy.

So bureaucrats regulate the fishing season. They limit the number of boats, their size, and how long they may fish. The result: fishing is now America's most dangerous job. Fishermen race out in all kinds of weather to get as many fish as they can in the narrow time window allowed by regulators. They try to game the system to make more money. Sometimes they still deplete the fish stock.

But Anderson points out that there is an alternative. "In places like New Zealand and Iceland . . . we've created individual fishing quotas, which are tradable, which are bankable, which give people an incentive to invest in their fisheries."

Because the fisherman "owns" his fishing quota, he is careful to preserve it. He doesn't overfish because he wants "his" fish to be there next year.

The moral of the story: when possible, let markets and property protect nature. That avoids the tragedy of the commons.

Critical Thinking

1. Do you think the author's argument holds merit? Why or why not?
2. Do you think people are poor stewards of commonly held resources?
3. Debate with a colleague or fellow student how best to protect the environment.

Create Central

www.mhhe.com/createcentral

Internet References

Economist
http://www.economist.com/node/9136122
Ludwig von Mises Institute
http://mises.org/daily/5978/The-Libertarian-Manifesto-on-Pollution
The Atlantic
http://www.theatlantic.com/business/archive/2012/05/how-property-rights-could-help-save-the-environment/257756/

Unit 4

UNIT

Prepared by: Eric Teoro, *Lincoln Christian University*

Ethics and Social Responsibility in the Marketplace

Marketing is a process in which goods and services move from concept to the customer. Whether a marketing program focuses on a product, service, person, place, cause, event, or an organization, it consists of the four "Ps": product, price, place, and promotion. Organizations have translated the four Ps into the four Cs in an attempt to place the customer at the center of their business: customer solution, customer cost, convenience, and communication. Marketing enables the meeting of human needs and wants. Marketers have an ethical duty to ensure their practices do not harm consumers or their companies.

The articles in this unit explore issues related to marketing ethics. They describe examples of failed innovations and provide recommendations to promote ethical new product development. They look at how companies should respond to unfair customers, questioning the maxim that the customer is always right. One article examines the nature of marketing to children. Who is primarily responsible for the marketing

messages children receive—companies or parents? What is the impact of marketing efforts on children? Is it ethical for a business to socialize children regarding values? Another article explores the nature of social-media marketing. The author presents ethically questionable examples of the use of likes, retweets, replies, and shares. He raises questions about the use of product placement in ads that, on the surface, appear to convey a different message. When a company expresses concern regarding a tragedy, is it unethical for it to place its products at the center of the communication? The author provides guidelines for the ethical use of social-media marketing. A couple of the articles consider the balance between focusing on profits and focusing on meeting social needs. Can meeting social needs be profitable? What benefits can result for the company and employees from meeting social needs? Do businesses have a responsibility to meet social needs if doing so hurts them in terms of profitability?

Article   Prepared by: Eric Teoro, *Lincoln Christian University*

Honest Innovation

Ethics issues in new product development could be stalling innovation growth.

CALVIN L. HODOCK

Learning Outcomes

After reading this article, you will be able to:

- Recognize errors associated with flawed innovation.
- Implement steps to promote ethical product and service development.

Product innovation is the fuel for America's growth. Two Harvard economists described its importance as follows: "Innovation is no mere vanity plate on the nation's economic engine. It trumps capital accumulation and allocation of resources as the most important contributor to growth."

Innovative initiatives are a high risk game; failures widely outnumber successes. While enthusiasm, conviction, and creativity should flourish in the hearts and minds of the innovation team, judgments must remain totally, even brutally, objective. But unconscious and conscious marketing dishonesty may make this easier said than done.

Unconscious Marketing Dishonesty

People fall in love with what they create, including movies, television pilots, novels, art, and new products. And all too often that love is blind: As objectivity eludes the creator, normally rational people become evangelical rather than practical, rational marketing executives.

The Coca-Cola executive suite was convinced that New Coke was the right thing to do. Procter & Gamble's research and development (R&D) believed that Citrus Hill was a better-tasting orange juice than Tropicana and Minute Maid. The spirited Pepsi Blue team overlooked the obvious knowledge that colas should be brown. Ford's MBA crowd believed in a "cheap Jag" strategy. And Motorola's engineers were misguided in their devotion to the Iridium satellite telephone system.

Crest Rejuvenating Effects was fake innovation: It basically was just regular Crest with a great cinnamon vanilla flavor and feminine packaging, positioned for the "nip and tuck" generation of women aged 30 to 45. Similar to Rice Krispies' famous "snap, crackle, and pop" campaign, it encountered a tepid reception, but the brand's custodians believed that America was ready for "his and hers" tubes of toothpaste in their medicine cabinets.

These were well-meaning people who wandered off course because they became enamored with what they created. But let's face it, optimism has limits. The marketplace disagreed, and that's the only vote that counts in any innovation effort.

Conscious Marketing Dishonesty

Conscious marketing dishonesty is more insidious. Blinded passion may still be part of the equation, but in this case the innovation team consciously pushes the envelope across the line of propriety. Before long, there are disquieting signs or signals that all is not well with the new product.

Unfavorable data or information might be ignored, perhaps even suppressed. There might be the blithe assumption that some miracle will surface, and make it all right. Successful innovation initiatives are not products of miracles, but simply take a good idea and execute all the basic steps that are part of the discovery process. The reward goes to those who excel in executing the thousands of details associated with the dirt of doing.

Either way, conscious or unconscious, marketing dishonesty means resources are wasted, valuable time and energy are lost forever and shareholder value may be diminished (depending on the magnitude of the mistake). Often, nobody takes the blame—and many get promoted, because activity gets rewarded over achievement.

There's often no accountability, even though the new product blueprint is peppered with the fingerprints of many. New product assignments are similar to a NASCAR pit stop. The players are constantly moved around the chess board. The brand manager working on a new product for 6 to 9 months moves to mouthwash. The mouthwash brand manager moves to shampoos. And what we have is a game of musical chairs, with no accountability. It is understandable why innovation teams are willing to "run bad ideas up the flag pole" in lassiez-faire-type innovation environments.

While there are supposed to be security checkpoints in the development process, the marketing "id" finds ways to maneuver around them. When important marketing research findings are ignored or rationalized away, because the innovation team is racing toward a launch date promised to management, the spigot of objectivity is turned off because reality might get in the way. Innovation initiatives build momentum to the point where nothing will stop the new product from being launched—not even dire news.

Marketing Dishonesty

There are eight recurring errors associated with flawed innovation. The most disingenuous is marketing dishonesty, where the innovation team consciously engages in deception—even though there is a red flag flapping in the breeze, indicating that a new product is ill. Six marketing dishonesty scenarios are outlined here.

Campbell's Souper Combo

Souper Combo was a combination frozen soup and sandwich for microwave heating; it tested extremely well as a concept. The product was test marketed, and national introduction was recommended.

Two forecasts surfaced. The new product team estimated that Souper Combo would be a $68 million business. The marketing research department viewed it differently: It would be a $40 to 45 million business, due to weak repeat purchase rates. Nobody challenged the optimistic forecast. Senior management trusted what they heard, while being fed a bouillabaisse of marketing dishonesty. The national introduction was a disaster, and Souper Combo died on the altar of blemished innovation in 9 months.

Crystal Pepsi

Pepsi's innovation team ignored focus group participants who hated the taste of this clear cola. It was forced through the Pepsi distribution system on its journey to failure. When was the last time you saw Crystal Pepsi on the store shelves?

Apple Newton

The Newton was the first (but flawed) PDA rushed to market, because then-CEO John Scully viewed it as his signature product—knowing that Apple loyalists were dismayed that a "Pepsi guy" was running the company. Scully wanted to establish a technical legacy that endured long after he left the Apple campus.

The first Newtons were shipped to market with more than a thousand documented bugs. Nobody had the courage to tell Scully and the Apple board about this.

Arthritis Foundation Pain Relievers

This was a line of parity analgesics, involving a licensing agreement where the company paid the Atlanta-based Arthritis Foundation $1 million annually for trademark use. This analgesic line was a positioning gimmick destined for a law and order encounter, and that doesn't mean the NBC television program. Nineteen states attorney generals said the proposition was deceptive. The drugs contained analgesics common to other pain relievers, and were developed without assistance from the Arthritis Foundation. The Foundation was paid handsomely for the use of its name.

Although McNeil Consumer Healthcare admitted no wrong doing, the case was settled for close to $2 million.

Pontiac Aztek

This was considered the ugliest car ever, and the research verified this. While the research predicted that the Aztek was a hopeless cause, the project team sanitized the research sent to senior management to make the situation look better than it was. Decisions about the Aztek's fate were based on intelligence that was heavily modified and edited. Get it out became more important than "get it right."

Aztek-type decisions became regrettably common in the General Motors culture. John Scully never heard the bad news about the Newton, and the General Motors executive suite didn't want to hear any bad news about their cars. It is a heck of way to run one of America's largest corporations and a bad deal for General Motors shareholders, when a culture of intimidation fuels marketing dishonesty. No wonder things are grim at GM these days.

Polaroid Captiva

This camera was similar to Polaroid's original goldmine product the SX 70, but with a smaller film format. It was priced at $120, although marketing research indicated it would not sell if priced over $60. In this scenario, marketing sold a bad idea supported with a specious assumption; marketing research couldn't sell the truth.

Captiva's potential sales were inflated with an assumption about high levels of repeat purchases after introduction. Selling cameras is different than selling cookies or shampoo, products that need replacement. Captiva perished in the marketplace, as the company violated its cardinal principle: Make the cash register ring selling film, while offering the cameras at cost.

Ethics Issues

While these new products had varied product deficiencies, they all share a common denominator: an optimistic sales forecast. An innovation team can manipulate the numbers to get any sales level it wants. It's easy to do, use optimistic assumptions. New product teams can, and do, cook the books with creative number crunching.

Most new product failures are heavily researched. It is used to justify moving a bad new product forward. In a recent *Advertising Age* article, Bob Barocci, the CEO of the Advertising Research Foundation, remarked, "There is a general belief that over 50 percent of the research done at companies is wasted." He attributed this to the desire to "support decisions already made." All too often, innovation teams push questionable new products through the pipeline with the support of "justification research."

Another ethical issue is targeting. It is difficult to imagine that ad agencies and their clients did not know Vioxx and Celebrex were overprescribed drugs, sold to consumers with minor aches and pains who could have used less expensive alternatives like Advil and Aleve. Both clients and agencies mutually formulated target strategies with Celebrex and Vioxx as examples. These drugs were developed for senior citizens with chronic pain. But the target segment was too small, so the focus shifted to aging baby boomers with clients and agencies in agreement on the reconfiguration.

Prescriptives

Here are seven recommendations:

1. *Innovation committee.* Boards have finance, audit, nominating and compensation committees. Why not an innovation committee composed of outsiders who are not board members? Their role is to assist the board in assessing innovation initiatives. The board can then decide what action should be taken, including pressing the "kill button."

    Companies sometimes do postmortems after failure. The innovation committee should perform premortems early in the development process, before bad ideas soak up lots of money. There is a rich reservoir of people resources to serve on innovation committees (e.g., academics, retired senior executives, industrial designers, and product and industry specialists). But one thing that they should not be is cronies of professional management.

2. *Find a value-added marketing research department.* The prior case histories illustrate that bad research news often is ignored or rationalized away. Hire a research director who knows how to develop and steward a value-added research department, and that has senior management's respect. The respect factor will protect the function from retribution, should the news be bad. Such a person will not be easy to find. One company's solution was to hire a consultant from McKinsey & Company to steward their research department.

    In the early days, pioneer researchers such as Alfred Politz and Ernest Dichter presented their findings to boards of directors. Marketing research lost it status on its journey from infancy to maturity. Today's market research is frequently unseen by the board. The right person in the function—think one with management respect—gives marketing research an influential voice in the innovation process that it currently does not have.

3. *Reinforce the unvarnished truth.* Senior management needs to embrace skeptics, rather than surround themselves with "yes people." Before management reviews a new product plan, key players—manufacturing, finance, marketing, and marketing research—should sign off that the plan's assumptions, the underlying source for rosy sales forecasts, are truthful.

4. *Ethics boot camp.* Corporations spend millions on employee training, but how much is focused on ethics to help marketers navigate through gray areas? The innovation team should attend an ethics boot camp early in the development process. This should include everybody, including the ad agencies. Manipulating the forecast for a new product is unethical. It cheats the shareholders even more than it cheats the public.

5. *Teaching new product development.* In academia, new product courses are taught with a focus on best practices; a different perspective is required. The abysmal failure rate is due to worst practices. Classroom discussions of

best practices aren't doing much to reduce failure. Class lectures should focus on ethics issues, like manipulating forecasts and justification research used to keep bad ideas afloat.

6. *Ethics test.* Business schools screen candidates based on their graduate management admission test (GMAT) scores. But there is another much-needed test that business schools should implement: an ethics test. Ethics scores should carry equal weight with GMATs. This demonstrates to candidates that ethics are important, and represent a significant prerequisite for admission. As evidenced in new product cases, ethics is more than simply the despicable acts of WorldCom's Bernie Ebbers and Enron Corporation's Andrew Fastow. And, most important, this should help business schools turn out students with a stronger moral compass—ones who don't feed management a duplicitous forecast for a flawed new product.

7. *Corporate endowments.* Corporations interact with business schools on many different levels. They make sizable donations, fund basic research, and send their executives to workshops and seminars. They also need to endow ethics chairs with dedicated academics who are interested in ethics scholarship. Corporations should not hesitate to open up their vaults of information to these academics. What are the ethical patterns that underscore an endless stream of new product failures?

Final Thoughts

Failure is inevitable in product innovation. Perfect success is impossible, even undesirable, because it impedes reaching for the stars like Apple did with iPhone or Toyota with the Prius. Perfect success would be a dull agenda of safe bets like a new fragrance or a new flavor. This means the company has elected to play small ball.

This was the trap that Procter & Gamble fell into for close to three decades, despite having 1,250 PhD scientists churning out a treasure chest of patents—leading to 250 proprietary technologies. Despite all this patent activity, very few market-place hits that made the company famous—think Tide or Pampers as examples—had surfaced from this scientific capability. The innovation focus had drifted to minor product improvements, until the newly anointed CEO A. G. Lafley came along to change all that.

Lafley mandated that P&G be more aggressive, expect failures, and shoot for an innovation success rate in the range of 50 to 60 percent. And that means having only 4 out of 10 new products fail at Procter & Gamble, well below the industry norm.

The statistic—9 out of 10 new products fail—has hovered over the marketing landscape for six decades. It is estimated that the food industry loses $20 billion to $30 billion annually on failed new products. Would it not be refreshing to attempt to scale this back with a healthy dose of marketing honesty?

Critical Thinking

1. What is the difference between optimism and lying?
2. In what ways does product innovation lend itself to deceptive practices?

Create Central

www.mhhe.com/createcentral

Internet References

Canadian Business
http://www.canadianbusiness.com/blogs-and-comment/the-ethics-of-innovation/

Institute for Corporate Ethics
http://www.corporate-ethics.org/pdf/innovation_ethics.pdf

Stanford Social Innovation Review
http://www.ssireview.org/blog/entry/the_ethics_of_innovation

CALVIN L. HODOCK is former chairperson of the American Marketing Association board, author of *Why Smart Companies Do Dumb Things* (Prometheus Books, 2007), and professor of marketing at Berkeley College, based in West Paterson, N.J. He may be reached at calhodock@hotmail.com.

Reprinted with permission from *Marketing Management*, March/April 2009, pp. 18–21, published by the American Marketing Association. Copyright © 2009 by American Marketing Association.

Article

Prepared by: Eric Teoro, *Lincoln Christian University*

Serving Unfair Customers

LEONARD L. BERRY AND KATHLEEN SEIDERS

Learning Outcomes

After reading this article, you will be able to:

- Recognize that the customer is not always right.
- Describe ways in which customers behave badly.
- Implement steps to respond to unfair customers.

1. Changing Focus: From Unfair Companies to Unfair Customers

Ten years ago, we published an article titled "Service Fairness: What It Is and Why It Matters" (Seiders & Berry, 1998). Therein, we argued that poor service is not always linked to unfair company practices, but that unfair company practices are always linked to customer perceptions of poor service. We also argued that companies can pay a heavy price when customers believe they have been treated unfairly because customers' responses to perceived injustice often are pronounced, emotional, and retaliatory. We concluded by providing guidelines for managers on preventing unfairness perceptions and effectively managing those that do arise.

Fairness remains a critically important topic today, for it is essential to a mutually satisfactory exchange between two parties. Perceived unfairness undermines trust and diminished trust undermines the strength of relationships. Perceived unfairness is always a negative development. The focus of our original article was company unfairness to customers. Fairness, however, is a two-way street; thus, our present focus is customer unfairness to companies. This time, we examine how customers can be unfair, why it is important, and what companies can do about it.

We are ardent champions of the customer, but we do *not* believe in the maxim that "the customer is always right." Sometimes, the customer is wrong and unfairness often results. That the customer is sometimes wrong is a dirty little secret of

marketing, known to many but rarely discussed in public—or in print. What better occasion to broach this unmentionable topic than *Business Horizons'* 50th anniversary?

2. What Is Customer Unfairness and Why Does it Matter?

Customer unfairness occurs when a customer behaves in a manner that is devoid of common decency, reasonableness, and respect for the rights of others, creating inequity and causing harm for a company and, in some cases, its employees and other customers. Customer unfairness should be viewed independent of illegality because unfair customer behavior frequently is legal; repugnant, perhaps, but not necessarily illegal. Our focus in this article is legal customer behavior that is unfair, falling in the so-called "gray area" of company response.

When does a customer's bad judgment (or, when do bad manners) cross the line to "unfairness"? Three concepts are particularly useful in considering this question. The first is the severity of the harm the customer causes. The second is the frequency of the customer's problematic behavior. Figure 1 shows increasing levels of these two factors: "minor," "moderate," and "extreme" for severity of harm and "uncommon," "intermittent," and "recurrent" for frequency of occurrence. Customer behavior that reaches either the "moderate" or "intermittent" level would usually earn the unfairness label. At these levels, the customer crosses a threshold.

The third concept is intentionality. The customer who seeks to take advantage and inflict harm, who willfully disrespects the rights of other parties, will almost always deserve the unfairness label. In some cases, customers may seek to harm a company that they believe has harmed them. The customers' behavior in this case is an act of retaliation. When customers blame a company for unfair treatment, there are fair and unfair ways of responding. Intentionally unfair behavior is usually indefensible.

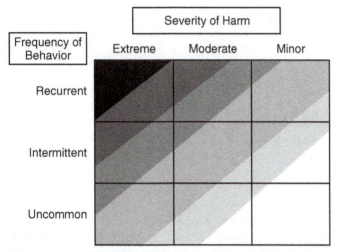

Figure 1 The threshold of customer unfairness. Adapted from Seiders and Berry (1998).

How do companies deal with unfair customers? We contacted executives from a variety of service organizations to solicit their opinions on the topic and to document examples drawn from their experiences. (We restricted our inquiries to consumer services executives based on the assumption that business-to-business services merit a separate exploration.) Our preliminary research reveals that some executives struggle with how to respond to customer unfairness. They don't want to respond in a way that confounds the company's commitment to quality service, which they and others worked hard to instill. Nor do they want to risk offending a still-profitable, albeit problematic, and customer. The following comments from four executives illustrate:

- "I think there is a subservient or servant mentality to all service, and to stray from that causes confusion in taking clear and concise action that should be positive for the customer."
- "The lifetime cost of losing a guest exceeds $500, so we go to great lengths to avoid losing them, even when they're wrong. Rather than risk offending guests, we tend to let 'little things' go."
- "My philosophy is that the customer is always right to some degree. It is that matter of degree that determines the action of the company. I believe that if we ever think that the customer is 100 percent wrong, then we have a high risk of becoming arrogant and not being customer-focused. I know that this may sound crazy, but if we crack open the door to this idea, then I think we can very quickly go down the slippery slope."
- "We are just not used to thinking of guests 'crossing the line.' I don't know that I have ever set up

boundaries. I always feel that guests have the right to say what they want and to do what they want, short of inconveniencing another guest or physically harming another guest or employee."

Our position is that companies cannot afford to ignore customer unfairness and should devise a plan to deal with it. Unfair customer behavior can exact a significant toll on employees' job satisfaction and weaken a company's overall service quality. We are not just speculating about this. Recent research by Rupp and Spencer (2006) found that customer injustice increased the degree of effort required for employees to manage their emotions in inter-personal transactions. This increased effort in what is termed *emotional labor* produces added stress, and contributes to employee turnover and overall unwillingness to perform (Grandey, Dickter, & Sin, 2004). Moreover, the injustice of one customer can negatively affect employee behavior toward other customers.

The effects of customer unfairness are often magnified because employees find it difficult to deal with customers who have treated their coworkers disrespectfully, even if the same customers treated them fairly (Rupp, Holub, & Grandey, 2007). Unfair acts are more memorable than typical encounters (Lind & Tyler, 1988), and employees may respond to customer unfairness by discussing incidents with other sympathetic employees, fostering negative word of mouth about customers.

When some customers systematically abuse company policies, such as retail return policies, companies are inclined to either clamp down with tougher rules or increase prices to cover losses. In effect, fair customers are penalized by the actions of unfair customers. Employees are put on the defensive and can become more sensitive to customer manipulation, and more inclined to question the sincerity of customers' communications and the motives that lie behind their actions (Tyler & Bies, 1990). The dynamic can turn adversarial. In short, both employees and customers pay for other customers' misdeeds.

3. Types of Unfair Customers

Over the last 30 years, justice research has focused on three types of justice. *Distributive justice* relates to the outcomes of decisions or allocations; *procedural justice* relates to the procedures used to arrive at those outcomes; and *interactional justice* relates to interpersonal treatment and communication. Interactional justice is demonstrated by interpersonal fairness (i.e., when individuals are treated with dignity and respect) and informational fairness (i.e., when communications are truthful and important decisions are explained) (Rupp & Spencer, 2006). Many studies have found that interactional injustice produces particularly strong responses.

Our exploration of customer unfairness led us to identify distinct types of problem customers. The categories we discuss are neither mutually exclusive nor comprehensive, but describe the most common and problematic types of unfair customers. Each category highlights a different facet of customer unfairness, although some behaviors may logically fit into more than one category. We exclude customers who use stolen credit cards, manipulate price tags, steal merchandise, and stage "accidents" in service facilities (see, for example, Fullerton & Punj, 2004). The scenarios we consider involve more ambiguity than clear-cut illegality.

3.1. Verbal Abusers

Verbal abusers lash out at employees in a blatantly offensive and disrespectful manner whether in face-to-face transactions, over the telephone, or via the Internet. The verbal abuser capitalizes on the power imbalance commonly present in service encounters: the customer who is "always right" has the upper hand by default and an opportunity to push the boundaries of fair behavior. One healthcare executive profiled this customer type as "patients and family members who belittle, demean, intimidate, and abuse staff members, and threaten litigation at the slightest lapse in service." Verbal abusers bully front-line employees who typically lack the freedom to defend themselves and, in fact, are expected not to react visibly to unfair treatment by customers. Given the importance of interactional injustice, it is no surprise that the verbal abuser's behavior can have such negative effects on employees.

Customers' verbal abuse of employees is probably more pervasive than most service industry executives would want to admit. There is no accepted protocol for managing a verbal abuse episode, and we suspect that most often this type of incident is not managed. Our favorite story involves the owner of a bicycle store well known for its dedication to customer service. A father was picking up a repaired bicycle for his daughter, who, without telling him, had approved the recommended replacement of both tires (a $40 service). Although the employee patiently and repeatedly explained that the purchase was approved and offered to further verify it, the customer made accusatory remarks and yelled at her angrily, saying at one point, "Either you think I'm stupid or you're stupid. You're trying to rip me off." At that point. Chris Zane, the store's owner, walked up to the customer and said, "I'm Chris Zane; get out of my store and tell all your friends!" After the customer wordlessly slapped $40 on the counter and stormed out, the besieged employee looked at Zane and asked "'. . . and tell all your friends'?"

Zane explained to her, and other employees who had gravitated to the front of the store, that he wanted it to be clear that he valued his employee infinitely more than a rude, belligerent customer. "I also explained that this was the first time I had ever thrown a customer out of the store and that I would not tolerate my employees being mistreated by anyone. . . . I believe that my employees need to know that I respect them and expect them to respect our customers. Simply, if I am willing to fire an employee for mistreating a customer (and I have), then I must also be willing to fire a customer for mistreating an employee."

Verbal abusers can also have a profound effect on other customers. This is illustrated by a customer who, during a lunch rush at a very busy restaurant location, insisted that his steak be prepared rare. Although a manager apologized and explained that each steak is prepared uniformly in order to maintain the best quality (and said there would be no charge for the lunch), the customer continued to voice his disapproval to the staff, creating a disturbance that distracted them and degraded the overall experience of the surrounding customers.

In another incident, two customers in a bar loudly criticized the bartender for assisting other patrons before them and then rebuked the restaurant manager who intervened to try to calm them down. The manager then went to the kitchen to check on the progress of their food; when he returned, the two customers were leaving and shouting obscenities as they walked out. A common device of the verbal abuser is the threat to report employees and/or their facility "to corporate," a way to prolong employee unease after the offensive incident is over.

3.2. Blamers

Whereas verbal abusers bring misery primarily to customer contact employees, blamers will indict a company's products, policies, and people at all levels for any perceived shortfall. With blamers, "the company is always wrong."

Because customers play a coproducer role in many services, they affect the service quality and final outcome. Blamers, however, never see themselves in any way responsible for the outcome, regardless of the scenario. Causal inferences or attributions individuals use to assess the failure of a product or service performance are based on the locus of blame and whether or not the incident could have been controlled (Sheppard, Lewicki, & Minton, 1992). From the blamer's perspective, not only is the company always at fault, but the perceived problem is always controllable.

Blamers are not discriminate about where they voice discord, and every service provider is familiar with this type of customer. A tennis coach had been working with an adult student for about 6 months when the student learned that an opponent in an upcoming match had worked briefly with the same coach in the past. The student asked for and received specific advice from the coach on how to win the match by attacking the opponent's greatest weaknesses. However, the opponent had corrected these weaknesses and much to the student's chagrin, she could find no way to beat her. In the clubhouse immediately after the match, she raged at her coach for not preparing her well, giving her poor information and lousy lessons, and causing her to lose the match.

In another example, a customer called the headquarters of a national casual dining chain to complain about the price of its cocktails. It seems the gentleman had spent $86 in the bar of this restaurant having drinks and appetizers after work the previous evening. He wanted to talk to someone about what he considered the excessive price of the drinks and how unfair he thought the cost. The switchboard operator noted the caller's angry tone and put him through to the president of the company.

The man reexplained to the president and said he could not believe the restaurant had charged him $7.50 for each of the beverages that he ordered. When asked how many he had consumed, the man said that was beside the point. The president asked the number in the man's party, and the man said only two. The president asked the man when he learned that the drinks were $7.50, which he said was after he paid the bill. The president then asked what the company might do to make it right. The customer replied that he wanted all of his money back; the president responded that this was unfair, as the customer and his guest had consumed enough appetizers and drinks to total $86. A full refund would not be equitable.

The customer became extremely angry, threatening to go online and destroy the company, report it to the Better Business Bureau, and picket in front of its restaurants for the next month. He raised his voice and asserted, "You will feel the effects of my negative PR efforts for a long time to come." Frustrated at the angry customer's threats, the president asked the customer how he could resolve this negative situation without giving the customer his money back for the food and drinks he consumed. The customer calmed down, thought about it, and told the president that if the company donated double the amount of the bill to the customer's favorite charity, he would consider the situation resolved. The president agreed to do so in order to move past the situation and end the disagreement.

The blamer is a particularly difficult type of customer for the healthcare industry. Patients who fail to take responsibility for their own health status often are blamers. Many such patients believe that a treatment cure exists for every condition and thus see no need to take measures to improve their own health. In one case, a patient was referred to a hospital's patient relations department after lodging serious complaints with the president's office. The patient claimed that his wound from surgery failed to heal because the staff ignored his complaints. In reality, the patient was noncompliant with recommended diet and wound care, refused to follow his doctor's recommendations for exercise and physical therapy, and failed to return for a follow-up appointment. At each point of contact, the patient threatened to hire a malpractice attorney.

This example may sound extreme, but in fact we heard a number of such stories. One healthcare professional noted, "I have been in patient relations for more than 10 years now, and I can attest to the fact that these patients are a huge burden on the healthcare system. They tie up resources that could be used to improve services for all of our patients." An executive from a different healthcare institution expressed a similar view: "I hear from the same patients over and over again, and once a resolution is offered, many times it's a prolonged argument because it's their way or no way. Unfortunately, these cases are no longer rare."

3.3. Rule Breakers

Rule breakers readily ignore policies and procedures when they find them to be inconvenient or at odds with their own goals. Rule breakers generally ignore the honor code by which other customers abide. In chronic cases, a rule breaker may be a mild version of a con artist. Rule breakers are not concerned with equity, which is the first principle of distributive justice. Equity exists in an exchange when participants' rewards equal their contributions; rule breakers seek to optimize their rewards at the expense of the company. This not only harms the company, but also puts company employees in a tenuous and uncomfortable situation as they attempt to protect their employer from customer wrongdoing.

The damage done by rule breakers varies, of course, based on the nature of the rules and polices that are being broken. A restaurant that offers "all you can eat" shrimp entrees encounters some patrons who share with their tablemates, even though the menu clearly states that the price is per person. Managers are not quick to put servers in the awkward position of having to remind guests they are breaking the rule, but will do so if the "sharing" gets out of hand.

A retailer with a catalog operation is subject to "customers who bend the facts" (in the words of one executive) when post-delivery complainers assert that a telephone sales associate told them that shipping was free. When this happens, a company representative will listen to a tape of the original call and will usually hear the shipping charges discussed. For smaller transactions with first-time customers, the retailer apologizes, deducts the shipping charge, and restates the shipping fee policy for future transactions. For larger transactions, the customer is told that the call was reviewed and the company is not sure why there was confusion. Once customers realize that a company representative has reviewed the call and knows what actually was said, they rarely demand a shipping refund. "It's a nice way of saying we know what happened without becoming confrontational," explains a company manager.

One type of rule breaker can be termed a *rule maker*. Rule makers expect to be exempted from the rules and demand special treatment because of perceived superior status. Both rule breakers and rule makers demonstrate unfairness to other customers who are behaving according to norms and convention. When certain customers are allowed to break the rules because of their social or financial status, the equality principle of distributive justice is defied (Grover, 1991). A hospital executive describes the rule maker in this way:

"We have had patients who believe that there is some special level of care that we are constantly holding back, and if we knew how special they were that they would get this special executive level care. This is common in the family of trustees and board members. These are families that expect to be cared for only by departmental chairmen. We have coined the concept *chairman syndrome*."

Often, it is the family-member-turned-advocate who demands to make the rules. For example, a patient's daughter insisted, "I want all of the labs printed out each day and handed to me when I walk in in the morning." A patient's son threatened, "I am an attorney and I demand to know what is going on with my mother!" A corporate chairman transferred his child by private jet to a hospital in another city when his company's physicians (nonpediatric, without privileges to practice in the hospital) were not allowed to direct the team of hospital physicians who were treating the child. These scenarios seem almost amusing until one considers the extent to which medical staff members and other hospital patients may be adversely affected by this disregard for the rules.

3.4. Opportunists

Opportunists have their antennae up for easy paths to personal financial gain. This customer's modus operandi can be demanding compensation by fabricating or exaggerating problems or flaws in a product or service. While this type of opportunist stiffs the company, there is a second type that stiffs "the little guy." These penny-ante opportunists, for example, don't tip (or don't adequately tip) service employees because they don't have to; that is, they can get away with it. This behavior is distasteful because, like many cases of verbal abuse, it hurts front-line employees whose tips often represent a significant percentage of their pay.

Opportunists frequently use gamesmanship to optimize their gain. A customer observed a plumbing problem in a restaurant restroom and complained to the manager, who called a plumbing service for the repair, and sent an employee to clean up. The customer contacted the company's customer relations office, complained about the state of the restroom, and requested a refund for his party's $80 meal. In response, the company sent $30 in gift certificates, in addition to an $80 check and an apology. The customer called the company again, stating that $30 was not enough to cause him to return to the restaurant because it would not cover the cost of his dining companions' meals. He was persistent, calling several times to express his displeasure in the amount of the gift certificates. In turn, the company sent an additional $50 in gift certificates, bringing the total compensation to $160, a nice return for encountering a plumbing problem.

The opportunist may not be a chronic gold digger, but rather just someone who recognizes an opportunity to take financial advantage of a company's service failure and recovery efforts. For example, when an ambulatory surgery patient complained to her hospital that her lingerie had been lost, she was offered reimbursement. She claimed that the cost was $400 and, because this was an unusually high amount, the hospital inquired about the value of the items. The patient said she had not kept the receipts. To maintain good will, the hospital paid the $400 and apologized.

The opportunist doesn't require a service failure to take action. Some users of professional services, for example, maneuver to gain pro bono consultation from a prior provider. A communications coach periodically receives "pick your brain" phone calls from former clients. Because these customers don't intend to pay for this "informal" advice, the consultant is forced into an awkward position by clients attempting to exploit the relationship.

3.5. Returnaholics

This customer is a hybrid, with traits common to rule breakers and opportunists but engaged in a specific type of activity: returning products to stores. Returnaholics are rule breakers in that they don't adhere to the spirit of the company's return policies, whereby returns are accepted for defective products, a postpurchase change of mind, and gift exchange. In many cases, the returnaholic never intends to keep the product to begin with. Returnaholics are opportunists because they exploit retailer return policies for their own benefit. There are two types of returnaholics: situational and chronic.

Situational returnaholics become active under certain conditions. For example, one retailer's sales of equipment such as snow blowers, generators, and chainsaws would spike just before a major weather event but then fall precipitously shortly thereafter when many customers returned new *and* used equipment, and even products such as ice melt and flashlights, demanding refunds. It was not unusual for a store to see more than half the generators sold the week before a storm returned within 2 weeks after the storm. This phenomenon was a painful and expensive exercise for the retailer and its vendors. Reluctantly, the company adopted a stricter return policy covering specific items to better manage after-the-storm return rates.

Some situational returners use an item until it is damaged or worn out and then return it for a full refund or new item, claiming it is defective because it "should have held up better." They expect the refund to be 100 percent of purchase price because they believe that retailers carry a manufacturer's warranty for all items indefinitely.

Chronic, or serial, returnaholics are referred to by some store operators as "rental" customers. One customer of a men's shoe and accessories chain started shopping at two of the company's stores in 2001. The customer would often buy a product in store A and return it (after wearing it) to store B, using a different name for the return transaction. He also would complain to upper management about quality or the service he received in hopes of getting discounts on future purchases. The company realized this pattern of behavior spanned 6 years, once it figured out that all of this activity involved one customer rather than two. In that period, the customer had purchased 23 pairs of shoes and returned 17 for net sales of $381 (which obviously did not come close to covering the cost of 17 pairs of worn and returned shoes). When the customer was contacted about his serial returning behavior, he became angry; he was told it was obvious the company could not please him and that it could no longer afford to do business with him.

Chronic returnaholics can be very crafty. Some purchase expensive items with credit cards to earn rewards or airline points and then return the merchandise during certain periods of the billing cycle when the points will not be removed from their account. Some purchase large quantities of items, try to sell them on the Internet or in private shops, and then return them for a refund if they don't sell. Some interior designers will purchase items for a specific event, such as an open house or a staged model home, and then return the items for a refund. These are but a few examples of how chronic returnaholics operate.

4. What Managers Can Do

Unfair customers need to be dealt with effectively. They can be a big problem for poorly managed companies with customer unfriendly policies and practices that provoke retaliatory customer behavior. Unfair customers also can bedevil well-managed companies that devote considerable energy and investment to serving customers superbly. After all, these companies build their culture on delivering an excellent experience and value to customers. As a long-time operations executive of one of America's most admired supermarket chains told us:

"I think companies that are truly committed to customer service have a difficult time dealing with unfair customers. We always [tell] our store managers that we will give the unfair customer the benefit of the doubt one or two times. The third time, we [will] fire them as a customer."

So, what should managers do about unfair customers?

4.1. Manage Customers to a Standard of Behavior

Companies cannot build a reputation for service excellence unless, in addition to serving customers competently, they treat them with respect and commitment. Treating customers with respect and commitment requires an organizational culture in which employees, themselves, are treated with respect and commitment. Managers that allow customers to behave badly (e.g., to verbally abuse employees, to create a disturbance, to rip off the company) in the name of "customer service" undermine the organizational culture upon which excellent service depends. Appeasing a customer who doesn't deserve appeasement does not go unnoticed within the organization. The bicycle shop owner who ordered an abusive customer out of the store strengthened his culture that day, rather than weakened it.

Just as managers need to manage employees, they should also "manage" customers when the situation warrants. A good manager certainly would intervene if made aware of an employee who treated customers rudely or broke important company policies. Likewise, a manager should be ready to intervene when made aware of customer misbehavior. Effective "customer management," as illustrated by the manager's intervention in the bar ruckus, demonstrated to employees and nearby customers that the disruptive party's behavior was unacceptable and would not be allowed to continue. If the customers did quiet down, the bartender could more easily interact with them because the manager, and not he, addressed their misbehavior.

4.2. Don't Penalize Fair Customers

Companies should design their business operations for the vast majority of their customers who are fair and responsible, rather than for the unfair minority. Firms should not allow unfair customer behavior to instigate needlessly restrictive policies that disrespect the good intentions of most customers. The better approach, for the business culture and reputation, is to deal fairly but firmly with unfair customers specifically.

The retailer experiencing heavy returns of outdoor power equipment following a major storm illustrates this guideline. The retailer could have done nothing, in effect enabling unreasonable customer behavior. Alternatively, the company could have installed a more restrictive return policy for all merchandise, which would have affected all customers, not just returnaholics, and likely hurt the company's reputation for customer service. The company's implementation of a more restrictive return policy for specific products with high afterstorm return rates made returns more difficult for situational returnaholics. The new policy was designed specifically to deal with opportunistic customers.

The goodwill created by *not* treating all customers as untrustworthy is an investment worth making. A supermarket operations executive illustrates this lesson with the following story:

"When I was at [Company X], we had a policy that if customers forgot their checkbook, we would let them leave with their groceries after filling out a simple IOU. The great majority of customers would immediately return to pay the amount. This policy created a great deal of positive goodwill. However, every year we had to write off a significant amount of loss because some customers would not come back to pay off the IOU. I remember 1 year it was in excess of $30,000. We would make attempts to recover the money, but I don't recall trying to prosecute anyone for it. Our CFO wanted to stop giving the IOUs, but I would not let him. I treated it as a marketing expense because it created so much goodwill. Interestingly, when we started accepting credit, I thought that the loss number would plunge, assuming customers would carry their credit card and use that instead of a check. However, the loss number remained the same. I believe there will always be customers who will take advantage of you. They are very intentional about their unfairness. The loss incurred by them has to be built into your financial model because you should not penalize the great customers for the deeds of a few bad customers."

4.3. Prepare for Customer Unfairness

Companies should strive to both reduce the frequency of unfair customer episodes and effectively manage specific incidents. This requires advance planning. Managers need to determine the kinds of situations that are most likely to produce unfair customer behavior, given the nature of the company's business. Managers can determine at-risk situations for unfairness by: (1) using past experiences to identify conditions in which customer and company goals might conflict; (2) soliciting employee input on causes of customer unfairness; and (3) surveying customers previously involved in unfairness incidents to gain their perspective on what happened and why. Once at-risk exchanges are identified, managers can evaluate the firm's existing practices to consider needed changes. Employee and customer input can again be helpful at this stage (Seiders & Berry, 1998).

Preparing for customer unfairness also involves investing in education and training of front-line employees and managers on how to prevent and manage the most likely types of incidents. Particular emphasis should be placed on the rationale for company policies that respond to customer misbehavior, or that may encourage it. Employees who intervene need to be able to explain the company's position effectively, which makes communications training for dealing with problem customers a priority. Contact personnel (and their managers) would benefit from focused training on the best ways to interact with verbal abusers,

rule breakers, returnaholics, and other problem customers. Organizational justice researchers recommend the use of explanation as an impression management strategy (Sitkin & Bies, 1993). Explanations have been found to diffuse negative reactions and convey respect, among other positive outcomes (Seiders & Berry, 1998), although they will not always be effective with unfair customers.

Collecting pertinent information is another way to prepare for customer unfairness. Information can clarify the appropriate company response to a customer incident. The catalog retailer which captures information on every shipping transaction is better prepared to assess posttransaction claims. Has the customer complained about this issue before? If so, did the company explain its policy? What is the customer's purchase history? "Research is a great way to keep things on the up and up," explains a company executive. "It's on a case-by-case basis."

4.4. Don't Reward Misbehavior

As mentioned, companies that take pride in the quality of their service often struggle to satisfactorily resolve acts of customer opportunism. Such companies are so culturally focused on serving customers well and giving them the benefit of the doubt when problems arise that they may offer more than they should to reach resolution. Doing more than should be done for an unfair customer rewards misbehavior and encourages future incidents.

Companies need to respond to customer unfairness with fairness—and firmness. They should respond to unreasonableness with reason. It isn't easy. The case of the restaurant bathroom plumbing problem is instructive. The customer had a legitimate complaint about the state of the restroom, but then used the incident opportunistically to extract as much as possible from the restaurant. The company's first response of a full refund for the party's meal, a small gift certificate, and an apology was fair. The additional gift certificates went beyond fair. The second helping of gift certificates was excessive, reinforcing customer opportunism. Companies need to be willing to cut the cord with unfair customers.

Sometimes unfair customers recant when dealt with appropriately, as shown by a postscript to the bicycle story. The abusive customer phoned the owner to apologize three hours after being told to leave the store, explaining that he had argued with his wife prior to visiting the store. Once he returned home and verified the accuracy of the store employee's explanation, he realized he had been unreasonable. He asked that the store not blame the daughter for his actions and that he be allowed to shop in the store again. He also commented that he respected the owner for supporting his employee, even if it might mean losing a customer. The owner thanked him for the call, welcomed him back to the store, and indicated that the apology would be conveyed to the employee.

5. Rethinking Old Wisdom

Following the old wisdom—the customer is always right—has operated as the basic rule in business for so long that it has become entrenched as an "absolute truth." The practical reality, however, is that sometimes the customer is wrong by behaving unfairly.

Customer unfairness can exact a heavy cost. Company goodwill, employee relations, financial position, and service to responsible customers can deteriorate when customers engage in unfair tactics such as verbal abuse, blaming, rule breaking, opportunism, and "returnaholism."

Companies must acknowledge the unfair behavior of certain customers and manage them effectively. Some customers may need to be fired. Denying the existence and impact of unfair customers erodes the ethics of fairness upon which great service companies thrive.

References

Fullerton, R. A., & Punj, G. (2004). Repercussions of promoting an ideology of consumption: Consumer misbehavior. *Journal of Business Research, 57*(11), 1239–1249.

Grandey, A. A., Dickter, D. N., & Sin, H. P. (2004). The customer is not always right: Customer aggression and emotion regulation of service employees. *Journal of Organizational Behavior, 25*(3), 397–418.

Grover, S. L. (1991). Predicting the perceived fairness of parental leave policies. *Journal of Applied Psychology, 76*(2), 247–255.

Lind, E. A., & Tyler, T. R. (1988). *The social psychology of procedural justice.* New York: Plenum Press.

Rupp, D. E., & Spencer, S. (2006). When customers lash out: The effects of customers' interactional injustice on emotional labor and the mediating role of discrete emotions. *Journal of Applied Psychology, 91*(4), 971–978.

Rupp, D. E., Holub, A. S., & Grandey, A. A. (2007). A cognitive–emotional theory of customer injustice and emotional labor. In D. De Cremer (Ed.), *Advances in the psychology of justice and affect* (pp. 199–226). Charlotte, NC: Information Age Publishing.

Seiders, K., & Berry, L. L. (1998). Service fairness: What it is and why it matters. *Academy of Management Executive, 12*(2), 8–21.

Sheppard, B. H., Lewicki, R. J., & Minton, J. W. (1992). *Organizational justice: The search for fairness in the workplace.* New York: Lexington Books.

Sitkin, S. B., & Bies, R. J. (1993). Social accounts in conflict situations: Using explanations to manage conflict. *Human Relations, 46*(3), 349–370.

Tyler, T. R., & Bies, R. J. (1990). Beyond formal procedures: The interpersonal context of procedural justice. In J. Carroll (Ed.), *Advances in applied social psychology: Business settings* (pp. 77–98). Hillsdale, NJ: Lawrence Erlbaum Associates.

Critical Thinking

1. Which ethical philosophy or perspective underlies the insistence on fairness?

2. Which party has more "right" to fair treatment—the customer or the employee? Under what circumstances would you fire a customer?

Create Central

www.mhhe.com/createcentral

Internet References

Association of Consumer Research
http://www.acrwebsite.org/search/view-conference-proceedings.aspx?Id=8065

Bermuda Sun
http://www.bermudasun.bm/Content/Default/Homepage-Article-Rotator/Article/Consumer-Affairs--How-to-combat-unethical-customers/-3/1288/74219

International Excess
http://www.ourinfoshare.com/tag/unethical-customers/

Article

Prepared by: Eric Teoro, *Lincoln Christian University*

Marketing to Children: Accepting Responsibility

GAEL O'BRIEN

Learning Outcomes

After reading this article, you will be able to:

- Describe the debate between McDonald's and industry watchdogs regarding McDonald's marketing practices to children.

- Understand the potential impact of marketing to children.

- Discuss who is primarily responsible for the marketing messages children receive—parents or companies.

For all the significant achievements companies are making as corporate citizens, the issue of their real impact on society—and what as a result society may actually need back from them—raises the question of whether we are adequately defining what is expected by being socially responsible.

The issue of marketing to children really brings that into focus; with food marketing a timely lens, the issue of **obesity** a hot health care crisis, and McDonald's handling of responsibility, as one of the world's largest fast food chains, a case in point.

As background, McDonald's Happy Meals for children with toys has come under attack. San Francisco is one of the cities that has voted to **ban selling toys with fast food** for children that exceed certain levels of salt, fat, calories and sugar. McDonald's was accused of **deceptive marketing practices to children** over the lure of toys as an inducement to buy Happy Meals. Healthy alternatives are available, apple slices in place of fries and milk instead of soda—if kids are willing to eat them. But, there is still the issue of **high sodium content in burgers**.

At McDonald's May 17, 2011 shareholder meeting, activists focused attention on McDonald's marketing to children. In February 2011, in anticipation of McDonald's shareholder meeting, **Corporate Accountability International** launched a campaign to fire Ronald McDonald, the clown mascot for the last nearly 50 years, and encourage headquarters to stop marketing to children by delivering petitions to individual restaurants. They also asked the chain to address directly the relationship of fast food to obesity. Beginning the campaign in a **Portland, Oregon suburb**, by May they had gathered 20,000 parents' and community residents' signatures on petitions which they delivered to the shareholder meeting.

In Oregon, McDonald's threw down the gauntlet, and **affirmed Ronald's job security**, saying he is "the heart and soul of Ronald McDonald House Charities, which lends a helping hand to families in their time of need." The response demonstrated how McDonald's infuses the emotional and the marketing: Ronald, the symbol to families dealing with sick and dying children, is also the brand, signifying the food and fun atmosphere to eat it in.

A letter signed by 600 health professionals and organizations, critical of the link between fast food and obesity, was read at the shareholder meeting. It had run as full page ads in newspapers across the country. In addition, **shareholder Proposal 11**, by the Sisters of St. Francis of Philadelphia, requested McDonald's undertake a report on its "policy responses to public concerns about the linkage of fast food to childhood obesity, diet-related diseases and other impacts on children's health." The proposal was soundly defeated.

In **his remarks at the meeting**, CEO Jim Skinner asserted the company's right to advertise freely, to offer its menu and lifestyle selections, and leave to parent's the right to chose what their children eat, saying it is up to personal responsibility. McDonald's **Corporate Social Responsibility (CSR) information indicates** the company serves "a balanced array of quality food products and provides the information to make individual choices."

Marketing to children, whether the subject is food, toys, clothes or anything else raises enormous concerns for Susan Linn, director and cofounder of a national coalition of health care professionals, educators, parents, and others called the **Campaign for a Commercial-Free Childhood**.

"There is no ethical, moral, social, or spiritual justification for targeting children in advertising and marketing, said Linn recently at a **Conscious Capitalism Conference**. Linn, who also teaches psychiatry at Harvard Medical School, cited obesity and a number of other issues impacting children and society that stem from targeting kids, including youth violence, sexualization, underage drinking and smoking, excessive materialism, and the erosion of creativity.

"Kids are inundated with advertising in a way never before," she said in an interview. "I don't believe in any advertising to children."

The food industry has been effective in limiting the Federal Trade Commission's ability to regulate marketing to children, and unless Congress changes the rules, companies self-regulate. I asked Linn what protection the **Children's Food and Beverage Initiative** provides. Linn indicated it didn't provide any because it has no actual authority and the standards are voluntary.

The Coalition advocates that children be able to develop a healthy relationship to food, but McDonald's, Linn says, entices kids not because of the food but because of the toys and the message of happiness that is part of their advertising.

Marketing to children is inherently deceptive because kids take things literally and media characters play a big role in their lives, Linn says. They don't understand persuasive intent until they are 8 years old; and the brain's capacity for judgment isn't developed until their 20s which makes them very vulnerable as marketing targets.

Of course parents are accountable for educating their children about responsible choices and healthy foods. And, they have the choice not to take their kids to McDonald's. Except . . . if you serve **more than 64 million people in 117 countries each day** and many of your restaurants are open 24/7, the chain has created a compelling draw.

Add to that, a **recent report** by Yale University's Rudd Center for Food Policy and Obesity that more fast food marketing dollars for toys are being spent (to get kids in the door) while marketing efforts to promote healthy meals haven't really increased.

I asked Cheryl Kiser, the former managing director of Boston College's Center for Corporate Citizenship for her take on marketing to kids. "CSR has had an enormous influence helping companies reduce their global footprint by addressing human rights and other issues," said Kiser, now the managing director of **Babson College's Lewis Institute**. But "companies are socializing kids and the imprint on those kids is not necessarily creating common good outcomes."

"Having a young over-sexualized population of kids who have no awareness of the implications or consequences of their choices is unhealthy," she adds. "Foods appealing to kids because they are tasty, high fat and zero nutrition is also unhealthy. When we start to imprint early in behaviors and consumer choices things that don't lead to personal and common good, and that need to be corrected in teen years by good CSR programs, is CSR doing its job?"

Critical Thinking

1. What limits, if any, should be imposed on businesses regarding marketing to children? Explain your rationale.

2. To what degree are parents responsible for the marketing messages to which their children are exposed? Why are they thusly responsible?

3. Debate with a colleague or fellow student on the permissibility of marketing to children.

Create Central

www.mhhe.com/createcentral

Internet References

Association for Consumer Research
http://www.acrwebsite.org/search/view-conference-proceedings.aspx?Id=11328
Campaign for a Commercial-Free Childhood
http://www.commercialfreechildhood.org/
Wall Street Journal
http://online.wsj.com/news/articles/SB10001424052748703509104576329610340358394?mod=dist_smartbrief&mg=reno64-wsj&url=http%3A%2F%2Fonline.wsj.com%2Farticle%2FSB10001424052748703509104576329610340358394.html%3Fmod%3Ddist_smartbrief

---

GAEL O'BRIEN is a *Business Ethics Magazine* columnist. Gael is a thought leader on building leadership, trust, and reputation and writes **The Week in Ethics**.

Article   Prepared by: Eric Teoro, *Lincoln Christian University*

First, Make Money. Also, Do Good

Steve Lohr

Learning Outcomes

After reading this article, you will be able to:

- Recognize that profits are good and that they should be a priority of any business.

- Recognize that there are profitable ventures in addressing social concerns.

Corporate social responsibility efforts have always struck me as the modern equivalent of John D. Rockefeller handing out dimes to the common folk. They may be well intentioned, but they often seem like small gestures at the margins of what companies are really trying to do: make money.

As well they should, an argument most famously made by the Nobel laureate Milton Friedman decades ago. He called social responsibility programs "hypocritical window-dressing" in an article he wrote for The New York Times Magazine in 1970, titled "The Social Responsibility of Business Is to Increase Its Profits."

But Michael E. Porter, a Harvard Business School professor, may have an answer to the Friedman principle. Mr. Porter is best known for his original ideas about corporate strategy and the economic competition among nations and regions. Recently, however, he has been promoting a concept he calls "shared value."

Earlier this year, Mr. Porter and Mark R. Kramer, a consultant and a senior fellow in the corporate social responsibility program at the Kennedy School of Government at Harvard, laid out their case in a lengthy article in the Harvard Business Review, "Creating Shared Value: How to Reinvent Capitalism—and Unleash a Wave of Innovation and Growth." Since then, Mr. Porter and Mr. Kramer have been championing the shared-value thesis in conferences, meetings with corporate leaders, and even a conversation with White House advisers.

Shared value is an elaboration of the notion of corporate self-interest—greed, if you will. The idea that companies can do well by doing good is certainly not new. It is an appealing proposition that over the years has been called "triple bottom line" (people, planet, profit), "impact investing," and "sustainability"—all describing corporate initiatives that address social concerns including environmental pollution, natural-resource depletion, public health, and the needs of the poor.

The shared-value concept builds on those ideas, but it emphasizes profit-making not just as a possibility but as a priority. Shared value, Mr. Porter says, points toward "a more sophisticated form of capitalism," in which "the ability to address societal issues is integral to profit maximization instead of treated as outside the profit model."

Social problems are looming market opportunities, according to Mr. Porter and Mr. Kramer. They note that while government programs and philanthropy have a place—beyond dimes, Mr. Rockefeller created a path-breaking foundation—so, increasingly, does capitalism.

The shared-value concept is not a moral stance, they add, and companies will still behave in their self-interest in ways that draw criticism, like aggressive tax avoidance and lobbying for less regulation. "This is not about companies being good or bad," Mr. Kramer says. "It's about galvanizing companies to exploit the market in addressing social problems."

The pair point to promising signs that more and more companies are pursuing market strategies that fit the shared-value model.

Several years ago, executives at General Electric began looking across its portfolio of industrial and consumer businesses, eyeing ways to apply new technology to reduce energy consumption. They were prompted by corporate customers voicing concerns about rising electrical and fuel costs, and by governments pushing for curbs on carbon emissions.

The result was G.E.'s "ecomagination" program, a business plan as well as a marketing campaign. In recent years, the company has invested heavily in technology to lower its products' energy consumption, and the use of water and other resources in manufacturing.

To count in the program, a product must deliver a significant energy savings or environmental benefit over previous designs. G.E. hired an outside environmental consulting firm, GreenOrder, to help in measuring performance. To date, more than 100 G.E. products have qualified, from jet engines to water filtration equipment to light bulbs. In 2010, such products generated sales of $18 billion, up from $10 billion in 2005, when the program began.

"We did it from a business standpoint from Day 1," says Jeffrey R. Immelt, G.E.'s chief executive. "It was never about corporate social responsibility."

Technology has opened the door to markets that have shared-value characteristics. For decades, I.B.M. sold its computers, software, and services to city governments around the world, though mainly for back-office chores like managing payrolls. But the Internet, the Web, electronic sensors, and steady advances in computing have helped transform I.B.M.'s role, as it now helps cities track and analyze all kinds of data to improve services.

"We've moved from the back office to the core mission of cities—managing traffic, monitoring public health, optimizing water use, and crime-fighting," says Jon C. Iwata, a senior vice president.

I.B.M. is now working with about 2,000 cities worldwide as part of its "Smarter Cities" business, which began 3 years ago. One advanced project is in the sprawling city of Rio de Janeiro, where I.B.M. is designing a computerized command center. It is intended to pull data from dozens of city agencies, as well as weather stations and webcams. One assignment is to closely track heavy rainfall and to predict its impact—where flooding might occur, how traffic should be rerouted, and what neighborhoods may need to be evacuated. The goal is to predict and prepare for the kind of mudslides and floods that killed hundreds of people in April 2010 and left 15,000 homeless.

The evolution of low-cost Internet and mobile phone technology has also let Intuit pursue opportunities with shared-value attributes. The company offers free online income-tax preparation software and filing services for lower-income households (now earning $31,000 or less). Since 1999, nearly 13 million people have taken advantage of the service.

The cost is relatively inexpensive for Intuit, as the service exploits the efficiency of online distribution; the charge for paying customers is $20 to $50. And the program blurs the line between charity and marketing, because millions of

people who are sampling the company's product, may well become paying customers as their incomes rise.

In India, Intuit has begun offering a free information service for farmers that can be accessed on any cellphone. Part-time workers check crop prices at local markets and send the information to Intuit. The company then relays the latest, local price quotations in text messages to subscribing farmers. As a result, the farmers can make smarter decisions about when and where to sell their produce.

The service in India began last year, and 300,000 farmers now use it. In follow-up surveys, farmers report that their earnings are up 25 percent, says Scott Cook, the founder of Intuit and chairman of the executive committee. The company, he adds, is testing ways to make money off the service, perhaps with text ads for simple tractors and fertilizers.

Mr. Cook points to other new business forays that are part of the same strategy. One is an Intuit health debit card for American small businesses that want to pay for some of their employees' medical care but cannot afford conventional health insurance.

"We look for places we can use our strengths as a company to help solve big problems," he says. "You can call that shared value if you like. But I look at it as the business we're in."

Critical Thinking

1. Explain the concept of making money first while doing good along the way.
2. What is Porter's "shared value" concept?
3. How is the shared value concept an elaboration of corporate self-interest?

Create Central

www.mhhe.com/createcentral

Internet References

Forbes
http://www.forbes.com/sites/csr/2012/06/04/what-is-creating-shared-value/
Harvard Business Review
http://hbr.org/2011/01/the-big-idea-creating-shared-value
Shared Value Iniative
https://www.sharedvalue.org

Article   Prepared by: Eric Teoro, *Lincoln Christian University*

Doing Good to Do Well

Corporate Employees Help and Scope Out Opportunities in Developing Countries.

ANNE TERGESEN

Learning Outcomes

After reading this article, you will be able to:

- Describe initiatives by companies sending "volunteers" overseas to address social needs.

- Recognize the value to companies and employees in engaging in meeting social needs.

L ast fall, Laura Benetti spent 4 weeks in rural India, helping women examine stitchery and figure out prices for garments to be sold in local markets.

After working nine-hour days, she and nine colleagues would sleep in a lodge frequented by locals that had spotty access to hot water and electricity. Ms. Benetti, a 27-year-old customs and international trade coordinator for Dow Corning Corp., considered it a plum assignment.

Dow Corning is among a growing number of large corporations—including PepsiCo Inc., FedEx Corp., Intel Corp., and Pfizer Inc.—that are sending small teams of employees to developing countries such as India, Ghana, Brazil, and Nigeria to provide free consulting services to nonprofits and other organizations. A major goal: to scope out business opportunities in hot emerging markets.

Despite the promise of long workdays in less-than-cushy surroundings, many employees consider the stints prize postings. There are usually many more applicants than spaces: Intel, for example, says about 5 percent of its applicants win spots in its Education Service Corps.

Though referred to as "volunteer" posts, employees usually continue to receive their regular salaries during the stints, which typically last 2 to 4 weeks. They appeal to employees looking to develop new skills and donate time and expertise to those in need—or simply take a break from their routines.

"It gives more meaning to your career," Ms. Benetti says.

At least 27 Fortune 500 companies currently operate such programs, up from 21 in April and six in 2006, according to a survey by CDC Development Solutions, a Washington, DC, nonprofit that designs and manages these programs.

At a cost of $5,000 to over $20,000 per employee, the programs require a significant investment. It costs International Business Machines Corp., which has the largest such corporate volunteer operation, roughly $5 million a year.

IBM has sent 1,400 employees abroad with its Corporate Service Corps since 2008. Its projects have produced plans to reform Kenya's postal system and develop an eco-tourism industry in Tanzania.

IBM credits its program with generating about $5 million in new business so far, including a contract, awarded in April 2010, to manage two public service programs for Nigeria's Cross River State, says Stan Litow, vice president for corporate citizenship.

Silicone supplier Dow Corning plans to evaluate 15 new business-related ideas generated by the 20 employees it has sent to India since September 2010, says Laura Asiala, director of corporate citizenship. Ms. Asiala declined to discuss specifics, but says the company has "identified opportunities" in affordable housing, energy, and other sectors, thanks to volunteers' observations.

The programs drum up good public relations, both internally and externally, via positive media coverage and blogs many participants write from the field.

Companies "gain local name recognition" in the markets they wish to break into, says Deirdre White, president and CEO of CDC Development Solutions.

Company officials also say the popular programs can help them recruit in-demand talent and retain valued employees.

Dow Corning accepted about 10 percent of the approximately 200 prospective volunteers who applied online for the trips it sponsored in 2010 and 2011. The company says it selects those with strong performance evaluations, and seeks a diverse mix of participants with varying tenure.

The overseas assignments can act as a training ground for future leaders. Caroline Roan, vice president of corporate responsibility and president of the Pfizer Foundation, says some of the 270 people the pharmaceutical giant has sent abroad describe the experience "as a mini-MBA."

"They build skills, in part because they are sometimes thrust into situations outside of their comfort zone, which tends to make people more creative," she says.

Chris Marquis, an associate professor at Harvard Business School, was hired by IBM in 2009 to survey its volunteers. His subsequent research shows that alumni of the program remain on the job longer than peers with similar performance and tenure.

"These are the stars at IBM," he says. "If by offering something like this they can retain these people for longer, it is a very smart investment."

Critical Thinking

1. Develop a brief report about the good-works projects of one of the companies named in the article. How do the good-works projects help the company to do well in the marketplace?

2. The article mentions that a major goal of sending employees abroad on good-works projects is "to scope out business opportunities in hot emerging markets." What do you think of this goal? Develop arguments defending the goal as well as denouncing the goal. Bring your arguments to class for class discussion.

3. Beyond the example given in the article of the various good-works projects, can you think of other good things companies might do in order to do well in the marketplace? Make a list of the other good things and bring your list to class discussion.

Create Central

www.mhhe.com/createcentral

Internet References

Fast Company Co.Exist
http://www.fastcoexist.com/1679510/corporate-volunteerism-should-be-part-of-corporate-social-responsibility

Itasca Project
http://www.theitascaproject.com/

Points of Light
http://www.pointsoflight.org/corporate-institute

Tergesen, Anne. From *The Wall Street Journal*, January 9, 2012. Copyright © 2012 by Dow Jones & Company, Inc. Reprinted by permission via Rightslink.

Unit 5

UNIT

Prepared by: Eric Teoro, *Lincoln Christian University*

Developing the Future Ethos and Social Responsibility of Business

Ethos can be defined as the fundamental character, spirit, or disposition of an individual, group, or culture. It informs, and is manifested in, one's beliefs, customs, aspirations, or practices. For business ethics ultimately to be meaningful, it must transcend momentary reactions or responses to ethical scandals. For business ethics ultimately to be meaningful, they must become part of an organization's ethos. They should guide member behavior on a daily, on-going basis. They should impact strategic decision-making, and shape an organization's interactions with all stakeholders. Business ethics should start at the top of an organization and filter throughout every level. They do not serve as a tactic to prevent legal action against an organization, though they might result in fewer lawsuits or governmental regulations and interventions. By their very nature, ethics should be proactive and normative, promoting good for its own sake.

The articles in this last unit explore how organizations can embed ethics into their corporate ethos. They provide examples of two business leaders, and how they set the tone for ethical behavior in their companies. They provide guidance on developing an ethical culture, from the types of questions one can ask of potential hires during an interview process to inculcating an ethical framework throughout the seven levels of corporate values. One article asks whether diversity should be a strategic goal, and if so, what should be the nature of that strategic goal be. Another article presents a history of fiduciary theory, and examines the relationship between fiduciary and corporate social responsibilities. How do business ethics guide board members when making decisions among competing stakeholder claims? The unit concludes with an article that poses the following question. When you look in the mirror, what kind of person do you want to see? It shares some of the managerial philosophy of Peter Drucker who believed that "management always deals with the nature of Man and (as all of us with any practical experience have learned), with Good and Evil as well."

Article   Prepared by: Eric Teoro, *Lincoln Christian University*

Creating an Ethical Culture

Values-based ethics programs can help employees judge right from wrong.

DAVID GEBLER, JD

Learning Outcomes

After reading this article, you will be able to:

- Describe the seven levels of corporate values and how they relate to each other.

- Develop a program for creating an ethical corporate culture.

While the fate of former Enron leaders Kenneth Lay and Jeffrey Skilling is being determined in what has been labeled the "Trial of the Century," former WorldCom managers are in jail for pulling off one of the largest frauds in history.

Yes, criminal activity definitely took place in these companies and in dozens more that have been in the news in recent years, but what's really important is to take stock of the nature of many of the perpetrators.

Some quotes from former WorldCom executives paint a different picture of corporate criminals than we came to know in other eras:

"I'm sorry for the hurt that has been caused by my cowardly behavior."
—*Scott Sullivan, CFO*

"Faced with a decision that required strong moral courage, I took the easy way out. . . . There are no words to describe my shame."
—*Buford Yates, director of general accounting*

"At the time I consider the single most critical character-defining moment of my life, I failed. It's something I'll take with me the rest of my life."
—*David Myers, controller*

These are the statements of good people gone bad. But probably most disturbing was the conviction of Betty Vinson, the senior manager in the accounting department who booked billions of dollars in false expenses. At her sentencing, US District Judge Barbara Jones noted that Vinson was among the lowest-ranking members of the conspiracy that led to the $11 billion fraud that sank the telecommunications company in 2002. Still, she said, "Had Ms. Vinson refused to do what she was asked, it's possible this conspiracy might have been nipped in the bud."

Judge Jones added that although Ms. Vinson "was among the least culpable members of the conspiracy" and acted under extreme pressure, "that does not excuse what she did."

Vinson said she improperly covered up expenses by drawing down reserve accounts—some completely unrelated to the expenses—and by moving expenses off income statements and listing them as assets on the balance sheet.

Also the company's former director of corporate reporting, Vinson testified at Bernie Ebbers's trial that, in choosing which accounts to alter, "I just really pulled some out of the air. I used some spreadsheets." She said she repeatedly brought her concerns to colleagues and supervisors, once describing the entries to a coworker as "just crazy." In spring 2002, she noted, she told one boss she would no longer make the entries. "I said that I thought the entries were just being made to make the income statement look like Scott wanted it to look."

Standing before the judge at her sentencing, Vinson said: "I never expected to be here, and I certainly won't do anything like this again." She was sentenced to 5 months in prison and 5 months of house arrest.

Pressure Reigns

While the judge correctly said that her lack of culpability didn't excuse her actions, we must carefully note that Betty

Vinson, as well as many of her codefendants, didn't start out as criminals seeking to defraud the organization. Under typical antifraud screening tools, she and others like her wouldn't have raised any red flags as being potential committers of corporate fraud.

Scott Sullivan was a powerful leader with a well-known reputation for integrity. If any of us were in Betty Vinson's shoes, could we say with 100 percent confidence that we would say "no" to the CFO if he asked us to do something and promised that he would take full responsibility for any fallout from the actions we were going to take?

Today's white-collar criminals are more likely to be those among us who are unable to withstand the blistering pressures placed on managers to meet higher and tougher goals. In this environment, companies looking to protect themselves from corporate fraud must take a hard look at their own culture. Does it promote ethical behavior, or does it emphasize something else?

In most companies, "ethics" programs are really no more than compliance programs with a veneer of "do the right thing" messaging to create an apparent link to the company's values. To be effective, they have to go deeper than outlining steps to take to report misconduct. Organizations must understand what causes misconduct in the first place.

We can't forget that Enron had a Code of Ethics. And it wasn't as if WorldCom lacked extensive internal controls. But both had cultures where engaging in unethical conduct was tacitly condoned, if not encouraged.

Building the Right Culture

Now the focus has shifted toward looking at what is going on inside organizations that's either keeping people from doing the right thing or, just as importantly, keeping people from doing something about misconduct they observe. If an organization wants to reduce the risk of unethical conduct, it must focus more effort on building the right culture than on building a compliance infrastructure.

The Ethics Resource Center's 2005 National Business Ethics Survey (NBES) clearly confirms this trend toward recognizing the role of corporate culture. Based on interviews with more than 3,000 employees and managers in the United States the survey disclosed that, despite the increase in the number of ethics and compliance program elements being implemented, desired outcomes, such as reduced levels of observed misconduct, haven't changed since 1994. Even more striking is the revelation that, although formal ethics and compliance programs have some impact, organizational culture has the greatest influence in determining program outcomes.

The Securities & Exchange Commission (SEC) and the Department of Justice have also been watching these trends. Stephen Cutler, the recently retired SEC director of the Division of Enforcement, was matter of fact about the importance of looking at culture when it came to decisions of whether or not to bring an action. "We're trying to induce companies to address matters of tone and culture. . . . What we're asking of that CEO, CFO, or General Counsel goes beyond what a perp walk or an enforcement action against another company executive might impel her to do. We're hoping that if she sees that a failure of corporate culture can result in a fine that significantly exceeds the proverbial 'cost of doing business,' and reflects a failure on her watch—and a failure on terms that everyone can understand: the company's bottom line—she may have a little more incentive to pay attention to the environment in which her company's employees do their jobs."

Measuring Success

Only lagging companies still measure the success of their ethics and compliance programs just by tallying the percentage of employees who have certified that they read the Code of Conduct and attended ethics and compliance training. The true indicator of success is whether the company has made significant progress in achieving key program outcomes. The National Business Ethics Survey listed four key outcomes that help determine the success of a program:

- Reduced misconduct observed by employees,
- Reduced pressure to engage in unethical conduct,
- Increased willingness of employees to report misconduct, and
- Greater satisfaction with organizational response to reports of misconduct.

What's going to move these outcomes in the right direction? Establishing the right culture.

Most compliance programs are generated from "corporate" and disseminated down through the organization. As such, measurement of the success of the program is often based on criteria important to the corporate office: how many employees certified the Code of Conduct, how many employees went through the training, or how many calls the hotline received.

Culture is different—and is measured differently. An organization's culture isn't something that's created by senior leadership and then rolled out. A culture is an objective picture of the organization, for better or worse. It's the sum total of all the collective values and behaviors of all employees, managers, and leaders. By definition, it can only be measured by criteria that reflect the individual values of all employees, so understanding cultural vulnerabilities that can lead to ethics issues requires knowledge of what motivates employees in the organization. Leadership must know how the myriad human behaviors and interactions fit together like puzzle pieces to create a whole picture. An organization moves toward an ethical culture only if it understands the full range of values and behaviors needed to meet its ethical goals. The "full-spectrum" organization is one that creates a positive sense of engagement and purpose that drives ethical behavior.

> **Leadership must know how the myriad human behaviors and interactions fit together like puzzle pieces to create a whole picture. An organization moves toward an ethical culture only if it understands the full range of values and behaviors needed to meet its ethical goals.**

Why is understanding the culture so important in determining the success of a compliance program? Here's an example: Most organizations have a policy that prohibits retaliation against those who bring forward concerns or claims. But creating a culture where employees feel safe enough to admit mistakes and to raise uncomfortable issues requires more than a policy and "Code training." To truly develop an ethical culture,

the organization must be aware of how its managers deal with these issues up and down the line and how the values they demonstrate impact desired behaviors. The organization must understand the pressures its people are under and how they react to those pressures. And it must know how its managers communicate and whether employees have a sense of accountability and purpose.

Categorizing Values

Determining whether an organization has the capabilities to put such a culture in place requires careful examination. Do employees and managers demonstrate values such as respect? Do employees feel accountable for their actions and feel that they have a stake in the success of the organization?

How does an organization make such a determination? One approach is to categorize different types of values in a way that lends itself to determining specific strengths and weaknesses that can be assessed and then corrected or enhanced.

The Culture Risk Assessment model presented in Figure 1 has been adapted from the Cultural Transformation Tools® developed by Richard Barrett & Associates. Such tools provide a comprehensive framework for measuring cultures by mapping values. More than 1,000 organizations in 24 countries have used this technique in the past 6 years. In fact, the international management consulting firm McKinsey & Co. has adopted it as its method of choice for mapping corporate cultures and measuring progress toward achieving culture change.

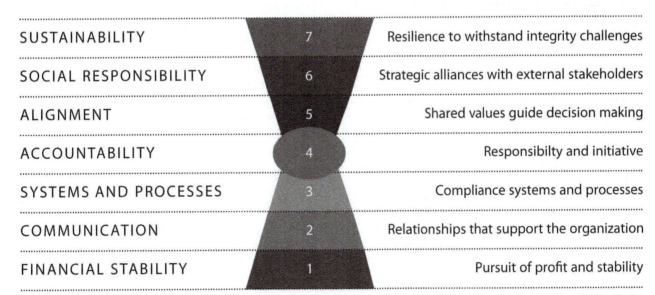

SUSTAINABILITY	7	Resilience to withstand integrity challenges
SOCIAL RESPONSIBILITY	6	Strategic alliances with external stakeholders
ALIGNMENT	5	Shared values guide decision making
ACCOUNTABILITY	4	Responsibilty and initiative
SYSTEMS AND PROCESSES	3	Compliance systems and processes
COMMUNICATION	2	Relationships that support the organization
FINANCIAL STABILITY	1	Pursuit of profit and stability

Based on Cultural Transformation Tools Seven Levels of Consciousness Model, Copyright Barrett Values Centre

Figure 1   Seven levels of an ethical organization.

The model is based on the principle, substantiated through practice, that all values can be assigned to one of seven categories:

Levels 1, 2, and 3—The Organization's Basic Needs

Does the organization support values that enable it to run smoothly and effectively? From an ethics perspective, is the environment one in which employees feel physically and emotionally safe to report unethical behavior and to do the right thing?

Level 1—Financial Stability. Every organization needs to make financial stability a primary concern. Companies that are consumed with just surviving struggle to focus enough attention on how they conduct themselves. This may, in fact, create a negative cycle that makes survival much more difficult. Managers may exercise excessive control, so employees may be working in an environment of fear.

In these circumstances, unethical or even illegal conduct can be rationalized. When asked to conform to regulations, organizations do the minimum with an attitude of begrudging compliance.

Organizations with challenges at this level need to be confident that managers know and stand within clear ethical boundaries.

Level 2—Communication. Without good relationships with employees, customers, and suppliers, integrity is compromised. The critical issue at this level is to create a sense of loyalty and belonging among employees and a sense of caring and connection between the organization and its customers.

The most critical link in the chain is between employees and their direct supervisors. If direct supervisors can't effectively reinforce messages coming from senior leadership, those messages might be diluted and confused by the time they reach line employees. When faced with conflicting messages, employees will usually choose to follow the lead of their direct supervisor over the words of the CEO that have been conveyed through an impersonal communication channel. Disconnects in how local managers "manage" these messages often mean that employees can face tremendous pressure in following the lead established by leadership.

Fears about belonging and lack of respect lead to fragmentation, dissension, and disloyalty. When leaders meet behind closed doors or fail to communicate openly, employees suspect the worst. Cliques form, and gossip becomes rife. When leaders are more focused on their own success, rather than the success of the organization, they begin to compete with each other.

Level 3—Systems and Processes. At this level, the organization is focused on becoming the best it can be through the adoption of best practices and a focus on quality, productivity, and efficiency.

Level 3 organizations have succeeded in implementing strong internal controls and have enacted clear standards of conduct. Those that succeed at this level are the ones that see

internal controls as an opportunity to create better, more efficient processes. But even those that have successfully deployed business processes and practices need to be alert to potentially limiting aspects of being too focused on processes. All organizations need to be alert to resorting to a "check-the-box" attitude that assumes compliance comes naturally from just implementing standards and procedures. Being efficient all too often leads to bureaucracy and inconsistent application of the rules. When this goes badly, employees lose respect for the system and resort to self-help to get things done. This can lead to shortcuts and, in the worst case, engaging in unethical conduct under the guise of doing what it takes to succeed.

Level 4—Accountability

The focus of the fourth level is on creating an environment in which employees and managers begin to take responsibility for their own actions. They want to be held accountable, not micromanaged and supervised every moment of every day. For an ethics and compliance program to be successful, all employees must feel that they have a personal responsibility for the integrity of the organization. Everyone must feel that his or her voice is being heard. This requires managers and leaders to admit that they don't have all the answers and invite employee participation.

Levels 5, 6, and 7—Common Good

Does the organization support values that create a collective sense of belonging where employees feel that they have a stake in the success of the ethics program?

Level 5—Alignment. The critical issue at this level is developing a shared vision of the future and a shared set of values. The shared vision clarifies the intentions of the organization and gives employees a unifying purpose and direction. The shared values provide guidance for making decisions.

The organization develops the ability to align decision making around a set of shared values. The values and behaviors must be reflected in all of the organization's processes and systems, with appropriate consequences for those who aren't willing to walk the talk. A precondition for success at this level is building a climate of trust.

Level 6—Social Responsibility. At this level, the organization is able to use its relationships with stakeholders to sustain itself through crises and change. Employees and customers see that the organization is making a difference in the world through its products and services, its involvement in the local community, or its willingness to fight for causes that improve humanity. They must feel that the company cares about them and their future. Companies operating at this level go the extra mile to make sure they are being responsible citizens. They support and encourage employees' activities in the community by providing time off for volunteer work and/or making a financial contribution to the charities that employees are involved in.

Level 7—Sustainability. To be successful at Level 7, organizations must embrace the highest ethical standards in all their interactions with employees, suppliers, customers, shareholders, and the community. They must always consider the long-term impact of their decisions and actions.

Employee values are distributed across all seven levels. Through surveys, organizations learn which values employees bring to the workplace and which values are missing. Organizations don't operate from any one level of values: They tend to be clustered around three or four levels. Most are focused on the first three: profit and growth (Level 1), customer satisfaction (Level 2), and productivity, efficiency, and quality (Level 3). The most successful organizations operate across the full spectrum with particular focus in the upper levels of consciousness—the common good—accountability, leading to learning and innovation (Level 4), alignment (Level 5), social responsibility (Level 6), and sustainability (Level 7).

Some organizations have fully developed values around Levels 1, 2, and 3 but are lacking in Levels 5, 6, and 7. They may have a complete infrastructure of controls and procedures but may lack the accountability and commitment of employees and leaders to go further than what is required.

Similarly, some organizations have fully developed values around Levels 5, 6, and 7 but are deficient in Levels 1, 2, and 3. These organizations may have visionary leaders and externally focused social responsibility programs, but they may be lacking in core systems that will ensure that the higher-level commitments are embedded into day-to-day processes.

Once an organization understands its values' strengths and weaknesses, it can take specific steps to correct deficient behavior.

Starting the Process

Could a deeper understanding of values have saved WorldCom? We will never know, but if the culture had encouraged open communication and fostered trust, people like Betty Vinson might have been more willing to confront orders that they knew were wrong. Moreover, if the culture had embodied values that encouraged transparency, mid-level managers wouldn't have been asked to engage in such activity in the first place.

The significance of culture issues such as these is also being reflected in major employee surveys that highlight what causes unethical behavior. According to the NBES, "Where top management displays certain ethics-related actions, employees are 50 percentage points less likely to observe misconduct." No other factor in any ethics survey can demonstrate such a drastic influence.

So how do compliance leaders move their organizations to these new directions?

1. *The criteria for success of an ethics program must be outcomes based.* Merely checking off program elements isn't enough to change behavior.

2. *Each organization must identify the key indicators of its culture.* Only by assessing its own ethical culture can a company know what behaviors are the most influential in effecting change.

3. *The organization must gauge how all levels of employees perceive adherence to values by others within the company.* One of the surprising findings of the NBES was that managers, especially senior managers, were out of touch with how nonmanagement employees perceived their adherence to ethical behaviors. Nonmanagers are 27 percentage points less likely than senior managers to indicate that executives engage in all of the ethics-related actions outlined in the survey.

4. *Formal programs are guides to shape the culture, not vice versa.* People who are inclined to follow the rules appreciate the rules as a guide to behavior. Formal program elements need to reflect the culture in which they are deployed if they are going to be most effective in driving the company to the desired outcomes.

Culture may be new on the radar screen, but it isn't outside the scope or skills of forward-thinking finance managers and compliance professionals. Culture can be measured, and finance managers can play a leadership role in developing systematic approaches to move companies in the right direction.

Critical Thinking

1. Whose values should guide an organization? Senior management? Middle management? "Workers"? Investors?

2. What might happen in an organization that switched "resilience to withstand integrity challenges" and "pursuit of profit and stability" on the right hand side of the seven levels of an ethical organization, while leaving the left hand side as is?

Create Central

www.mhhe.com/createcentral

Internet References

AZ Central
  http://yourbusiness.azcentral.com/ethical-behavior-culture-14949.html
Corporate Compliance Insights
  http://www.corporatecomplianceinsights.com/guarding-the-slippery-slope-what-can-hr-do-to-create-an-ethical-culture/
Houston Chronicle
  http://smallbusiness.chron.com/create-ethical-workplace-10543.html

---

DAVID GEBLER, JD, is president of Working Values, Ltd., a business ethics training and consulting firm specializing in developing behavior-based change to support compliance objectives. You can reach him at dgebler@workingvalues.com.

From *Strategic Finance*, May 2006, pp. 29–34. Copyright © 2006 by Institute of Management Accountants-IMA. Reprinted by permission via Copyright Clearance Center.

Article Prepared by: Eric Teoro, *Lincoln Christian University*

Barclays Tells Staff to Uphold New Values or Leave

Margot Patrick

Learning Outcomes

After reading this article, you will be able to:

- Describe Barclays' CEO's position on upholding corporate values.

- Recognize that working for a given company is a choice— you can choose to leave if you find its policies disagreeable.

Barclays PLC's Chief Executive Antony Jenkins Thursday told staff they should uphold the company's new values or leave. The comments come 7 months after a scandal over trying to rig interest rates.

In a memorandum to employees, Mr. Jenkins said bonuses will now be based in part on how employees and business units uphold five values, rather than "just on what we deliver."

"We must never again be in a position of rewarding people for making the bank money in a way which is unethical or inconsistent with our values," Mr. Jenkins said.

Barclays is attempting to repair its reputation with regulators, investors, customers, and the broader public after acknowledging in June that some staff had tried to manipulate interest rates. It paid around $450 million in regulatory fines and its chief executive, chairman, and chief operating officer resigned. Mr. Jenkins became CEO in August after having run the group's global retail and business banks. He pledged to make reforms.

"Having a firm commitment throughout the business to strong values is not something I want to do for public relations or political benefit. It is simply how I will run Barclays," Mr. Jenkins told staff.

"There might be some who don't feel they can fully buy in to an approach which so squarely links performance to the upholding of our values," Mr. Jenkins said. "My message to those people is simple: Barclays is not the place for you. The rules have changed. You won't feel comfortable at Barclays and, to be frank, we won't feel comfortable with you as colleagues."

Mr. Jenkins is to address staff to expand upon the memo later Thursday and will present the outcome of a strategic review of the bank Feb. 12, the day Barclays is to report full-year results. He has previously said every part of the bank would be reviewed by considering its contribution to both returns and reputation.

He said there are plans to train more than 1,000 staff to spread the new values across the bank in an effort to "embed them throughout our business at every level."

The values are: respect, integrity, service, excellence and stewardship.

Critical Thinking

1. Would you like to work for Antony Jenkins? Why or why not?
2. Would you have taken a similar or different approach to what Jenkins did? Why?
3. Did Jenkins behave ethically in issuing his charge? Why or why not?

Create Central

www.mhhe.com/createcentral

Internet References

Barclays
http://www.barclays.com/about-barclays/barclays-values.html
Choose
http://www.choose.net/money/guide/features/how-ethical-banking.html

Article — Prepared by: Eric Teoro, *Lincoln Christian University*

Hiring Character

In their new book, ***Integrity Works,*** authors Dana Telford and Adrian Gostick outline the strategies necessary for becoming a respected and admired leader. In the edited excerpt that follows, the authors present a look at business leader Warren Buffett's practice of hiring people based on their integrity. For sales and marketing executives, it's a practice worth considering, especially when your company's reputation with customers—built through your salespeople—is so critical.

DANA TELFORD AND ADRIAN GOSTICK

Learning Outcomes

After reading this article, you will be able to:

- Describe the ethicality of Warren Buffet.
- Determine if résumés are accurate.
- Ask ethics-based questions during hiring interviews.

This chapter was the hardest for us to write. The problem was, we couldn't agree on whom to write about. We had a number of great options we were mulling over. Herb Brooks of the Miracle on Ice 1980 US hockey team certainly put together a collection of players whose character outshined their talent. And the results were extraordinary. We decided to leave him out because we had enough sports figures in the book already. No, we wanted a business leader. So we asked, "Who hires integrity over ability?"

The person suggested to us over and over as we bandied this idea among our colleagues was Warren Buffett, chairman of Berkshire Hathaway Inc.

Sure enough, as we began our research we found we had not even begun to tell Buffett's story. But we were reluctant to repeat his story. Buffett had played an important part in our first book. And yet, his name kept coming up. So often, in fact, that we finally decided to not ignore the obvious.

Perhaps more than anyone in business today, Warren Buffett hires people based on their integrity. Buffett commented, "Berkshire's collection of managers is unusual in several ways. As one example, a very high percentage of these men and women are independently wealthy, having made fortunes in the businesses that they run. They work neither because they need the money nor because they are contractually obligated to—we have no contracts at Berkshire. Rather, they work long and hard because they love their businesses."

The unusual thing about Warren Buffett is that he and his longtime partner, Charlie Munger, hire people they trust—and then treat them as they would wish to be treated if their positions were reversed. Buffett says the one reason he has kept working so long is that he loves the opportunity to interact with people he likes and, most importantly, trusts.

Buffett loves the opportunity to interact daily with people he likes and, most importantly, trusts.

Consider the following remarkable story from a few years ago at Berkshire Hathaway. It's about R.C. Willey, the dominant home furnishings business in Utah. Berkshire purchased the company from Bill Child and his family in 1995. Child and most of his managers are members of the Church of Jesus Christ of Latter-day Saints, also called Mormons, and for this reason R.C. Willey's stores have never been open on Sunday.

Now, anyone who has worked in retail realizes the seeming folly of this notion: Sunday is the favorite shopping day for many customers—even in Utah. Over the years, though, Child had stuck to his principle—and wasn't ready to rejigger the formula just because Warren Buffett came along. And the formula was working. R.C.'s sales were $250,000 in 1954 when Child took over. By 1999, they had grown to $342 million. Child's determination to stick to his convictions was what attracted Buffett to him and his management team. This was a group with values and a successful brand.

Arnie Ferrin, longtime friend of Child, said, "I believe that [Child] is a man of extreme integrity, and I believe that Warren Buffett was looking to buy his business because he likes to do business with people like that, that don't have any shadows in their lives, and they're straightforward and deal above-board."

This isn't to say Child and Buffett have always agreed on the direction of the furniture store.

"I was highly skeptical about taking a no-Sunday policy into a new territory, where we would be up against entrenched rivals open seven days a week," Buffett said. "Nevertheless, this was Bill's business to run. So, despite my reservations, I told him to follow both his business judgment and his religious convictions."

Proving once again that he believed in his convictions, Child insisted on a truly extraordinary proposition: He would personally buy the land and build the store in Boise, Idaho—for about $11 million as it turned out—and would sell it to Berkshire at his cost if—and only if—the store proved to be successful. On the other hand, if sales fell short of his expectations, Berkshire could exit the business without paying Child a cent. This, of course, would leave him with a huge investment in an empty building.

You're probably guessing there's a happy ending to the story. And there is. The store opened in August of 1998 and immediately became a huge success, making Berkshire a considerable margin. Today, the store is the largest home furnishings store in Idaho.

Child, good to his word, turned the property over to Berkshire—including some extra land that had appreciated significantly. And he wanted nothing more than the original cost of his investment. In response, Buffett said, "And get this: Bill refused to take a dime of interest on the capital he had tied up over the two years."

And there's more. Shortly after the Boise opening, Child went back to Buffett, suggesting they try Las Vegas next. This time, Buffett was even more skeptical. How could they do business in a metropolis of that size and remain closed on Sundays, a day that all of their competitors would be exploiting?

But Buffett trusts his managers because he knows their character. So he gave it a shot. The store was built in Henderson, a mushrooming city adjacent to Las Vegas. The result? This store outsells all others in the R.C. Willey chain, doing a volume of business that far exceeds any competitor in the area. The revenue is twice what Buffett had anticipated.

As this book went to print, R.C. Willey was preparing to open its third store in the Las Vegas area, as well as stores in Reno, Nevada, and Sacramento, California. Sales have grown to more than $600 million, and the target is $1 billion in coming years. "You can understand why the opportunity to partner with people like Bill Child causes me to tap dance to work every morning," Buffett said.

Here's another example of Buffett's adeptness at hiring character. He agreed to purchase Ben Bridge Jeweler over the phone, prior to any face-to-face meeting with the management.

Ed Bridge manages this 65-store West Coast retailer with his cousin, Jon. Both are fourth-generation owner-managers of a business started 89 years ago in Seattle. And over the years, the business and the family have enjoyed extraordinary character reputations.

Buffett knows that he must give complete autonomy to his managers. "I told Ed and Jon that they would be in charge, and they knew I could be believed: After all, it's obvious that [I] would be a disaster at actually running a store or selling jewelry, though there are members of [my] family who have earned black brits as purchasers."

Talk about hiring integrity! Without any provocation from Buffett, the Bridges allocated a substantial portion of the proceeds from their sale to the hundreds of coworkers who had helped the company achieve its success.

Overall, Berkshire has made many such acquisitions—hiring for character first, and talent second—and then asking these CEOs to manage for maximum long-term value, rather than for next quarter's earnings. While they certainly don't ignore the current profitability of their business, Buffett never wants profits to be achieved at the expense of developing ever-greater competitive strengths, including integrity.

It's an approach he learned early in his career.

Warren Edward Buffett was born on August 30, 1930. His father, Howard, was a stockbroker-turned-congressman. The only boy, Warren was the second of three children. He displayed an amazing aptitude for both money and business at a very early age. Acquaintances recount his uncanny ability to calculate columns of numbers off the top of his head—a feat Buffett still amazes business colleagues with today.

At only 6 years old, Buffett purchased six-packs of Coca-Cola from his grandfather's grocery store for 25 cents and resold each of the bottles for a nickel—making a nice five-cent profit. While other children his age were playing hopscotch and jacks, Buffett was already generating cash flow.

Buffett stayed just 2 years in the undergraduate program at Wharton Business School at the University of Pennsylvania. He left disappointed, complaining that he knew more than his professors. Eventually, he transferred to the University of Nebraska–Lincoln. He managed to graduate in only 3 years despite working full time.

Then he finally applied to Harvard Business School. In what was undoubtedly one of the worst admission decisions in history, the school rejected him as "too young." Slighted, Buffett applied to Columbia where famed investment professor Ben Graham taught.

Professor Graham shaped young Buffett's opinions on investing. And the student influenced his mentor as well. Graham bestowed on Buffett the only A+ he ever awarded in decades of teaching.

While Buffett tried working for Graham for a while, he finally struck out on his own with a revolutionary philosophy: He would research the internal workings of extraordinary companies. He could discover what really made them tick and why they held a competitive edge in their markets. And then he would invest in great companies that were trading at substantially less than their market values.

Ten years after its founding, the Buffett Partnership assets were up more than 1,156 percent [compared to the Dow's 122.9 percent], and Buffett was firmly on his way to becoming an investing legend.

In 2004, Warren Buffett was listed by Forbes as the world's second-richest person (right behind Bill Gates), with $42.9 billion in personal wealth. Despite starting with just $300,000 in holdings, Berkshire's holdings now exceed $116 billion. And Buffett and his employees can confidently say they have made thousands of people wealthy.

We often ask business leaders one simple question: Which is more dangerous to your firm—the incompetent new hire or the dishonest new hire? It's the part of our presentation where attendees sit up straight and start thinking.

We always follow the question with an exercise on identifying and hiring integrity. Though it becomes obvious that many of the executives and managers haven't given employee integrity much thought, most of the CEOs in the audiences are increasingly concerned about hiring employees with character.

So, how do you hire workers with integrity? It's possible, but not easy. It is important to spend more time choosing a new employee than you do picking out a new coffee machine. Here are a few simple areas to focus on:

It is important to spend more time choosing a new employee than you do picking out a new coffee machine.

First, ensure educational credentials match the resume. Education is the most misrepresented area on a resume. Notre Dame football coach George O'Leary was fired because the master's degree he said he had earned did not exist, the CEO of software giant Lotus exaggerated his education and military service, and the CEO of Bausch & Lomb forfeited a bonus of more than $1 million because he claimed a fictional MBA.

Job candidates also often claim credit for responsibilities that they never had. Here's a typical scenario:

Job candidate: "I led that project. Saved the company $10 million." Through diligent fact checking, you find an employee at a previous employer who can give you information about the candidate:

Coworker: "Hmm. Actually, Steve was a member of the team, but not the lead. And while it was a great project, we still haven't taken a tally of the cost savings. But $10 million seems really high."

How do you find those things out? Confer with companies where the applicant has worked—especially those firms the person isn't listing as a reference. Talk to people inside the organization, going at least two levels deep (which means you ask each reference for a couple more references). Talk to the nonprofit organizations where the person volunteers. Tap into alumni networks and professional associations. Get on the phone with others in the industry to learn about the person's reputation. Check public records for bankruptcy, civil, and criminal litigation (with the candidate's knowledge). In other words, check candidates' backgrounds carefully (but legally, of course).

We find that most hiring managers spend 90 percent of their time on capability-related questions, and next to no time on character-based questions. In your rush to get someone in the chair, don't forget to check backgrounds and be rigorous in your interviewing for character. Hiring the wrong person can destroy two careers: your employee's—and your own.

Ask ethics-based questions to get to the character issue. We asked a group of executives at a storage company to brainstorm a list of questions they might ask candidates to learn more about their character. Their list included the following questions:

- Who has had the greatest influence on you and why?
- Who is the best CEO you've worked for and why?
- Tell me about your worst boss.
- Who are your role models and why?

- How do you feet about your last manager?
- Tell me about a time you had to explain bad news to your manager.
- What would you do if your best friend did something illegal?
- What would your past manager say about you?
- What does integrity mean to you?
- If you were the CEO of your previous company, what would you change?
- What values did your parents teach you?
- Tell me a few of your faults.
- Why should I trust you?
- How have you dealt with adversity in the past?
- What are your three core values?
- Tell me about a time when you let someone down.
- What is your greatest accomplishment, personal or professional?
- What are your goals and why?
- Tell me about a mistake you made in business and what you learned from it.
- Tell me about a time when you were asked to compromise your integrity.

It's relatively easy to teach a candidate your business. The harder task is trying to instill integrity in someone who doesn't already have it.

Of course, we don't want to imply that it's impossible. Sometimes people will adapt to a positive environment and shine. Men's Wearhouse has certainly had tremendous success hiring former prison inmates, demonstrating everyone should have a second chance.

But integrity is a journey that is very personal, very individual. An outside force, such as an employer, typically can't prescribe it. It's certainly not something that happens overnight. That's one reason many of the CEOs we have talked with prefer promoting people from inside their organizations when possible.

Don Graham, chairman and CEO of the Washington Post Company, said, "There's a very good reason for concentrating your hires and promotions on people who already work in your organization. The best way to predict what someone's going to do in the future is to know what they've done in the past—watch how people address difficult business issues, how they deal with the people who work for them, how they deal with the people for whom they work. You may be able to put on a certain face for a day or even a week, but you're not going to be able to hide the person you are for five or ten years."

Graham tells a story about Frank Batten, who for years ran Landmark Communications and founded The Weather Channel. "Frank is a person of total integrity," Graham says. "Frank once said, 'When you go outside for hire you always get a surprise. Sometimes it's a good surprise. But you never hire quite the person you thought you were hiring.'"

What do you look for in a job applicant? Years of experience? College degree? Specific skill sets? Or do you look for character? If so, you're in good company.

Years ago, Warren Buffett was asked to help choose the next CEO for Salomon Brothers. "What do you think [Warren] was looking for?" Graham asks. "Character and integrity—more than even a particular background. When the reputation of the firm is on the line every day, character counts."

Don't like surprises? Then hire people who have integrity. Want to ensure a good fit with the people you hire? Then hire people who have integrity. Want to ensure your reputation with customers? Then hire people who have integrity.

Are we saying that nothing else matters? No. But we are saying that nothing matters more.

Critical Thinking

1. Describe Warren Buffett's hiring practices that assure he is hiring integrity.
2. What are the top three characteristics that an ethical leader must exhibit (from your perspective)?

Create Central

www.mhhe.com/createcentral

Internet References

Entrepreneur
http://www.entrepreneur.com/article/235101

Montana State University Billings
http://www.msubillings.edu/BusinessFaculty/larsen/MGMT452/HR%20 Articles/Can%20You%20Interview%20for%20Integrity%20-%20Across%20 the%20Board%20%28MarApr%2007%29.pdf

Recruiterbox
http://recruiterbox.com/blog/what-warren-buffett-wants-to-know-before-he-hires-you/

From *Integrity Works: Strategies for Becoming a Trusted, Respected and Admired Leader* by **Dana Telford** and **Adrian Gostick**.

Article

Prepared by: Eric Teoro, *Lincoln Christian University*

Strategic Organizational Diversity: A Model?

Frederick Tesch and Frederick Maidment

Learning Outcomes

After reading this article, you will be able to:

- Describe the benefits of diversity within an organization.

- Understand that diversity should be driven by an organization's goals and needs.

- Describe the application of La Modigliani to HR diversity management.

U sing resources, especially human ones, effectively is a key issue facing organizations and their managers, especially the human resource management staffs. Diversity is about the human resources available to an organization, about recognizing and using the breadth and depth of differences in its employees' experiences, backgrounds, and capabilities, and about viewing these differences as assets to the organization (Watson & Kumar, 1992). A key assumption is that diversity in a population should produce a similar diversity in our labor markets and in turn in the workforces derived from those labor markets.

Organizations that pursue workforce diversity are more likely to be successful than ones that do not (Cox & Blake, 1991; Marquez, 2005). Human diversity can actually drive business growth (Robinson & Dechant, 1997). An organization that manages diversity well can, for example, understand its markets better, increase its creativity and innovation, and improve its problem solving, thereby reducing its exposure to risk and increasing its chances of higher returns on investment. Clearly, these effects make workforce diversity a goal worth pursuing.

The major problem encountered in pursuing diversity is the lack of agreement on a definition. A recent study by the Society for Human Resource Management found that "Almost three-quarters of the HR professionals who responded said their organizations had no official definition of diversity. Those who had a definition said it was very broad and included an extensive set of differences and similarities among individuals, such as race, gender, age, etc." (Hastings, 2008, p. 34). How are we to manage what we have yet to define conceptually or operationally?

Given the potential benefits of workforce diversity, discussion of possible theoretical linkages between diversity and organizational goals has been minimal. What paradigm could account for the range of positive effects? What ideas move diversity from a practical concept to a management principle? Most discussion has focused on the practical matters and applications. Pragmatically, diversity works. Research (Parkhe, 1999) shows that managing diversity well gives organizations a competitive edge and reduces business risk. Given these robust, positive effects, we need not examine nor debate the mechanisms producing them. Do it; don't analyze it!

Unguided diversity, however, might lead an organization to a state of confusion and to actions not consistent with its strategic goals. Much diversity training appears to promote diversity for diversity's sake, often as a moral or ethical imperative. A stance of maximizing all types of human diversity as an end in itself might lead an organization to some dysfunctional thinking and actions. For example, would having recently hired someone from University X with a degree in Discipline Y prohibit hiring another such applicant? Hiring the second, similar applicant could be seen as promoting intellectual and academic homogeneity. Should an applicant be hired because her constellation of skills, knowledge, abilities, and background is unlike that of any other employee, even if her attributes have no relevance to the organization's goals?

Developing a Model for Diversity

Our thesis is that an organization's quest for diversity should be guided by the organization's goals and needs, not by a diffuse concept of diversity as the means to social responsibility or good citizenship.

There are two paths to building a theory. The first path is developing a model to explain the observed events, just as scientists build constructs to explain the phenomena they study (Kuhn, 1970). The second path, typically used by business disciplines, is borrowing a model or paradigm from another discipline and modifying it to the new phenomena. Ideas from economics, psychology, engineering, and mathematics abound in finance, marketing, and management. For example, in finance, portfolio analysis is a tool for managing stock purchases and sales, but marketing borrowed it to use in managing a portfolio of products (Hedley, 1977). Borrowing and using what works is characteristic of the business disciplines and of business people.

Following the second path, there is a theory of diversity in investments that can be applied to diversity in human resources. This application becomes especially clear when organizations view their employees not as an expense but rather as an asset—a view fundamental to human resources, as opposed to personnel, management. Employees, when viewed as an asset, are the equivalent of stocks in a portfolio.

Modigliani's Theory of Diversity in Investments

Franco Modigliani won the Nobel Prize in Economics for this theory of diversity in investments. He began by distinguishing between systematic and unsystematic risks. Systematic risk, also called market risk, is the risk that affects all securities. "Unsystematic risk is the risk that is unique to a company. It can be eliminated by diversifying the portfolio. Thus, systematic risk and unsystematic risk are referred to as non-diversifiable and diversifiable risk, respectively" (Fabozzi & Modigliani, 1992, pp. 154–155).

Building on this difference, he discusses how risk can be reduced or removed. "[U]nsystematic" risk . . . can be washed away by mixing the security with other securities in a diversified portfolio . . . Increasing diversification gradually tends to eliminate the unsystematic risk, leaving only systematic, i.e., market related risk. The remaining variability results from the fact that the return on every security depends to some degree on the overall performance of the market" (Fabozzi & Modigliani, 1992, p. 135).

There will always be some market (systematic) risk: such is the nature of capitalism where organizations compete with one another in the marketplace. Eliminating these risks requires a centrally planned or monopolistic economy.

The case of unsystematic risk is different since it is unique to a company and can be eliminated by diversifying the portfolio. Modigliani's point is that people can control the amount of risk they accept and that the risk can be eliminated if there is enough diversity. The goal is to maximize the long-term results while minimizing, if not eliminating, unsystematic risk. Individually risky stocks remain in the portfolio, but holding a variety of stocks in a variety of industries minimizes risk. Simply stated, "Don't put all your eggs in one basket."

Joe Watson, a diversity expert, captured the argument when he said "Think about diversity in terms of your stock portfolio. If someone came to you and said they were going to put everything you own in Southeast Asian bonds, that's probably not what you would want to do. People want a balanced portfolio with 10 percent in this and 20 percent in that because it's understood in business that over time that is what will give you the best possible outcome. Well, how is the workforce any different? It also needs to be diverse to give companies the best possible outcome" (Harris et al., 2008). The organization's goals and strategy should determine the specific securities/people (i.e., differences) in which it needs to invest and which it should ignore.

Human Resources a La Modigliani

Building a parallel from how investors view their stocks in a portfolio, managers should view employees as assets to be managed, not a cost to minimize. With this perspective, Modigliani's concept of diversity for investments becomes a model for human resources diversity. Diversifying an organization's workforce should reduce the unsystematic (nonmarket) risk unique to the organization's human resources. The greater the diversity, the lower the organization's controllable risk, and the greater the likelihood of higher financial return as a result of the efforts of the employees.

Diversity in an organization's human resources can, for example, reduce the possibility of groupthink (Janis, 1982), "A mode of thinking that people engage in when they are deeply involved in a cohesive [perhaps homogenous] group, when the members, striving for unanimity, override their motivation to realistically appraise alternative courses of action." Groupthink diminishes the group's capabilities to consider, thoroughly, all realistic courses of action. Groups of people with similar backgrounds, experiences, and educations are more likely to fall prey to groupthink than groups having diversity of those factors. Diversity, when properly managed, brings a richer, stronger set of individuals who should be more resistant to the groupthink trap when dealing with organizational issues.

A classic example of the lack of diversity as a tactical organizational weakness is the famous incident of General Motors introducing their "Chevrolet Nova" into the Latin American market (Schnitzier, 2005). In Spanish the phrase "No va!" translates to "No go!," a costly blunder in marketing to the Spanish speaking countries of Latin America. Had the groups involved in this decision at GM contained diversity that was representative of Latin America the episode could have been avoided.

Strategic diversity is not diversity for diversity's sake (i.e., simply maximizing all differences randomly), but is rather diversity aligned to the organization's goals, strategies, mission, and vision (Bonn, 2005). Strategic diversity encourages developing a pool of relevant diversity and not developing differences that are not strategically relevant. For example, an organization doing business in China should probably not hire people from Argentina to conduct its business in Hong Kong. Diversity makes business sense when it is done strategically, not when it is done simply for the sake of diversity or in the name of moral or philosophical agendas. Doing business in the United State of America requires a diverse workforce because it is such a diverse country. To operate in any other way would not only be illegal (e.g., EEO) but also illogical and detrimental to its long-term success. Similarly, doing business in Norway requires a workforce reflecting the Norwegian stakeholders and having an understanding of Norwegian markets, practices, and laws.

The only sustainable competitive edge that can be unique to an organization is its workforce (Pfeffer, 1995). Most organizations have access to the same technology, transportation and communication systems, and financial markets. Managers exert little influence on their organization's external environments, but do have some control over internal ones. Diversifying the organization's human resources promotes controlling, minimizing, and perhaps even eliminating unsystematic (nonmarket) risk. This is the theoretical base for workforce diversity.

A strong corporate culture, one that embraces diversity, is one approach to reducing risks. When an organization's operations are scattered across distances, time zones, and cultures, a strong corporate culture is a significant element of the glue holding the pieces together. But no glue can overcome missing pieces. All the cultural variables surrounding the organization must be adequately represented within that organization. Recruiting, selecting, hiring, promoting, training, and compensating must all reflect the drive for diversity. Not doing so would leave the organization vulnerable in an increasingly competitive marketplace and subject to unsystematic risk. Managing diversity well brings the advantage of reduced unsystematic risk in a factor that is controllable and has the most potential for competitive advantage, that is, its human resources.

Human Resources Implications

The HR diversity model based on Modigliani's thinking supplies an additional base, a business justification, to the case for workforce diversity. Arguing for diversity based on legal compliance, ethical posture, or simple cost reduction cannot carry the day. HR executives and managers need the stronger theoretical position this model provides by eliminating or at least reducing unsystematic or nonmarket risk to the organization in the area of human resources. Let's look at some typical applications.

As organizations go global, those drawing only on their home countries to staff senior positions practice a form of discrimination that severely limits their long-term capabilities. As corporations, for example, become more globalized, their management staff must do the same in order to reduce the unsystematic risks (Bell & Harrison, 1996). One example would be the few non-USA nationals who lead or have led US corporations (e.g., Ford Motor Company, NCR).

Diversity as a risk management strategy means that we must go beyond simply having people of diverse backgrounds in our organizations. It argues, as does EEO, that the strategy requires offering everyone the same opportunities for movement and advancement within the organization. No department, division, unit, or level can be permitted to be too homogenous, but its diversity must be structural, not random. And that structural linkage should derive from and reflect the organization's strategic goals.

Workforce diversity promotes the achievement of excellence in human resources and the concurrent reduction of organizational risk leading to enhanced competitiveness and performance. Under these conditions of risk management the cream of the organization's human resources can perform exceptionally. The cream of the workforce that rises to the top is made of richer ingredients and is a better grade of cream (Ng & Tung, 1998).

Diversity's Challenge to Human Resource Management

In today's highly turbulent and hyper-competitive environments, organizations simply cannot afford to allow their competitors the competitive advantage of better workers, managers, and executives, that is, better human resources. To do so is to risk becoming second rate—or even becoming extinct (Collins, 2001; Olson & van Bever, 2008). HR professionals need to develop action plans that are strongly linked to the organization's goals and that guide their recruiting, succession planning, career development, and compensation activities. They must create workforces having diversity that is congruent with the organization's strategic goals and that promotes and ensures equitable treatment and opportunities for all employees.

References

Bell, M. P. & Harrison, D. A. (1996). Using intra-national diversity for international assignments: A model of bicultural competence and expatriate adjustment, *Human Resource Management Review,* Spring, 6(1), 47–74.

Bonn, I. (2005). Improving strategic thinking: A multilevel approach, *Leadership & Organizational Development Journal,* 25(5), 336–354.

Collins, J. (2001). *Good to Great: Why Some Companies Make the Leap—and Others Don't,* New York: Harper Business.

Cox, T. H. & Blake, S. (1991). Managing cultural diversity: Implications for organizational competitiveness, *Academy of Management Executive,* August, 5(3), 45–56.

Fabozzi, F. J., & Modigliani, F. (1992). *Capital Markets: Institutions and instruments,* Englewood Cliffs, NJ: Prentice Hall.

Harris, W., Drakes, S., Lott, A., & Barrett, L. (2008). The 40 best companies for diversity, *Black Enterprise,* 38(12), 94–112.

Hastings, R. (2008). SHRM diversity report a call to action: Majority of companies say they haven't defined diversity, *HRMagazine,* 53(4), April, 34.

Hedley, B. (1977). Strategy and the business portfolio, *Long Range Planning,* February.

Janis, I. (1982). *Groupthink: Psychological studies of policy decisions and fiascos,* Boston: Houghton-Mifflin.

Kuhn, T. (1970). *The structure of scientific revolutions,* Chicago: University of Chicago Press.

Marquez, J. (2005). SHRM survey shows diversity contributes to bottom line (Society for Human Resource Management), *Workforce Management,* 84.12, November 7, 8. Retrieved February 26, 2007, from General Reverence Center Gold database.

Ng, E. S. & Tung, R. L. (1998). Ethno-cultural diversity and organizational effectiveness: A field study, *International Journal of Human Resource Management,* December, 9(6), 980–995.

Olson, M. S. & van Bever, D. (2008). *Stall Points: Most Companies Stop Growing—Yours Doesn't Have To,* New Haven, CT: Yale University Press.

Parkhe, A. (1999). Interfirm diversity, organizational learning, and longevity in global strategic alliances, *Journal of International Business Studies,* Winter, 22(4), 579–601.

Pfeffer, J. (1995). Producing sustainable competitive advantage through the effective management of people, *Academy of Management Executive,* February, 9(1), 55–72.

Robinson, G. & Dechant, K. (1997). Building a business case for diversity, *Academy of Management Executive,* August, 21–31.

Schnitzier, P. (2005). Translating success: Network of language experts key to Pangea Lingua's growth, *Indianapolis Business Journal,* 26(21), August 1, 3.

Watson W. E. & Kumar, K. (1992). Differences in decision-making regarding risk-taking: A comparison of culturally diverse and culturally homogeneous task groups, *Journal of Intercultural Relations,* 16(1), 53–65.

Critical Thinking

1. Explain what you think "strategic organizational diversity" means.

2. Come up with weaknesses of "strategic organizational diversity" and explain how these weaknesses can be ameliorated.

Create Central

www.mhhe.com/createcentral

Internet References

Colorado Technical University
http://www.coloradotech.edu/resources/blogs/march-2013/ethics-cultural-diversity

Houston Chronicle
http://smallbusiness.chron.com/cultural-diversity-business-ethics-26116.html

Huffington Post
http://www.huffingtonpost.com/natalia-lopatniuk-brzezinski/diversity-ethics-keys-to-_b_4901755.html

FREDERICK TESCH, Western Connecticut State University, USA.
FREDERICK MAIDMENT, Western Connecticut State University, Connecticut, USA.

Article   Prepared by: Eric Teoro, *Lincoln Christian University*

Fiduciary Principles: Corporate Responsibilities to Stakeholders

SUSAN C. ATHERTON, MARK S. BLODGETT, AND CHARLES A. ATHERTON

Learning Outcomes

After reading this article, you will be able to:

- Describe the history of fiduciary theory and court opinion.
- Understand the relationship between fiduciary and corporate social responsibilities.

Introduction

The lack of trust in American corporations and in corporate management over the recent scandals and financial crisis has increased public and legislative outcry for accountability in business decisions. Frustration is rampant, with "seemingly unending examples of mismanagement, ethical misconduct, and patterned dishonesty of a society dubbed 'the cheating culture.'"[1] International competition created tremendous risks and rewards but forced companies to attract investors through creative accounting practices to raise share value. As a result, 3 decades of corporate greed, inappropriate financial risk-taking and personal misconduct eroded trust in corporate decision-making.[2]

Corporate governance reform initiatives beginning in 2002 were designed to increase financial disclosure and responsibility; however, such legislation is insufficient to rebuild public trust in business. Restoring trust requires that those individuals who manage corporations, that is, the board of directors and senior officers, comply with requirements for greater accountability and transparency, *and* abide by the legal norms to which boards of directors and management are already subject, as directors and officers are legally bound as fiduciaries owing duties of care and loyalty to the corporation.[3] However, centuries of legal and religious formalization and codification have diminished the actual meaning and

purpose of fiduciaries, with the result that modern corporate fiduciaries have limited responsibility toward stakeholders and the greater society. Restoring the original definitions and roles of fiduciaries may legitimize and guide the corporation in developing new relationships with stakeholders.

This paper does not focus on illegal conduct by corporate individuals, although many criminal violations of fiduciary norms involve intentional assessment of the risk of penalties versus potential profits.[4] Rather, the paper examines the limitations of today's corporate fiduciary duties given the original intent of the fiduciary relationship. In particular, we examine the definitions of fiduciaries and fiduciary responsibilities to determine the extent to which formalization and codification have led to avoidance of corporate responsibility. We then revisit the historical and religious origins of fiduciaries in commercial transactions that defined and shaped the integration of moral and ethical duties in business today yet were so narrowly defined that corporate liability became increasingly limited. We propose a modest but well-defined, consistent and universal definition of "fiduciary duties," that could offer corporate managers guidance in developing new approaches to stakeholder relationships—relationships built on expectations of corporate trust and decision-making that maximize shareholder wealth while protecting stakeholders.

The Modern Fiduciary

Most business students and executives today are introduced to the concept of a "fiduciary" in the context of agency law, where a fiduciary is defined as "one who has a duty to act primarily for another person's benefit," and agency is generally defined as "the fiduciary relation that results from the manifestation of consent by one person (a 'principal') to another (an 'agent') that the agent shall act on the principal's behalf and subject to the principal's control, and the agent manifests or otherwise consents so to act."[5] Restatement (Third) of Agency states that proof of an agency relationship requires the existence of the manifestation by the principal that the agent shall act for him; the agent's acceptance of the undertaking; and, the understanding that the principal is in control of the undertaking. The agency relationship that results is founded on trust, confidence, and good faith by one person in the integrity and fidelity of another, creating certain duties owed by each party established in the agency agreement and implied by law.[6] Within the relationship, fiduciaries have a duty of loyalty—the duty to act primarily for another in matters related to the activity and not for the fiduciary's own personal interest.

Fiduciaries also have a duty of good faith—the duty to act with scrupulous good faith and candor; complete fairness, without influencing or taking advantage of the client. The fiduciary relationship, as defined by history and case law, exists in every business transaction. Moreover, the relationship is defined by the specific role or function of the agent toward the principal, that is, the relationship of corporate management and boards of directors to shareholders, lawyer to client, or broker to client, and governed by the laws associated with those transactions, including criminal and labor law, securities and corporate law, contracts, partnerships, and trusts.[7] The roles of trustees, administrators, and bailees as fiduciaries were of ancient origin, whereas agents appeared only at the end of the eighteenth century.[8] Partners, corporate boards of directors, and corporate officers held fiduciary duties originating with the formation of modern partnerships and corporations, as did majority shareholders, while union leaders held fiduciary roles only when unions were granted power by statute to represent workers in negotiations with management.[9] While modern definitions of these duties remain intact, the scope of the duties greatly varies based on the fiduciary's role, which increases the complexity of analysis required to understand violations of those duties.

The modern definition of "agent" as a fiduciary was first rationalized and clarified as a legal doctrine in 1933:[10] "When the person acting is to represent the other in contractual negotiations, bargainings or transactions involved in business dealings with third persons, or is to appear for or represent the other in hearings or proceedings in which he may be interested, he is termed an 'agent,' and the person for whom he is to act is termed the 'principal.'" The element of continuous subjection to the will of the principal distinguishes the agent from other fiduciaries and the agency agreement from other agreements.[11] This implies that corporate officers and directors are also agents. However, in law and practice today, the fiduciary roles of corporate officers and directors are not "continuous subjection to the will of the principal (shareholders)" but more flexible as officers and directors make many decisions not approved by shareholders.

Further, the duties of officers and directors are distinct from those of other corporate employees. Corporate officers and directors owe fiduciary duties to shareholders (as defined by state case law and Delaware corporate law) while employees as agents owe duties to employers, suppliers, vendors, or customers in a wide variety of relationships involving trust.[12] This distinction has created a two-tiered definition of fiduciaries, each with different duties, and varying liabilities for breaches of those duties, and is supported by economic theory. Such differentiation in fiduciary roles does not appear to be the intention, either historically or in modern corporate law. In 1928, Judge Benjamin Cardozo, then Chief Judge of the New York Court of Appeals, eloquently recognized the significance and sanctity of fiduciary principles in *Meinhard v. Salmon*:[13]

> [J]oint adventurers, like copartners, owe to one another . . . the duty of the finest loyalty . . . and the level of conduct for fiduciaries has been kept at a higher level than that trodden by the crowd. It will not consciously be lowered by any judgment of this court.

Cardozo's opinion reflects three important principles that reinforce a long line of precedent in defining a *special level of fidelity for all fiduciaries:* (1) fiduciary matters demand a higher standard than normal marketplace transactions; (2) exceptions to the fiduciary standard undermine the duty of loyalty; and (3) neither courts nor regulators who interpret, enforce or modify the fiduciary standard should consciously weaken it.[14] Supreme Court Justice Brandeis later noted that a fiduciary "is an occupation which is pursued largely for others and not merely for oneself . . . in which the amount of financial return is not the accepted measure of success."[15]

Fiduciary Duties: The Required Triad

The Delaware Supreme Court, renowned for its corporate governance decisions and the source of the primary legal standards for the duties and liabilities of corporate officers, ruled in 1993, re-affirmed in 2006, and again in 2010, that the "triad" of duties includes the duty of loyalty, due care and good faith, where "good faith" and "full and fair disclosure" are considered to be the essential elements of, or prerequisites for proper conduct, by a director.[16] Violation of the duty of good faith could remove directors' protections from liability. The Delaware Court also ruled that corporate officers owe the same fiduciary duties as corporate directors, noting that it is not possible to discharge properly either the duty of care or the duty of loyalty without acting in good faith with respect to the interests of the companies' constituents.[17] Major legislation such as The Sarbanes-Oxley Act of 2002[18], or The Dodd–Frank Act[19] of 2010 support these legal standards *and* require that directors and their corporations return to these fundamental principles to which they were formally subject already: individual integrity and responsibility in corporate governance; and, accountable and transparent disclosure of important financial and other information on which investors and the stability of the capital markets depend.[20]

The Court has long held that the board of directors is ultimately responsible for the management of the corporation,[21] although boards often delegate major decisions to corporate officers with more expertise and information on a particular subject. Under Delaware corporate law, officers are granted titles and duties through the corporation's bylaws or the board's resolutions and employees who are not granted this power are deemed agents.[22] Additionally, Delaware law dictates that the terms "officers" or "agents" are by no means interchangeable: officers are the corporation, but an agent is an employee and does not have the equivalent status of an officer.[23] Agents' specific duties include loyalty, performance, obedience, notification, and accounting.

Again, we see this distinction between officers as managers of the corporation and agents as employees as contrary to the historical and case law definitions espoused by two leading Chief Justices. It is noteworthy that agents as employees (and fiduciaries) are not required to act in a manner that ensures that organizational activities are conducted in good faith and with care for stakeholder's interests. Also noteworthy is the omission in corporate law of the duty of obedience (to obey the law), which appeared to occupy a recognized place in corporations through 1946 but eventually was eliminated. As recent courts have made clear that corporate actors cannot consciously violate, or permit the corporation to violate, corporate and noncorporate norms, even when it may be profitable for the corporation, this duty may be resurfacing.[24] The recent *Disney* decision specifically defines the current required triad of fiduciary duties.[25]

The Duty of Loyalty

"[T]he duty of loyalty mandates that the best interests of the corporation and its shareholders takes precedence over any interest possessed by a director, officer or controlling shareholder and . . . is not limited to cases involving a financial or other cognizable fiduciary conflict of interest. It also encompasses cases where the fiduciary fails to act in good faith."[26] The duty of loyalty is often described as a obligation of directors to protect the interests of the company and its stockholders, to refrain from decisions that would injure the company or deprive the company of profit or an advantage that might properly be brought to the company for it to pursue, and to act in a manner that he or she believes is in good faith to be in the best interests of the company and its stockholders.[27] Recent case law also adds that the duty of loyalty requires boards to act *affirmatively and in good faith.*"[28]

The Duty of Care

The duty of care is defined as " . . . that amount of care which ordinarily careful and prudent men would use in similar circumstances."[29] Courts review the standard of care in directors' decision-making *process,* not the substance of decisions thus limiting director liability for failure in risky decisions. A breach of the duty of care may be found when a director is grossly negligent if the substance of the board's informed decision cannot be "attributed to any rational business purpose."[30] In response to the financial crisis, legislation has specifically addressed the need for increased risk assessment in our financial institutions, requiring increased disclosure to ensure that effective reporting systems are in place and that all relevant information has been evaluated to ensure financial and economic stability. The duty of care is often perceived as a minimal standard, but addressing the impact of risk could increase the importance of this standard.

The Duty to Act in Good Faith

In the *Disney* case, the court stated that "Good faith has been said to require an 'honesty of purpose,' and a genuine care for the fiduciary's constituents . . ."[31] A director acts in "subjective bad faith" when his actions are "motivated by an actual intent to do harm" to the corporation, and bad faith can take different forms with varying degrees of culpability.[32] The court clearly ruled that the duty of good faith cannot be satisfied if directors act in subjective bad faith, consciously disregard their duties, actually intend to harm the corporation, or cause the corporation to knowingly violated the law.[33]

Most legal scholars disagree as to the practical importance of the duty of good faith, but proponents of managerial accountability in corporate governance look to the doctrine of good faith because the traditional duties of care and loyalty do very little to discipline boards, even if allegations of self-dealing were made (i.e., violations of duty of loyalty).[34] The Disney decision was critical for corporate governance since the court recognized that conduct that benefits the corporation must be done with proper motives in order to satisfy the duty of good faith, thus making boards and senior managers more accountable for their decisions. Implicit in these recent cases is the assumption that new rules of "conduct" may be useful in restoring trust to a doubting public. To more fully understand these new rules of ethical conduct we must turn to the historical origins of fiduciary principles.

Origins of Fiduciary Principles
Biblical and Early History

If you would understand anything, observe its beginning and its development.

Aristotle, 4th Century BCE [35]

The historical definition of a "fiduciary" was stated in terms of "an essential code of conduct for those who have been entrusted to care for other peoples' property," carry out transactions, work for another, or aid persons who were vulnerable and dependent upon others.[36] The breadth and complexity of early trust relationships is implicit in today's corporate organizational structure and business relationships. As early as 1790 B.C., the Code of Hammurabi (a Babylonian code of laws) established rules of law governing business conduct, or fiduciary considerations, for the behavior of agents (employees) entrusted with property.[37] For example, a merchant's agent was required to keep receipts and to pay triple damages for failing to provide promised goods, although an exception was allowed if losses were due to enemy attack during a journey.[38] The insightful research of several scholars traces the religious roots of the fiduciary principle to the Old and New Testaments.[39] For example, the Lord told Moses that it is a sin not to restore that which is delivered unto a man to keep safely, and penalties must be paid for the violation,[40] (i.e., duties of loyalty and due care); the right to fair treatment in the marketplace,[41] implying a responsibility to conduct transactions in good faith; and the unjust steward who, expecting to be fired, curries favor with his master's debtors by allowing them to repay less than their full debts, illustrating the precept that one cannot serve two masters.[42] Additionally, the law on pledges obligates everyone to establish his own trustworthiness by carrying out the agreements he has made and by being sensitive to the needs of those who depend on him to meet their needs (i.e., loyalty of master to servant, employer to employee, seller to buyer, powerful to vulnerable).[43]

Fiduciary roles were likened to the roles of stewards in early religious and business history as well as in later corporate development. In this context, "Fiduciary law secularized a particular religious tradition and applied it to commercial pursuits," where the shepherd tending his flocks may be likened to a fiduciary (steward or employer) or an agent (servant or employee) tending the sheep for the owner of the flock.[44] The "steward," may be described as a moral agent or representative of "God," a corporate partner or stakeholder whose profits could be distributed by the steward to the poor at year's end.[45] Also, the King (as steward) was described as God's representative responsible for administering the covenant (agreements) for the people, and who must avoid preoccupation with the trappings of office while observing the law.[46] Thus, the king may be described as a model of godliness to the people by governing in a way that conforms to the requirements of the covenant.[47]

The increasing complexity in fiduciary relationships over time is equated to the increasing complexity in the relationship between man and God (as owner) in early biblical history. The relationships change as a function of the increase in the complexity of the duties demanded of the steward (manager of covenants). Similarly, the steward is the precursor to the modern professional fiduciary as well as to those corporate directors or officers who owe a duty of care to the owners (shareholders) of the corporation as well as a duty of loyalty to all stakeholders and to the larger society. Stewards, or fiduciaries, "hold offices with authority, power and privileges set by law or custom, separate from individual personalities, and such office demands moral duties in private conduct, requiring new decision-making habits and reflective capacities that transcend selfishness."[48] Similar to the descriptions of fiduciaries by Justices Cardozo and Brandeis, the description of stewards implies an inherent willingness to serve others (a moral duty), and a willingness to subordinate one's interests to that of others by acceptance of the duty to serve. Both in early law and today, the fiduciary, or steward, is evaluated and compensated for his performance and understands that failure to fulfill his duties will result in penalties. While today's corporations seldom attribute morality to a deity in fiduciary law, acceptance of fiduciary duties does require selflessness and a willingness to subordinate the fiduciary's interests to that of another. Aristotle, who lived from 384 B.C. to 322 B.C., influenced the development of fiduciary principles, recognizing that in economics and business, people must be bound by high obligations of loyalty, honesty and fairness, and that when such obligations aren't required or followed, society suffers.[49]

Fiduciaries in Ancient Law

Modern fiduciary law is traceable to developments in Ancient Roman law and early English law. Ancient Roman law defined fiduciary relationships as both moral and legal relationships of trust. For centuries until the end of the 18th Century, Roman law refined and formalized fiduciary law, recognizing various "trust" (*fiducia*) contracts in which a person held property in safekeeping or otherwise acted on another's behalf (the core duties of loyalty and due care), and acted in good "faith" (*fides*) (core duties of honesty, full disclosure and applied diligence). Failure to uphold such trust could result in monetary penalties as well as a formal "infamy" (*infamia*), in which one lost rights to hold public office or to be a witness in a legal case.[50] These fiduciary relationships in early Roman law were later incorporated into British courts of equity and then into Anglo-American law, providing standards for modern corporate law.[51]

Early English law established the role of steward or agent with the granting of the Magna Carta, an English legal charter issued in 1215 which allowed the King to grant charters (companies) yet retain sovereignty (ownership) in the charter while recognizing the recipient's limited rights.[52] The King served as steward, with fiduciary rights (ownership) in the management of his property but was required to place the interests of his subjects (inferior rights) above his own—a fiduciary relationship. Increasing population growth caused the King to transfer his role as steward to town leaders, creating an early form of agency (master to servant). Scholars describe the king's stewardship duties as similar to the legal or fiduciary duties ascribed primarily to boards of directors and senior officers.[53] Town leaders were similar to "agents" or employees who owed duties to their "stewards" or employers (managers). The continued development of Charter companies and later private companies, during the era of industrialization and specialization in business of the 1700–1800s, formalized the role of fiduciaries and their specific duties.

Early common law separated management from ownership (investors), creating the office of "manager" to protect the interests of investors and to prevent corporate self-dealing.[54] Subsequently, fiduciary duties were attached to such office, and stewardship duties were borrowed from early law and applied to positions of responsibility to promote financial goals. Thus, although a "fiduciary" is a term described by legal statute, case law or professional codes of conduct, this term also describes ethical obligations and duties in a wide variety of business and personal activities and encompasses a "legal or moral recognition of trust, reliance, or dependence and of responsibility often ignored." [55]

A Modest Proposal: New Rules of Fiduciary Conduct

Legal standards for management behavior can be traced to "deeply rooted moral standards" that shaped the "fiduciary principle, a principle of natural law incorporated into the Anglo-American legal tradition underlying the duties of good faith, loyalty and care that apply to corporate directors and officers."[56] Scholars examined early fiduciary history as a potential solution to understanding corporate misconduct, suggesting that revisiting those early fiduciary principles might answer the questions: To what standards should managers be held? What are the historical and conceptual bases for these standards?[57] Alternatively, if one assumes that fiduciaries are responsible to the company's shareholders as well as to a wider set of constituents, one might ask questions such as: In whose interests does the company presently function? In whose interests should it function in the future?[58] The latter set of questions not only asks who is served by the company, but also suggests that stakeholders bear some general rights as citizens, and should be protected against an abuse of power or violation that causes injury, as citizens.

If the role of a fiduciary is ascribed only to corporate boards and officers or to licensed professionals, corporate misconduct at other levels may go undetected. Despite this, corporate management argues that directors and officers are responsible only to shareholders, and that corporate management cannot serve two masters, that is multiple groups of stakeholders. To the contrary, history has demonstrated that fiduciary duties have been and can be the responsibility of all corporate members, and these duties may be extended to all stakeholders and the larger society. Research supports the theory that the corporation

should have one set of duties for multiple stakeholders, an argument made by managers in the 1990s that managers had the skills and independence to mediate fairly among the firm's stakeholders, and could assemble innovative teams capable of expanding wealth and economic opportunity.[59] Managers sustained this claim well into the 1990s, both within their firms and within their major business associations but by 1997 pressure from the global commodity and national financial markets persuaded managers to revise their stakeholder standard. The perception is that managers moved from a focus on a single duty of loyalty to shareholders, to a narrower focus on making their principals (shareholders) and themselves rich, while disassociating themselves from the ideal of widening economic opportunity and improving living standards for the many.[60] The Clarkson Principles, a set of principles for stakeholder management, are considered to be a critical academic effort to revive the idea that managers should be obligated to expand material opportunities for the many through economic growth.[61] Additionally, compliance with fiduciary duties can reduce the principal's costs of monitoring and disciplining agents and lessens the need for government regulation.[62]

Today, although most major corporations support the idea of corporate social responsibility (CSR), and believe that CSR and profit maximization work together, they continue to support the Freidman view that "The social responsibility of business is to increase its profits."[63] A top executive of a major oil company illustrates this view in the comment that "a socially responsible way or working is not . . . a distraction from our core business. Nor does it in any way conflict with our promise and our duty to deliver value to our shareholders."[64]

We propose that adherence to a *new understanding and rule* of fiduciary principles goes hand in hand with CSR and profit maximization and is perhaps the missing link in today's corporate governance. The essential definition of a fiduciary does not change—a fiduciary is a person who has a duty to act primarily for the benefit of another. However, the role of the fiduciary should extend to all corporate members, and the duties of the fiduciary should not differ regardless of the specific function or distinction in roles. The primary focus of all corporate members continues to be to the shareholders (owners of the corporation), but duties toward other stakeholders should be consistent with those duties to shareholders. Any differentiation lowers the high standard of fidelity required of fiduciaries. Thus, the duties of loyalty, good faith, due care and obedience to the law should be incorporated fully into all fiduciary relationships, regardless of role or function within the corporation.

Concluding Thoughts

"Many of the most shocking examples of corporate misbehaviors involve conduct that violates existing law."[65] This result occurs when most cost-benefit analysis weighs the potential harm and subsequent penalties against the potential profits, resulting in an ethical question often ignored because of the focus on maximizing shareholder profitability. Therefore, reform initiatives for boards of directors and corporate governance "without proper attention to ethical obligations will likely prove ineffectual."[66] Schwartz et al. found that board and officer leadership by example and action are roles central to the overall ethical and governance environment of their firms, a leadership role that is reinforced by board members' legal responsibilities to provide oversight of the financial performance of their firms—based on the assumption that ethical corporate leadership results in the best long-term interests of the firm.

Thus, Schwartz et al.'s study of corporate boards of directors demonstrated that boards have a professional duty expressed as a fiduciary duty to make ethics-based decisions. We contend that ethics and morals in line with fiduciary principles *must* permeate the entire corporate culture, if corporate governance reform is to succeed. A return to those central values inherent in ethical and fiduciary duties extended to the greater community as well as to shareholders may provide more socially responsible guidelines for corporations in this period of stakeholder demand for increased government regulation. Defining and providing examples of fiduciary values of honesty, loyalty, integrity responsibility, fairness, and citizenship can provide guidance for corporate fiduciary relationships with all stakeholders, and provide a more efficient voluntary control mechanism. Thus, we contend that consistent fiduciary principles should be implemented throughout the firm, regardless of the corporate member's function or role.[67] This view is consistent with Friedman's view, that a corporate executive is an employee of the owners of the business, owes responsibility to his employers to conduct the business in accordance with their desires, which generally will be to make as much money as possible while conforming to the basic rules of society, embodied both in law and ethical custom.[68]

Our review of the historical and religious origins of fiduciary relationships demonstrates that the concept of fiduciary was intended to be both a societal and a legal principle, and this is consistent with Friedman's view of obeying the law and social custom. The leaders of organizations, as stewards, were responsible to the whole organization, and to society, not just to themselves or shareholders. Perhaps a revitalization of the stewardship principle is part of the new perspective required to create sustainable competitive advantage in today's economy. We believe that there is room for stakeholder-focused management that does no harm to shareholder interests while also benefiting a larger constituency, *and* that fiduciary duties require the exercise of care, loyalty, obedience, and good faith with regard to shareholders as well as to all stakeholders and the larger community.[69]

References

1. See David Callahan, *The Cheating Culture: Why More Americans are Doing Wrong to Get Ahead* (Florida: Harcourt, Inc., 2004), 12.
2. See LaRue Tone Hosmer, *The Ethics of Management, 6th Ed.* (New York: McGraw-Hill, 2008).
3. Peter C. Kostant, *Meaningful Good Faith: Managerial Motives and the Duty to Obey the Law,* 55 N.Y.L.S.L. Rev., 421 (2010).
4. Alan R. Palmiter, *Duty of Obedience: The Forgotten Duty,* 55 N.Y.L.S.L. Rev., 457 (2010).
5. Restatement (Third) of Agency, 3rd Ed. §1(1). (2006), Restatement Third of Agency is a set of principles issues by the American Law Institute, frequently cited by judges as well as attorneys and scholars in making legal arguments.
6. Nancy Kubasek et al., *Dynamic Business Law* (New York: McGraw-Hill/Irwin, 2009), 856,857.
7. Tamar Frankel, *Fiduciary Law,* 71 Cal. L. Rev. 795, 797–802 (1983).
8. See Tamar Frankel, *Fiduciary Law,* 71 Cal. L. Rev., 801–802.
9. See note 8.
10. Deborah A. DeMott, "The First Restatement of Agency: What Was the Agenda?," 32 *S. Ill. U.L.J.,* (2007). Restatement (Second) of Agency, 1958, the American Law Institute, is now out of print and has been completely superseded and replaced by Restatement of the Law Third, Agency, 2006. However, some courts will continue to cite to The Restatement of the Law Second, Agency.
11. Deborah A. DeMott, "The First Restatement of Agency: What Was the Agenda?," 31.
12. Kenneth M. Rosen, *Meador Lecture Series 2005–2006: Fiduciaries,* 58 Ala. L. Rev., 1041 (2007).
13. Kenneth M. Rosen, *Meador Lecture Series 2005–2006: Fiduciaries,* citing *Meinhard v. Salmon,* 164 N.E. 545 (N.Y. 1928).
14. Kenneth M. Rosen, *Meador Lecture Series 2005–2006: Fiduciaries,* 1041.
15. See Kenneth M. Rosen, *"Meador Lecture Series 2005–2006: Fiduciaries."*
16. *See In re* Walt Disney Co. Deriv. Litig., 907 A.2d 693, 753–57 (Del. Ch. 2005) (identifying possible duty of good faith), *aff'd,* 906 A.2d 693 (Del. 2006) (affirming the decision of the Chancellor).
17. Michael Follett, "Note: *Gantler V. Stephens:* Big Epiphany or Big Failure? A look at the current state of officers' fiduciary duties and advice for potential protection," *35 Del. J. Corp. L.,* 563 (2010).
18. Sarbanes-Oxley Act of 2002, PL 107–204, 116 Stat 745. Sarbanes-Oxley requires corporate officers to be responsible for earnings reports, prohibits accounting firms from acting as consultants to accounting clients (a conflict of interest) and increases penalties for fraud.
19. The Dodd-Frank Wall Street Reform and Consumer Protection Act, Pub.L. 111–203, H.R. 4173, (2010).

20. Kilpatrick Stockton LLP, *Directors Fiduciary Duties After Sarbanes-Oxley* (Atlanta: Kilpatrick Stockton LLP), 2003.

21. Delaware General Corporation Law section 141(a) provides that "[t]he business and affairs of every corporation organized under this chapter shall be managed by or under the direction of a board of directors, except as may be otherwise provided in this chapter or in its certificate of incorporation." DEL. CODE ANN. Tit. 8, § 141(a)(2006).

22. See Michael Follett, note 57.

23. Michael Follett, note 57.

24. Alan R. Palmiter, citing *Stone v. Ritter,* 911 A.2d 362, 364–65 (Del. 2006), *Graham V. Allis-Chalmers Mfg. Co.,* 188 A.2d 125, 130 (Del. 1963), and *Caremark Int'l Inc. Deriv. Litig.,* 698 A.2d 959, 971 (Del. Ch. 1996), where directors breached the duty of care for "sustained or systematic failure" to assure existence of reporting systems that identify illegal corporate conduct, for example, medical referral kickbacks, 459.

25. *In re* Walt Disney Co. Deriv. Litig., 907 A.2d 693, 753 (Del. Ch. 2005), aff'd. 906 A.2d 27 (Del. 2006).

26. Thomas A. Uebler, "Shareholder Police Power: Shareholders' Ability to Hold Directors Accountable for Intentional Violations of Law," 33 Del. J. Corp. L., 199 (2008).

27. Thomas A. Uebler, "Shareholder Police Power: Shareholders' Ability to Hold Directors Accountable for Intentional Violations of Law," 201.

28. See Thomas A. Uebler.

29. *In re* Walt Disney Co. Deriv. Litig., 907 A.2d 693, 753–57 (Del. Ch. 2005), *aff'd,* 906 A.2d 693 (Del. 2006) .

30. *In re* Walt Disney Co. Deriv. Litig., 907 A.2d 693, 753 (Del. Ch. 2005), aff'd. 906 A.2d 27 (Del. 2006)), quoting *Sinclair Oil Corp. v. Levien,* 280 A.2d 717, 720 (Del. 1971), and *Smith v. Van Gorkom,* 488 A.2d 858, 873 (Del. 1985),

31. *In re* Walt Disney.

32. *In re* Walt Disney, at 55.

33. Peter C. Kostant , "Meaningful Good Faith: Managerial Motives and the Duty to Obey the Law," 424,426.

34. See Peter C. Kostant, 426–427.

35. Amanda H. Podany, "Why Study History? A View from the Past," Presented at The History Summit I, California State University Dominguez Hills, May 29, 2008.

36. See Kenneth Silber, "Fiduciary Matters," www.AdvisorOne.com/article/fiduciarymatters, June 28, 2011.

37. Joseph F. Johnston, Jr., "Natural Law and the Fiduciary Duties of Managers," *Journal of Markets & Morality* (2005), 8:27–51.

38. Kenneth Silber, "Fiduciary Matters."

39. See Brian P. Schaefer, "Shareholders Social Responsibility," *Journal of Business Ethics* (2008), 81:297–312; and Stephen B. Young, "Fiduciary Duties as a Helpful Guide to Ethical Decision-Making in Business," *Journal of Business Ethics* (2007), 74:1–15.

40. John H. Walton, Deuteronomy: An Exposition of the Spirit of the Law, *Grace Theological Journal* 8, 2(1987), 213–25, quoting Leviticus 6:2–5.

41. See John H. Walton, quoting Deuteronomy 25:13–16.

42. John H. Walton notes that the precept that one cannot serve two masters in Luke 16:1–13 was later cited by scholar Austin Scott in an influential 1949 paper "The Fiduciary Principle," which describes boards' and officers' responsibility to shareholders and not to other constituents.

43. John H. Walton, "Deuteronomy: An Exposition of the Spirit of the Law," quoting Deuteronomy 24:14–15.

44. See Stephen B. Young, "Fiduciary Duties as a Helpful Guide to Ethical Decision-Making in Business."

45. Sarah Key, "Toward a New Theory of the Firm: A Critique of Stakeholder 'Theory'," *Management Decision* (1999), 37:317–328.

46. John H. Walton, quoting Deuteronomy 17:14–20, 216.

47. Stephen B. Young details the link between fiduciary and ethical duties in the four covenants, or agreements, between God and man in the Old Testament that establishes and expands man's duties of care. These covenants allow stewards to impose ethical duties on those who obey them (i.e., agents or employees) and reflect the core of modern agency and fiduciary relationships: (1) The first covenant establishes Noah as steward of God's will to care for creation, and if Noah and his descendents take good care of creation it would not be destroyed (duty of care for the owner's property); (2) The second covenant requires Abraham to accept the duty to behave according to a code of holy behavior in return for protection (protection from liability for accepting the responsibilities of duty of loyalty and care); (3) The third covenant requires the children of Israel to behave morally with religious devotion in return for protection of all of society (extending fiduciary duties of loyalty and care from an individual to society, i.e., to all stakeholders); and (4) The fourth covenant expanded these promises–if the conduct of all mankind is ethical and moral and not based on material temptations, Jesus will protect them on earth and grant them entry into heaven (fiduciary duties are deeply rooted in moral principles).

48. See Stephen B. Young and Joseph F. Johnston, Jr.

49. John H. Walton, "Deuteronomy: An Exposition of the Spirit of the Law."

50. See Kenneth Silber, "Fiduciary Matters."

51. See Kenneth M. Rosen, *Meador Lecture Series 2005–2006: Fiduciaries.*

52. See Stephen B. Young, "Fiduciary Duties as a Helpful Guide to Ethical Decision-Making in Business."

53. See Kenneth M. Rosen, "Meador Lecture Series 2005–2006: Fiduciaries."

54. Richard Marens and Andrew Wicks, "Getting Real: Stakeholder Theory, Managerial Practice, and the General Irrelevance of Fiduciary Duties Owed to Shareholders," *Business Ethics Quarterly* (1999), 273–293.

55. Sarah W. Holtman, "Fiduciary Relationships," in The Encyclopedia of Ethics, 2nd Ed, eds. Lawrence C. Becker and Charlotte B. Becker (NY: Routledge, 2001), 545–49.

56. See Joseph F. Johnston, Jr., "Natural Law and the Fiduciary Duties of Business Managers."

57. See Joseph F. Johnston, Jr. "Natural Law and the Fiduciary Duties of Business Managers."

58. Sheldon Leader, "Participation and Property Rights," *Journal of Business Ethics* 21:97–109, (1999), 98–99.

59. Allan Kaufman, "Managers' Double Fiduciary Duty," *Business Ethics Quarterly* 12:189–214 (2002), 189.

60. Allan Kaufman, "Managers' Double Fiduciary Duty," 190.
61. Allan Kaufman, "Managers' Double Fiduciary Duty," 190–193.
62. Kaufman, "Managers' Double Fiduciary Duty."
63. See Peter C. Kolstad, 137–138, citing Milton Friedman, "The Social Responsibility of Business is to Increase Its Profits," The New York Times Magazine (New York: 1970).
64. See Allan Kaufman, 192.
65. See David Callahan, "The Cheating Culture: Why More Americans are Doing Wrong to Get Ahead."
66. Mark S. Schwartz et al., "Tone at the Top: An Ethics Code for Directors?," *Journal of Business Ethics* (2005), 58:79–100.
67. R. Edward Freeman, in "The Politics of Stakeholder Theory: Some Future Directors," *Business Ethics Quarterly* (1994) 4:409–421, suggested that "multi-fiduciary stakeholder analysis is simply incompatible with widely-held moral convictions about the special fiduciary obligations owed by management to stockholders. At the center of the objections is the belief that the obligations of agents to principals are stronger or different in kind from those of agents to third parties." This view is not supported by historical development of the fiduciary principle, and may be perceived more as a function of corporate management choosing those functions that support personal, not fiduciary, goals.
68. See Milton Friedman, 51.
69. Bradley R. Agle and Ronald K. Mitchell, "Introduction: Recent Research and New Questions," in Agle et al., "Dialogue: Toward Superior Stakeholder Theory," *Business Ethics Quarterly* (2008), 18:153–190.

Critical Thinking

1. What is a fiduciary?
2. What are the duties of a fiduciary?
3. Pick one of the duties of a fiduciary identified in the article and write a statement incorporating that duty into a code of ethics.
4. Explain the new rules of fiduciary conduct proposed in the article.
5. What are arguments in support as well as against use of the proposed new rules?

Create Central

www.mhhe.com/createcentral

Internet References

Business for Social Responsibility
http://www.bsr.org/reports/BSR_AW_Corporate-Boards.pdf

Forbes
http://www.forbes.com/sites/csr/2010/10/28/friend-or-foe-fiduciary-duties-meet-sociallyresponsible-investments/

United States Department of Labor
http://www.dol.gov/ebsa/publications/fiduciaryresponsibility.html

From *Journal of Religion and Business Ethics*, September 10, 2011. Copyright © 2011 by Journal of Religion and Business Ethics. Reprinted by permission.

Article

Prepared by: Eric Teoro, *Lincoln Christian University*

A Time for Ethical Self-Assessment

Peter Drucker's literature on business scruples and the Ethics of Prudence is newly timely, and not just because of the holidays.

RICK WARTZMAN

Learning Outcomes

After reading this article, you will be able to:

- Understand the importance and value of answering the following question: When you look in the mirror in the morning, what kind of person do you want to see?

- Recognize that management deals with the nature of "Man, and with Good and Evil."

This may be the season of giving, but it sure feels like everybody is suddenly on the take.

Siemens (SI), the German engineering giant, agreed this month to pay a record $1.6 billion to US and European authorities to settle charges that it routinely used bribes and kickbacks to secure public works contracts across the globe. Prominent New York attorney Marc Dreier—called by one US prosecutor a "Houdini of impersonation and false documents"—has been accused by the feds of defrauding hedge funds and other investors out of $380 million.

And then, of course, there's financier Bernard L. Madoff, who is said to have confessed to a Ponzi scheme of truly epic proportions: a swindle of $50 billion, an amount roughly equal to the GPD of Luxembourg.

All told, it begs the question that Peter Drucker first raised in a provocative 1981 essay in the journal *The Public Interest* and that later became the title of a chapter in his book, *The Ecological Vision*: "Can there be 'business ethics'?"

Drucker didn't pose this to suggest that business was inherently incapable of demonstrating ethical behavior. Nor was he positing that the workplace should somehow be exempt from moral concerns. Rather, his worry was that to speak of "business ethics" as a distinct concept was to twist it into something that "is not compatible with what ethics always was supposed to be."

What Drucker feared, specifically, was that executives could say they were meeting their social responsibilities as business leaders—protecting jobs and generating wealth—while engaging in practices that were plainly abhorrent. "Ethics for them," Drucker wrote, "is a cost-benefit calculation . . . and that means that the rulers are exempt from the demands of ethics, if only their behavior can be argued to confer benefits on other people."

It's hard to imagine that a Madoff or a Dreier would even attempt to get away with such tortured logic: an ends-justify-the-means attitude that Drucker labeled "casuistry." But we all know managers who've tried to rationalize an unscrupulous act by claiming that it served some greater good.

The Mirror Test

In his book *Resisting Corporate Corruption*, Stephen Arbogast notes that when Enron higher-ups sought an exemption from the company's ethics policy so that they could move forward with certain dubious financial dealings, the arrangement was made to "seem a sacrifice for the benefit of Enron." Reinhard Siekaczek, a former Siemens executive, told *The New York Times* (NYT) that the company's showering of foreign officials with bribes "was about keeping the business unit alive and not jeopardizing thousands of jobs overnight."

For Drucker, the best way for a business—indeed, for any organization—to create an ethical environment is for its people to partake in what he came to call in a 1999 article "the mirror test." In his 1981 piece, Drucker had a fancier name for this idea: He termed it "The Ethics of Prudence." But either way, it boils down to the same thing: When you look in the mirror in the morning, what kind of person do you want to see?

The Ethics of Prudence, Drucker wrote, "does not spell out what 'right' behavior is." It assumes, instead, "that what is wrong behavior is clear enough—and if there is any doubt, it is 'questionable' and to be avoided." Drucker added that "by following prudence, everyone regardless of status becomes a leader" and remains so by "avoiding any act which would make one the kind of person one does not want to be, does not respect."

Drucker went on: "If you don't want to see a pimp when you look in the shaving mirror in the morning, don't hire call girls the night before to entertain congressmen, customers, or salesmen. On any other basis, hiring call girls may be condemned as vulgar and tasteless, and may be shunned as something fastidious people do not do. It may be frowned upon as uncouth. It may even be illegal. But only in prudence is it ethically relevant. This is what Kierkegaard, the sternest moralist of the 19th century, meant when he said that aesthetics is the true ethics."

Time to Reflect

Drucker cautioned that the Ethics of Prudence "can easily degenerate" into hollow appearances and "the hypocrisy of public relations." Yet despite this danger, Drucker believed that "the Ethics of Prudence is surely appropriate to a society of organizations" in which "an extraordinarily large number of people are in positions of high visibility, if only within one organization. They enjoy this visibility not, like the Christian Prince, by virtue of birth, nor by virtue of wealth—that is, not because they are personages. They are functionaries and important only through their responsibility to take right action. But this is exactly what the Ethics of Prudence is all about."

Now is the time of year when many of us find ourselves sitting in church or in synagogue, or, if we're not religious, simply taking stock of who we are and where we want to be as the calendar turns.

But what's even more critical is that we continue this sort of honest self-assessment when we return to our jobs in early 2009.

"I have learned more theology as a practicing management consultant than when I taught religion," Drucker once said. This, he explained, is because "management always deals with the nature of Man and (as all of us with any practical experience have learned), with Good and Evil as well."

So take the mirror test now—and then keep taking it well after the Christmas ornaments have been packed away and the Hanukkah candles have burned down to the nub. In the meantime, happy holidays to all.

Critical Thinking

1. Explain the meaning of Drucker's question "can there be business ethics?"
2. Defend the position that there can be business ethics.
3. What is the mirror test?
4. What is the ethics of prudence?
5. What is meant by "aesthetics is the true ethics"?

Create Central

www.mhhe.com/createcentral

Internet References

American Management Association
  http://www.amanet.org/training/articles/Ethical-Leadership-Self-Assessment-How-Machiavellian-Are-You.aspx
National Association Medical Staff Services
  http://www.namss.org/Portals/0/Ethics%20Files/Self-assessment%20Tool.pdf

RICK WARTZMAN is the director of the Drucker Institute at Claremont Graduate University.